Epworth Commentaries

General Editor
Ivor H. Jones

The Second Epistle to the Corinthians

W0006484

The Second Epistle
to the Corinthians

NIGEL WATSON

EPWORTH PRESS

Copyright © Nigel M. Watson 1993

Extracts from the Revised English Bible are © 1989
by the Delegates of the Oxford University Press
and the Syndics of the Cambridge University Press
and are used by permission

ISBN 0 7162 0487 8

First Published 1993
by Epworth Press
1 Central Buildings
Westminster
London SW1H 9NR

Typeset by Regent Typesetting, London
and printed in Great Britain by
Mackays of Chatham, Kent

To the memory of my parents

Ronald Sinclair Watson
(1891–1959)

Clarice Evangeline Watson
(1894–1965)

CONTENTS

GENERAL INTRODUCTION

The *Epworth Preacher's Commentaries* that Greville P. Lewis edited so successfully in the 1950s and 1960s having now served their turn, the Epworth Press has commissioned a team of distinguished academics who are also preachers and teachers to create a new series of commentaries that will serve the 1990s and beyond. We have seized the opportunity offered by the publication in 1989 of the Revised English Bible to use this very readable and scholarly version as the basis of our commentaries, and we are grateful to the Oxford and Cambridge University Presses for the requisite licence and for granting our authors pre-publication access. They will nevertheless be free to cite and discuss other translations wherever they think that these will illuminate the original text.

Just as the books that make up the Bible differ in their provenance and purpose, so our authors will necessarily differ in the structure and bearing of their commentaries. But they will all strive to get as close as possible to the intention of the original writers, expounding their texts in the light of the place, time, circumstances, and culture that gave them birth, and showing why each work was received by Jews and Christians into their respective Canons of Holy Scripture. They will seek to make full use of the dramatic advance in biblical scholarship world-wide but at the same time to explain technical terms in the language of the common reader, and to suggest ways in which Scripture can help towards the living of a Christian life today. They will endeavour to produce commentaries that can be used with confidence in ecumenical, multiracial, and multifaith situations, and not by scholars only but by preachers, teachers, students, church members, and anyone who wants to improve his or her understanding of the Bible.

Ivor H. Jones

PREFACE

II Corinthians is in some ways both the most tantalizing and the most rewarding of all Paul's letters, since it raises historical and critical questions of extreme complexity, and yet at the same time contains reflections on the nature of Christian ministry and the Christian life which are as profound and as moving as anything he ever wrote.

When I first started lecturing on II Corinthians over twenty years ago, there was no commentary in English that could be described as outstanding. That is certainly no longer true. I consider Barrett's commentary on II Corinthians to be even better than his earlier volume on I Corinthians, and in the commentaries of Victor Paul Furnish and Ralph Martin we have two further works of outstanding scholarship.

As in the writing of the first volume, however, I have made it my invariable rule to attempt my own exegesis of a passage, before turning to the commentaries and other secondary literature.

In the preface to the earlier commentary, I observed that Paul's letters to the Corinthians have a great deal to teach us about the need for the message of the gospel to be embodied in the persons of its bearers. As I try to show in the Introduction, this theme comes more and more to the fore in II Corinthians.

During the whole of the time that I have been writing these commentaries, I have had an unusually direct and continuous exposure to the ambiguity of the church in its local embodiments and the frailty of its ministers. To follow Paul as he struggled with precisely the same problems has been no small comfort.

The book is dedicated to the memory of my parents, whose fidelity to their Christian and ministerial callings has always been a source of inspiration to me, as well as to hundreds of other people in the various parishes in New Zealand in which they served.

It remains for me to express my thanks to Geoff and Linda Thompson, for allowing me to type a large part of this commentary on their word processor, while spending a term at Wesley House, Cambridge.

ABBREVIATIONS

AusBR	*Australian Biblical Review*, Melbourne
AV	Authorized Version of the Bible, 1611
BJRL	*Bulletin of the John Rylands Library*, Manchester
ExpT	*Expository Times*, Edinburgh
ICC	International Critical Commentary
JBL	*Journal of Biblical Literature*, Philadelphia etc.
JSNT	*Journal for the Study of the New Testament*, Sheffield
MT	Masoretic text
NEB	New English Bible, 1970
NICNT	New International Commentary on the New Testament
NRSV	New Revised Standard Version of the Bible, 1990
NTD	Neue Testament Deutsch
NTS	New Testament Studies, Cambridge
REB	Revised English Bible, 1989
RevBib	*Revue Biblique*, Paris
RSR	*Recherches de Science Religieuse*, Paris
RSV	Revised Standard Version of the Bible, 1952
SBL	Studies in Biblical Literature
SJT	*Scottish Journal of Theology*, Edinburgh
TCNT	Twentieth Century New Testament, 1902
TNTC	Tyndale New Testament Commentary
ZNW	*Zeitschrift für die neutestamentliche Wissenschaft*, Berlin

BIBLIOGRAPHY

Commentaries

(normally cited by author's name only)

Allo, E.-B., *Seconde Épître aux Corinthiens*, Paris: Gabalda 1956.

Barrett, C. K., *The Second Epistle to the Corinthians* (Black's New Testament Commentaries), London: A. & C. Black 1973.

Best, Ernest, *Second Corinthians* (Interpretation Commentary), Atlanta: John Knox 1987.

Bruce, F. F., *1 and 2 Corinthians* (New Century Bible), London: Oliphants 1971.

Bultmann, Rudolf, *The Second Letter to the Corinthians*, Minneapolis: Augsburg 1985 (German original: 1976).

Denney, James, *The Second Epistle to the Corinthians* (The Expositor's Bible), London: Hodder & Stoughton 1894.

Furnish, Victor Paul, *II Corinthians* (Anchor Bible), New York: Doubleday 1984.

Klauck, H.-J., *2. Korintherbrief* (Neue Echter Bibel), Wurzburg: Echter Verlag 1986.

Kruse, Colin, *Second Corinthians* (TNTC), Grand Rapids: Eerdmans/Leicester: Intervarsity Press. 1987.

Lang, Friedrich, *Die Briefe an die Korinther* (NTD), Göttingen: Vandenhoeck & Ruprecht 1986.

Lietzmann, H., *An die Korinther 1/2* (Handbuch zum Neuen Testament 9), Tübingen: J.C.B. Mohr, 4th ed. 1949.

Martin, Ralph P., *2 Corinthians* (Word Biblical Commentary), Waco, Texas: Word Books 1986.

Plummer, Alfred, *A Critical and Exegetical Commentary on the Second Epistle of St Paul to the Corinthians* (ICC), Edinburgh: T. & T. Clark 1915.

Tasker, R.V.G., *The Second Epistle of Paul to the Corinthians* (TNTC), London: The Tyndale Press 1958.

Other books and articles

Badian, E., 'Triumph,' in N.G.L. Hammond and H.H. Scullard, eds, *The Oxford Classical Dictionary*, Oxford: OUP, 2nd ed 1970.

Baillie, John, *Invitation to Pilgrimage*, Oxford: OUP 1942.

Baird, W., 'Visions, Revelation and Ministry: Reflections on 2 Cor 12: 1–5 and Gal 1: 11–17,' *JBL* 104, 1985, pp. 651–62.

Barclay, William, *New Testament Wordbook*, London: SCM Press 1955.

Barrett, C.K., *The Signs of an Apostle*, London: Epworth 1970 (*Signs*).

—, 'Christianity at Corinth,' *BJRL* 46, 1964, pp. 269–97.

Bonhoeffer, Dietrich, *The Cost of Discipleship*, London: SCM Press, 6th ed 1959.

—, *Letters and Papers from Prison*, London: SCM Press, 3rd ed 1967.

Bornkamm, Günther, *Paul*, London: Hodder & Stoughton, 1971 (German original: 1969).

—, 'The History of the Origin of the So-Called Second Letter to the Corinthians,' *NTS* 8, 1961/62, pp. 258–64.

Bruce, F.F., *An Expanded Paraphrase of the Epistles of Paul*, Exeter: Paternoster 1965.

Buttrick, David, *Homiletic: Moves and Structures*, London: SCM Press, 1987.

Cadbury, H. J., *The Peril of Modernizing Jesus*, London: Macmillan 1937.

Carnley, Peter, *The Structure of Resurrection Belief*, Oxford: OUP 1987.

Carrez, M., 'Le "nous" en 2 Corinthiens,' *NTS* 26, 1979/80, pp. 474–86.

Cassidy, Sheila, *Audacity to Believe*, London: Collins 1978.

—, *Sharing the Darkness*, London: Darton, Longman and Todd 1988.

Chadwick, Henry, *The Enigma of St Paul*, London: The Athlone Press 1969.

Collange, Jean-François, *Énigmes de la deuxième épître aux Corinthiens. Étude exégétique de 2 Cor. 2: 14 – 7: 4*, Cambridge: CUP 1972.

Dalton, William J., S.J., 'Is the Old Covenant Abrogated (2 Cor 3: 14)?' *AusBR* 35, 1987, pp. 88–94.

Davies, W. D., *Invitation to the New Testament*, London: Darton, Longman and Todd 1967.

Didier, G., *Désintéressement du Chrétien: La Rétribution dans la Morale de Saint Paul*, Paris: Aubier 1955.

Dodd, C.H., *The Epistle of Paul to the Romans* (Moffatt NT Commentary), London: Hodder & Stoughton 1932.

—, *New Testament Studies*, Manchester: Manchester UP 1953.

Fee, Gordon D., *The First Epistle to the Corinthians* (NICNT), Grand Rapids: Eerdmans 1987.

Feuillet, A., 'Demeure céleste et Destinée des Chrétiens,' *RSR* 44, 1956, pp. 161–92, 360–402.

Forbes, Christopher, 'Comparison, Self-Praise and Irony: Paul's Boasting and the Conventions of Hellenistic Rhetoric,' *NTS* 32, 1986, pp. 1–30.

Georgi, Dieter, *The Opponents of Paul in Second Corinthians*, Philadelphia: Fortress 1986.

Glasson, T. Francis, '2 Corinthians v. 1–10 versus Platonism,' *SJT* 43, 1990, pp. 145–55.

Hanhart, K., 'Paul's Hope in Face of Death,' *JBL* 88, 1969, pp. 445–57.

Hock, Ronald F., *The Social Context of Paul's Ministry: Tentmaking and Apostleship*, Philadelphia: Fortress 1980.

Holladay, C. H., *Theios Aner in Hellenistic-Judaism* (SBL Series 40), Missoula: Scholars Press 1977.

Judge, Edwin A., 'The Conflict of Educational Aims in NT Thought,' *Journal of Christian Education* 9, 1966, pp. 32–45.

Käsemann, Ernst, 'Die Legitimität des Apostels,' *ZNW* 41, 1942, pp. 33–71.

Kingsbury, J. D., 'The "Divine Man" as the Key to Mark's Christology – The End of an Era?' *Interpretation* 35, 1981, pp. 243–57.

Knox, John, *Chapters in a Life of Paul*, London: A. & C. Black 1954 *(Chapters)*.

Koester, H., *Introduction to the New Testament* 2 Vols, Philadelphia: Fortress 1982.

Kubo, Sakae, *A Reader's Greek-English Lexicon of the New Testament*, Leiden: E. J. Brill 1971.

Lake, Frank, *Clinical Theology*, London: Darton, Longman and Todd 1966.

Lang, F. G., *2. Korinther 5, 1–10 in der neueren Forschung*, Tübingen: J. C. B. Mohr 1973.

Lüthi, Walter, *Der Apostel*, Munich and Hamburg: Siebenstern 1968.

Marshall, Peter, *Enmity in Corinth: Social Conventions in Paul's Relations with the Corinthians*, Tübingen: J. C. B. Mohr 1987.

Martyn, J. Louis, 'Epistemology at the Turn of the Ages: 2 Corinthians 5: 16,' in W. R. Farmer and others (eds), *Christian History and Interpretation: Studies presented to John Knox*, Cambridge: CUP 1967, pp. 269–87.

Metzger, Bruce M., *A Textual Commentary on the Greek New Testament*, London/New York: United Bible Societies 1971.

Moule, C. F. D., *The Meaning of Hope*, London: Highway Press 1953.

—, *The Birth of the New Testament*, London: A. & C. Black 1962.

Moulton, J. H., *A Grammar of New Testament Greek: Prolegomena*, Edinburgh: T. & T. Clark 1906.

Murphy-O'Connor, J., *The Theology of the Second Letter to the Corinthians*, Cambridge: CUP 1991.

—, 'Pneumatikoi and Judaizers in 2 Cor 2: 14 – 4: 6,' *AusBR* 34, 1986, pp. 42–58.

—, 'Relating 2 Corinthians 6. 14 – 7. 1 to its Context,' *NTS* 33, 1987, pp. 272–75.

—, 'Philo and 2 Cor 6: 14 – 7: 1,' *RevBib* 95, 1988, pp. 56–69.

—, 'The Date of 2 Corinthians 10–13,' *AusBR* 39, 1991, pp. 31–43.

Oestreicher, Paul, *The Double Cross*, London: Darton, Longman and Todd 1986.

Osei-Bonsu, Joseph, 'Does 2 Cor. 5. 1–10 teach the reception of the resurrection body at the moment of death?' *JSNT* 28, 1986, pp. 81–101.

Perkins, Pheme, *Resurrection: New Testament Witness and Contemporary Reflection*, New York/London: Doubleday/Geoffrey Chapman 1984.

Perrin, N. and Duling, D.C., *The New Testament: An Introduction*, New York: Harcourt Brace Jovanovich, 2nd ed 1982.

Schweizer, Eduard, *The Letter to the Colossians*, London: SPCK 1982 (German original: 1976).

—, *Theologische Einleitung zum Neuen Testament* (NTD), Göttingen: Vandenhoeck & Ruprecht 1989.

Shaw, Graham, *The Cost of Authority*, London: Collins 1983.

Snaith, N. H., 'Jealous, zealous,' in A. Richardson (ed.), *A Theological Word Book of the Bible*, London: SCM Press 1950, pp. 115f.

Sumney, Jerry L., *Identifying Paul's Opponents: the Problem of Method in 2 Corinthians*, Sheffield: JSOT Press 1990.

Theissen, Gerd, *The Social Setting of Pauline Christianity*, Edinburgh: T. & T. Clark 1982.

—, *Psychological Aspects of Pauline Theology*, Philadelphia: Fortress 1987.

Van Vliet, Hendrik, *No Single Testimony. A Study on the Adoption of the Law of Deut. 19: 15 Par. into the New Testament*, Utrecht: Kemink & Zoon 1958.

Watson, Francis, '2 Cor. x-xiii and Paul's Painful Letter to the Corinthians,' *JTS* 35 1984, pp. 324–46.

Watson, Nigel, *Easter Faith and Witness*, Melbourne: Desbooks 1990.

—, *The First Epistle of St. Paul to the Corinthians*, London: Epworth 1992.

—, 'The Interpretation of Romans VII,' *AusBR* 21, 1973, pp. 27–39.

—, '2 Cor 5: 1–10 in Recent Research,' *AusBR* 23, 1975, pp. 33–36.

—, 'Justified by faith; judged by works – an antinomy?' *NTS* 29, 1983, pp. 209–21.

'. . . To make us rely not on ourselves but on God who raises the dead,' in Ulrich Luz and Hans Weder, eds, *Die Mitte des Neuen Testaments* (Festschrift for Eduard Schweizer), Göttingen: Vandenhoeck & Ruprecht 1983, pp. 384–98.

Wedderburn, A. J. M., *The Reasons for Romans*, Edinburgh: T. & T. Clark 1988.

Young, B. H., 'The Ascension Motif of 2 Cors 12 in Jewish, Christian and Gnostic Texts,' *Grace Theological Journal* 9, 1988, pp. 73–103.

Young, Frances and Ford, David F., *Meaning and Truth in 2 Corinthians*, London: SPCK 1987.

Young, Frances, 'Note on 2 Corinthians 1. 17b,' *JTS* 37, 1986, pp. 404–15.

INTRODUCTION

For a brief account of Paul's founding of the church in Corinth and the circumstances leading up to the writing of I Corinthians the reader is referred to the beginning of the Introduction to our commentary on I Corinthians in this series. II Corinthians raises a number of complex, critical and historical questions.

One thing is clear: Paul's correspondence with the Christians of Corinth included more than the two letters that we know as I and II Corinthians.

The Previous Letter

In the first place, before writing I Corinthians, Paul had written a still earlier letter. He refers to this letter, usually known as the 'Previous Letter', in I Cor. 5. 9. Indeed, in that passage he seeks to correct a misunderstanding of the Previous Letter. He had been misunderstood as warning the Corinthians to have nothing to do with any immoral person. He now wishes to make it clear that by immoral persons he meant immoral Christians.

Can anything more be said about this Previous Letter? Many scholars have held that a fragment of it survives embedded in II Cor. 6.14 to 7.1. The transition from 6.13 to 6.14 is harsh, and, if one reads 7.2 straight after 6.13, one gets excellent sense and connection. Moreover, so it is argued, what is said in 6.14–7.1 could easily be understood (or misunderstood) in the way that the Previous Letter was misunderstood, according to I Cor. 5.9.

The view taken in this commentary, however, is that the section in question is more likely to be a non-Pauline interpolation.

For one thing, whereas the Previous Letter urged the Corinthians to have nothing to do particularly with those who were *sexually* immoral, there is no specific reference to sexual immorality in the paragraph in question.

Moreover, the theory that the paragraph is a fragment of the Previous Letter does not account for its many non-Pauline features.[1]

[1] For a fuller discussion of the question see our comments on 6.14–7.1 in the commentary proper; cf. also Victor Paul Furnish, *II Corinthians*, pp. 26f.

The Intermediate Letter

Something else of which we can be certain is that between writing
I Corinthians and the last of his letters to Corinth Paul wrote another
letter, sometimes known as the 'Intermediate Letter'. The writing of
this letter was bound up with certain other incidents which call for
some discussion.

The Painful Visit and its outcome

In II Cor. 2.1 Paul refers to a visit he had paid to Corinth which had
ended in a complete and devastating rebuff for him. He had left
Corinth thwarted, and with the feeling that he had been ill-treated by
those from whom he was entitled to expect kindness and loyalty. It
further appears from II Cor. 2.5–8 that on this occasion some member
of the church inflicted an injury not only on Paul but on the church as
a whole. These allusions suggest some sort of public vilification both
of Paul's person and his apostleship.

It seems quite likely that the offender in question had accused Paul
before the assembled church of not being a legitimate apostle and
that the church had not intervened.

At the time of writing this second chapter, relations between Paul
and the Corinthian church have been to a large extent restored to
normal. The wrongdoer has been punished, and punished sufficiently, and Paul asks that he be now reinstated.

This Painful Visit cannot have been Paul's first visit to Corinth, for
that was not particularly painful. It must have been a subsequent
visit. This conclusion is confirmed by II Cor. 12.14 and 13.1f., in
which Paul speaks of preparing to pay a third visit. It is clear then
that, after writing I Corinthians, Paul paid a second visit to Corinth,
which proved painful and unsuccessful.

It is from the same early chapters of II Corinthians that we learn
that, since the writing of I Corinthians, Paul has not only paid
another visit to Corinth but written another letter. More than once he
refers to a letter written only recently. In II Cor. 2.4 he has this to say:
*That letter I sent you came out of great distress and anxiety; how many tears I
shed as I wrote it!* Evidently it was a very severe letter. Indeed, it
caused the Corinthians so much heartburning that Paul for a time
half-regretted having sent it (2.2, 4; 7.8), though he now sees that it
has had the desired result (7.9). This is the letter which we referred to
earlier as the Intermediate Letter but which we will designate from
now on by its commoner name, the 'Severe Letter'. It is also referred
to sometimes as the 'Tearful Letter'.

The Severe Letter followed the Painful Visit

This Severe Letter cannot be our I Corinthians, which does not bear the marks of having been written 'out of great distress and anxiety' and with 'many tears'. It must therefore have been a subsequent letter. Furthermore, it must have been written after the Painful Visit, since we discover from 2.8 that it was only when Titus returned from a visit to Corinth that Paul learned of its effect. It had brought the Corinthian church to its senses and constrained them to submit to Paul's direction once more and discipline the offender. What Paul has to say in chapters 2 and 7 is a direct response to this good news. He now feels under some obligation to apologize for the severity of the letter's tone, and in 2.4 and 9 he assures his Corinthian readers that his object in writing it had been twofold: to demonstrate *the love, the more than ordinary love,* that he has for them and to test their loyalty and obedience to him.

II Corinthians a unity?

We move on now to consider II Corinthians in its entirety and note, to begin with, that the great majority of scholars do not consider it to be a unity. Most scholars by far believe that the last four chapters represent part, probably the major part, of a letter written at a different time from the first nine.

A number of scholars subdivide the letter still further. G. Bornkamm, for example, breaks up I and II Corinthians into seven separate letters.[2]

The strongest case can be made for partition after the end of chapter 9. The earlier chapters clearly imply that relations between Paul and the church in Corinth have been largely restored to normal after the estrangement that came to a head during the Painful Visit, but in chapters 10–13 we find Paul engaged in a desperate struggle to win back the allegiance of the community.

Barrett sums up well the difference in tone between the two parts of the letter, when he writes that the first nine chapters suggest that Paul 'expected that he would only have to remind his readers of the truth to ensure their acceptance of it,' whereas the last four chapters 'suggest his belief that the cause was as good as lost, and that little remained but to make a desperate counter-attack.'[3]

[2] G. Bornkamm, 'The History of the Origin of the So-Called Second Letter to the Corinthians,' *NTS* 8, 1961/62, pp. 258–64. His conclusions are stated more briefly in his book, *Paul* , pp. 244–46.

[3] C. K. Barrett, *The Second Epistle to the Corinthians* , pp. 243f.

Nothing in the last four chapters suggests that the conflict with the congregation has been settled and peace restored, although in the earlier chapters this is just what Paul is celebrating. To be sure, even in the first nine chapters everything is not yet in order in Corinth (see 3.1; 6.12f.; 7.2), yet Paul's mood is predominantly one of relief and reconciliation. The tone of the last four chapters, however, is predominantly one of vigorous remonstrance and irony.

How could Paul say, on the one hand, *How happy I am now to have complete confidence in you!* (7.16; cf. 7.11, 13; 9.13) and then, a few pages later, *Now I am afraid that, as the serpent in his cunning seduced Eve, your thoughts may be corrupted and you may lose your single-hearted devotion to Christ* (11.3; cf. 12.20)?

Moreover, the last four chapters refer to the presence in Corinth of *sham apostles, confidence tricksters masquerading as apostles of Christ* (11.13; cf. 11.4). There are also ironical references to *super-apostles* (11.5; 12.11), who, in our judgment, are to be identified with the 'sham apostles', though some distinguish them. What is important for our present purpose, however, is that, while there are some verses in the first nine chapters, like 2.17; 3.1; and 5.12 (discussed below under the heading of *Paul's Opponents*), which can be taken as evidence that the intruders were already present in Corinth, there is no suggestion of a conflict as sharp as this.

The conclusion seems inescapable that chapters 10–13 were written at a different time from chapters 1–9 and in response to different circumstances. It is conceivable that the first nine chapters were left lying around for a while, perhaps because the intended bearer of the letter was not yet able to travel, and that Paul then received new and disturbing news, but, had this happened, it is hardly likely that he would simply have added four chapters of remonstrance to the earlier draft and sent it all off as one letter. He would surely have put aside the earlier draft and written a completely new letter.[4] The view taken in this commentary is that the last four chapters represent part, and probably the most important part, of a separate letter, which we will refer to, from now on, as the 'Letter of Four Chapters'.

If this conclusion is accepted, the question inevitably arises, Where does this Letter of Four Chapters fit into the story of Paul's dealings with the Corinthian church?

---

[4] For a fuller statement of the case for partition at this point see Furnish, pp. 30–32. We pass over, as not worthy of serious consideration, the suggestion of Lietzmann that between writing chapter 9 and chapter 10 Paul had a bad night. See H. Lietzmann, *An die Korinther 1/2* , p. 139.

There is one answer to this question which has received a great deal of support, since it was first proposed over 100 years ago. A. Hausrath in 1870 and J. H. Kennedy in 1900 came independently to the conclusion that chapters 10–13 represent at least a substantial part of the Severe Letter referred to in II Cor. 2.4; 7.8f. During the first half of this century, this view was very widely accepted by British, American and German commentators and is still accepted in some commentaries and standard works of introduction.[5]

Certainly the tone of chapters 10–13 does match fairly well Paul's own description of the Severe Letter in 2.4 as the product of 'great distress and anxiety' and 'many tears'. As has already been indicated, these chapters contain his passionate self-defence against slanders which have been cast upon him by rivals who have intruded into the community and whom he describes as 'sham apostles'. To rebut their attacks, Paul asserts his apostolic status and authority at considerable length and with great vigour.

But his displeasure is directed not only at the 'sham apostles' but also at the members of the church in Corinth, whom he takes to task for allowing themselves to be swayed by the smear campaign of his opponents, as well as for being quarrelsome and malicious and persisting in sins of sensuality (12.19–21). He is facing a crisis in the relationship of the Corinthians to himself, their father in Christ (cf. I Cor. 3.15), which is threatening to lead to complete apostasy.

However, the theory which assigns chapters 10–13 to the Severe Letter is vulnerable to some serious criticisms.

There is first of all the problem of how to account for the two letters represented by chapters 1–9 and 10–13 being joined together in this way. Not only has the chronological order been reversed but the reassuring effect of the first nine chapters is destroyed, at least for any reader who reads II Corinthians right through.

Certainly there are parallel instances of the joining together of originally separate writings in the addition of Second and Third Isaiah to Isaiah 1–39 and in the addition of chapter 21 to the Fourth Gospel, but these examples do not entail the reversal of the original chronological sequence. However, it is possible that at the time when Paul's correspondence was being gathered together people no longer knew which was the earlier writing, which the later.

[5] See e.g. Friedrich Lang, *Die Briefe an die Korinther* p. 13; H.-J. Klauck, *2. Korintherbrief*, p. 9; N. Perrin & D. C. Duling, *The New Testament. An Introduction*, p. 130; H. Koester, *Introduction to the New Testament*, Vol. II, p. 129; E. Schweizer, *Theologische Einleitung zum Neuen Testament*, pp. 66f.

It is significant that the earliest witnesses to a Pauline correspondence, viz. I Clement, Ignatius and Polycarp, do not appear to know II Corinthians. In the letters of Ignatius and Polycarp's letter to the Philippians, some twenty clear echoes of I Corinthians can be found, but not a single clear echo of II Corinthians. The oldest reliable witness to the existence of II Corinthians is Marcion. It appears, therefore, that any letters of Paul to the Corinthians subsequent to our I Corinthians remained unknown outside Corinth and the neighbouring congregations until some time in the second century.

Bornkamm has suggested a reason why the order of the two writings may have been deliberately reversed. A number of early Christian compositions conclude with a warning against false teachers. They include the Sermon on the Mount, the Didache, Jude, I and II Peter, Hebrews and Revelation, as well as Galatians (6.11ff.) and Romans (16.17–20). This pattern reflects the belief that the appearance of false prophets is a sign of the last times. It is therefore conceivable that some later editor placed the earlier, more polemical letter at the end of II Corinthians in order to characterize Paul's opponents as false prophets of the last times and to characterize Paul himself as the fully legitimate apostle, defending the church from the danger of apostasy.[6]

A more serious objection to the identification of chapters 10–13 with the Severe Letter is that these four chapters are silent about something which is central to the Severe Letter and *vice versa*.

To begin with, nowhere in chapters 10–13 is there any mention of the person to whom Paul refers in II Cor. 2.5–11 as having insulted him in some particularly hurtful way. Supporters of the Hausrath-Kennedy theory have to make do with the rejoinder that chapters 10–13 cannot represent the Severe Letter in its entirety, and that the later collator may not have considered the references to the individual offender to be so important any longer, since he had subsequently repented.

But there is also the difficulty that there are no references to opponents in the first nine chapters that are of a comparable severity to the denunciations found in the last four. Supporters of the Hausrath-Kennedy theory can only account for this difference in tone by suggesting that by this time the opponents may have left

---

[6] See the article of Bornkamm's referred to in note 2. Barrett finds Bornkamm's theory unconvincing on the grounds that 'these chapters are not apocalyptic warnings of what is to be expected in the last days, but a straightforward attack upon contemporaries; not a paraenetic warning (comparable with Acts xx.29f.), but polemics' (p. 24). Barrett's view is shared by Furnish (pp. 39f.).

Corinth, so that Paul's main concern was now to consolidate the attachment of the community to himself and persuade them to forgive the individual offender.[7]

If chapters 10–13 were not written at the same time as chapters 1–9, and are not to be identified with the Severe Letter, then they must be assigned to a later date. There is some further evidence in chapter 12 which points to a later date for the last four chapters.

In 12.17f. Paul seeks to refute the aspersion that he had defrauded the Corinthians through the associates whom he had sent to Corinth, Titus in particular. In the same context he speaks of begging Titus to visit them and of sending 'the brother' (REB: *our friend*) with him. The visit to which he is referring here can hardly be the visit referred to in 2.13 and 7.5–9. On that occasion Titus evidently travelled on his own. Besides, since he brought back the welcome news that the community had had a change of heart and was now eager to take Paul's side (7.6–16), it is unlikely that that visit gave rise to the complaint that the community had been exploited.

In chapter 8, however, we learn that Paul has just 'asked' Titus (the same word as in 12.18) to return to Corinth to complete the organization of the collection for Jerusalem. This time Titus will not be travelling alone. It appears at first that he will be accompanied by one other person, described literally as 'the brother' (the REB translates *one of our company*, but it is the same word as is used in 12.18). Later in chapter 8, it transpires that Titus will also be accompanied by another companion who is also described as a brother (8.22).

There is much to be said for identifying the visit of Titus to Corinth referred to in 8.6–24, which at the time of writing still lies in the future, with the visit referred to in 12.17f., which now lies in the past. The linguistic parallels are striking, in spite of the fact that chapter 8 eventually mentions two brethren who are to accompany Titus, whereas chapter 12 only mentions one. Furthermore, it is precisely such a visit as is contemplated in chapter 8, viz. a visit to raise money, that would be likely to give rise to the complaint of exploitation, referred to in 12.17f.

Are there then any serious objections to dating chapters 10–13 later than chapters 1–9? There is one argument which Friedrich Lang has raised with me in conversation which at least deserves to be

---

[7] For a recent critique of the Hausrath-Kennedy theory see J. Murphy-O'Connor, 'The Date of II Corinthians 10–13,' *AusBR* 39, 1991, pp. 31–43. This article contains a judicious discussion of the fresh arguments advanced in favour of the theory by Francis Watson in his article, 'II Cor. x–xiii and Paul's Painful Letter to the Corinthians,' *JTS* 35, 1984, pp. 324–46.

mentioned. If chapters 10–13 are to be dated later, it follows that the Corinthians first of all failed to give Paul the support to which he felt entitled (2.1–4), then had a change of heart and renewed their commitment to him (7.6–16) and then succumbed to the propaganda of the sham apostles (chapters 10–13). Lang argues that if this was in fact the course that events took, we would expect to find Paul reproaching the Corinthians bitterly in chapters 10–13 for turning against him *a second time*, so soon after the reconciliation that he celebrates in 7.16. This is a not inconsiderable argument.

Whatever solution we adopt to the critical problems of II Corinthians, we would do well to ponder the comment that one of John Baillie's teachers once wrote on the margin of an essay of his: 'Every theory has its difficulties, but you have not considered whether any other theory has less difficulties than the one you have criticised.'[8]

The first nine chapters are often referred to by commentators as the 'Letter of Reconciliation.' In the Table of Contents we have retained this title, though a case could be made for calling it the 'Letter of Partial Reconciliation'.

If we do opt for the view that chapters 10–13 are later than chapters 1–9 (the view which is adopted by F. F. Bruce, C. K. Barrett, V. P. Furnish and Ralph Martin), then we need to note certain consequences, both historical and theological, which follow.

In the first place, it follows that the Severe Letter is not included among the extant correspondence of Paul's but has been lost, probably for ever.

It follows also that Paul's rejoicing over the success of Titus's visit to Corinth in 7.6–16 was premature. Perhaps Titus misread the situation. Perhaps the situation deteriorated after he left.

A further, more general, conclusion which follows is that the story of Paul's relationship with the church at Corinth was even less happy than we have been accustomed to thinking – a fact which affects profoundly Paul's contribution to our understanding of the nature of Christian ministry and the Christian life and serves as a salutary corrective to the picture of the success of the Gentile mission that is contained in Acts. As we note in our exegesis of 11.32f., Luke's account of the progress of the Gentile mission in Acts reads like the record of a triumphal procession. Whatever obstacles Paul meets, whatever his enemies may do, he always emerges victorious. The picture of Christian ministry and the Christian life that Paul presents in his own letters is a much more sombre one, which stresses much

[8] John Baillie, *Invitation to Pilgrimage* , p. 15.

more strongly the inevitability of suffering and humiliation. If the story of Paul's dealings with the Corinthians had in fact no happy ending, then that simply reinforces the truth of the picture of the Christian life that Paul presents.

However, it would be an exaggeration to suggest that the story of Paul's dealings with the church in Corinth ended in disaster and complete estrangement. While there is no direct evidence for the outcome of the visit that he is contemplating in chapters 10–13 (his third), there are at least some hints that it was not fruitless. There is good reason to think that Paul wrote Romans from Corinth or its vicinity during the final three months that he spent in Greece, according to Acts 20.2f. Cenchreae, mentioned in Rom. 16.1 as the home of Phoebe, the first person whom he commends to the Romans, is a suburb of Corinth. In Rom. 15.30f., Paul certainly expresses apprehension, but it is apprehension over his forthcoming visit to Jerusalem, and it is for that that he solicits the prayers of the Roman Christians, not for the situation in Corinth, where he probably was at the time. Could he even have given his mind to the composition of Romans, had there been an impasse between himself and the Corinthians at the time?

Moreover, in writing to the Romans, Paul is full of his plans for a mission to Spain, with Rome as his new base (15.17–30). But, as Martin observes, it is hard to imagine Paul being so eager to press westward, if the Corinthian church was still in disarray.[9] And from Rom. 15.26f. we may surmise that the Corinthians did finally contribute to the collection.

There is, however, evidence from I Clement, usually dated about 95 CE, that by then the church had reverted to its old contentious ways again.

Further subdivision?

We have seen that there is good reason to suppose that the last four chapters of II Corinthians were not composed at the same time as the first nine, whether we identify those four chapters with the Severe Letter or, as we prefer, assign them to a later date. We also noted earlier that a number of scholars subdivide the letter still further.

In 2.12f. Paul begins to tell his readers how agitated he was, on moving to Troas and finding that Titus, whom he had recently sent to Corinth, had not yet returned to tell him about the reaction of the Corinthians to the Severe Letter. Unable to bear the suspense, Paul

[9] Martin, p. 486.

had gone off to Macedonia, evidently hoping to meet Titus on the way, even though this meant turning his back on an opening to serve the Lord in Troas.

But did he meet Titus, on reaching Macedonia? We expect to find out in v. 14, but for the moment Paul does not tell us. He does break into a jubilant doxology, which suggests that he did receive good news, but we have to read through five more chapters before we discover, in 7.5ff., that Titus did eventually arrive with encouraging news. The sudden suspension of Paul's account of his movements in 2.14 and the equally sudden resumption of the account in 7.5 have led some scholars to the conclusion that originally 7.5 followed straight on after 2.13 and that the intervening section, viz. 2.14–7.4, derives from a separate letter (or letters, if 6.14–7.1 be assigned to the Previous Letter).

Johannes Weiss is often quoted as saying that 2.13 and 7.5 fit together 'like the fragments of a ring.'[10] Scholars who agree with Weiss's assessment that an insertion has been made after 2.13 often give to the separate letter which they identify in 2.14–7.4 the title of 'Paul's Apology for the Apostolic Office'. This would represent Paul's third letter to the Corinthians, following the Previous Letter and I Corinthians. The view taken in this commentary, however, is that the hypothesis that 2.14–7.4 derives from a separate letter, while certainly possible, is not necessary. For a fuller discussion see our commentary on 2.12–13.

The question of the integrity of II Corinthians also arises when we turn to chapters 8 and 9. At first sight, it seems incongruous that Paul should remark in 9.1, *About this aid for God's people, it is superfluous for me to write to you,* when he has just spent the whole of the previous chapter in commending the collection, to which he is obviously referring in 9.1. On this and other grounds, many scholars take the view that chapters 8 and 9 cannot have been written at the same time. Among those who separate the two chapters, however, there is no consensus. At least five different views have been advocated by different scholars about the relationship between the two chapters.

These can be summarized as follows:

(i) Chapters 8 and 9 are not to be separated from the previous chapters (Barrett, Furnish).

(ii) Chapter 8 belongs with the previous chapters, but chapter 9 is a commendation of the collection sent to Corinth a little earlier (Bultmann, Schmithals, Schweizer).

[10] See e.g. Günther Bornkamm, *Paul*, p. 245.

(iii) Chapter 9 is an independent writing sent after the letter or letters contained in the earlier chapters (Wendland).

(iv) Chapter 8 belongs with the previous chapters, but chapter 9 was sent at the same time and addressed to the other communities of Achaia (Windisch, Friedrich Lang, Martin).

(v) Both chapters were originally separate from the previous chapters. They are letters of commendation composed at about the same time, but chapter 8 was addressed to the church of Corinth, chapter 9 to the other communities of Achaia (Wilckens).

For our part, however, we do not find any of the arguments for separation entirely convincing and have no difficulty in reading both chapters 8 and 9 as the continuation and conclusion of the previous chapters. For a fuller discussion see our commentary on 9.1–5.

The likely sequence of events[11]

It would help to draw the argument of the preceding sections together, if we were to sketch what we consider to be the most likely sequence of events subsequent to Paul's writing of I Corinthians.

When Paul was writing I Cor. 16.10f., Timothy had left for Corinth and was expected back shortly. Timothy evidently returned with the bad news that he had received a hostile reception, so that Paul judged it imperative to pay a flying visit to Corinth in person from Ephesus. This was the Painful Visit, during which there took place a peculiarly painful collision with an individual (2.5–7; 7.12).

On returning from Corinth, Paul wrote the Corinthians, with many tears, a Severe Letter (2.4; 7.8). This letter has probably been lost. Paul also sent Titus to Corinth. Indeed, Titus may have carried the Severe Letter with him, but Paul's statement in 7.15 to the effect that the Corinthians met Titus *in fear and trembling* suggests that the letter may have preceded his arrival.

At about this time, while he was in Asia, and therefore probably in Ephesus, Paul's life was endangered (1.8f.).

Now half-regretting having written the Severe Letter, Paul moved to Troas, expecting to meet Titus there (2.12). Originally he had planned to travel via Corinth to Macedonia and, on his return, to pass through Corinth again on his way to Jerusalem (1.15f.), but the developments in Corinth induced him to abandon this plan (1.23–2.2).

On not finding Titus in Troas, Paul travelled on to Macedonia,

[11] For valuable chronological overviews of Paul's dealings with the Corinthians see Furnish, pp. 54f.; cf. pp.150f.; Martin, p. xlvi.

where he eventually did meet Titus, who brought the welcome news that the Corinthians had had a change of heart, had renewed their commitment to Paul and had taken disciplinary action against the individual offender. Thus the co-ordinated actions of writing a letter and sending Titus had had their effect. To which of the two the greater share of the success belongs, the blazing letter of protest or the mediating intervention of Titus, is an open question, but no doubt the personal integrity and diplomatic skill of Titus deserve to be rated very highly.

Paul then wrote chapters 1–9 of II Corinthians, as a sign of reconciliation and with the request that the Corinthians should now complete the organization of their contribution to the collection for the saints in Jerusalem. He also sent Titus, along with two trusted brethren, back to Corinth to supervise the raising of the Corinthian contribution (8.6, 16–24). Indeed, Titus could well have been the bearer of chapters 1–9.

We learn from 8.6 that Titus had enabled the Corinthians to make a beginning with the raising of their contribution. This can hardly mean that he had introduced the project to them, since I Cor. 16.1–4 implies that Paul had secured their support for it before writing I Corinthians. However, the Corinthians had obviously failed to follow through their original commitment, so that it fell to Titus to revive their interest. It is natural to assume that he did this during the visit referred to in 7.6–16. II Cor. 7.14 seems to imply that the visit from which Titus had just returned was his first.

Some scholars question whether Paul would have been likely to compound the difficulties Titus was facing on that occasion by giving him the additional responsibility of reviving their interest in the collection,[12] but it is perfectly conceivable that the initiative was taken by Titus himself. He had, after all, been present at the Jerusalem conference, at which Paul had acceded to the request of the 'pillar apostles' to prosecute the collection (Gal. 2.1, 10). Once it had become clear that the Corinthians were prepared to acknowledge Paul's authority once again, it would have been natural for Titus to remind them of their commitment to the collection.

The outcome of the visit of Titus and his two companions which is foreshadowed in 8.6, 16–24 was evidently not as successful as the outcome of his earlier visit referred to in 7.6–16. Indeed, the visit gave rise to the complaint that Paul was exploiting the Corinthians

---

[12] See Plummer, p. 364; Martin, p. 447. The argument of this paragraph is indebted to Murphy-O'Connor, 'The Date of II Corinthians 10–13.'

through his emissaries (12.17f.). Titus and his companions must have brought back the report that the Corinthian church was now dominated by intruding apostles, who were attacking Paul's character and apostleship. In great anxiety and distress, Paul then wrote chapters 10–13, refuting the attacks of his opponents and warning the Corinthians of the disciplinary action he would be forced to take, if they had not put their house in order before he paid his next visit, his third.

The impact of the Letter of Four Chapters, together with Paul's subsequent visit, was apparently sufficiently satisfactory to permit Paul to turn his attention soon afterwards to fresh mission fields in the west (Rom. 15.17–29).

Paul's opponents in II Corinthians
In the preceding discussion of the integrity of II Corinthians and the ensuing attempt to reconstruct the likeliest sequence of events, we have referred several times to evidence, mainly in the last four chapters, which points to the presence in Corinth of a group of opponents. The identity of these opponents calls for further discussion.[13]

First, it is no accident that in 11.4 Paul speaks of a *newcomer*, literally, 'one who comes', not 'one who is sent'. The actual expression he has used points to an individual rather than a group, but he seems to see this individual as the ringleader of a group. There is no need, however, to postulate a large group. Three or four itinerant missionaries would have been enough to precipitate a movement against Paul. Unlike Paul, these people have no mandate from Christ to come to Corinth. In Paul's eyes, they are intruders, who have invaded his God-given sphere of service. These charges are elaborated in 10.12–18. Paul believes himself to have been commissioned by Christ to carry the gospel to the Gentiles, and this commission was acknowledged as valid by the leaders of the Jerusalem church, James, Peter and John, when they met with Paul and Barnabas in Jerusalem at the conference referred to in Gal. 2.1–10. In Paul's view, the trouble-makers in Corinth have invaded his mission field, flouting the agreement reached in Jerusalem.

These intruding missionaries boast of their Jewish pedigree as

[13] For fuller accounts see Furnish, pp. 48–54, 532–35; Lang, pp. 12, 357–59; Martin, pp. 336–42, as well as my commentary on 10.7–11; 11.1–6, 21b–27. For a careful consideration of the methodological problems involved in identifying the nature of the opposition to Paul in II Corinthians, see Jerry L. Sumney, *Identifying Paul's Opponents*.

Hebrews, Israelites, Abraham's descendants (11.22). This could mean that they are Palestinian-Jewish Christians, but they could also be Diaspora Jews, formerly loyal to the tradition, who have become Christians. Indeed, the way that they make a special point of calling themselves descendants of Abraham, as well as the special importance that they attach to ecstatic experiences and other extraordinary powers, can be taken as supporting the view that they are Hellenistic-Jewish Christians.[14] They describe themselves as *servants of Christ* (11.23), probably also as *apostles* (11.13; cf. 11.5), and claim for themselves a particularly close relationship to Christ (10.7), possibly partly on the grounds that, unlike Paul, they have been personally acquainted with the earthly Jesus, or at least have been authorized by those who were.

In Paul's eyes, the intruders are preaching another Jesus, another Spirit and another gospel (11.4). In the light of the evidence of II Corinthians as a whole, we may surmise that the nub of Paul's objection to their message is their failure to put Christ crucified at the heart of it.

They rely on letters of recommendation (10.12) and engage in inordinate boasting (10.12–18; 11.12, 16–18, 21). They are freer to do this, since they do not measure themselves, as Paul does, by the standard of God but only by themselves (10.12–15).

As itinerant missionaries, they are accepting material support from the churches and are evidently contending that this practice legitimizes their claim to be servants of Christ (11.7–10, 23). They are probably claiming to be the legitimate heirs of the Twelve, whom Jesus bade accept whatever hospitality was offered them, when he sent them out as missionaries to Israel (Matt. 10.9–15).

It is also their boast that the Spirit is making its presence plain in their ministries in extraordinary ways, particularly through visions (12.1–10) and deeds of power (12.12).

As for their treatment of the community, that is not only patronising but insulting (11.11f., 20).

At the same time, they are conducting a smear campaign against Paul. They are accusing him of not being a spiritual person (10.2); of being feeble and timid in face-to-face encounter (10.1, 10); of being a woefully inadequate speaker (10.10; 11.6); and of failing to demonstrate 'the signs of an apostle' (12.12). They pride themselves, on the other hand, on being strong precisely where Paul appears to be weak – in charismatic gifts, personal presence and rhetorical virtuosity.

---

[14] See Furnish, pp. 534f.

Paul's unwillingness to accept material support shows that he is not a proper apostle, while his acceptance of support from the Macedonians, coupled with his refusal of it from the Corinthians, shows how little he cares for the Corinthians and how inconsistent he is.

On the basis of these allusions, some scholars have attempted quite elaborate reconstructions of the theology of Paul's opponents. The lack of anything like a consensus among scholars at this point, however, and the diversity of reconstructions that have been proposed should serve as a warning against the danger of outrunning the evidence.[15]

Nevertheless, relatively wide support has been given to the thesis of Dieter Georgi in his book, *The Opponents of Paul in Second Corinthians*.

Georgi argues that the opponents were representatives of a missionary movement among Hellenistic-Jewish Christians which was in turn influenced by the parent movement among Hellenistic-Jews. Central to both missions was the idea of the 'divine man', who participates in the power of God. In the Jewish wing of the movement, Moses was seen as the 'divine man' *par excellence*, whereas the Christians venerated both Moses and Jesus and also understood themselves in the same terms.

However, Georgi's view that they thought of Jesus pre-eminently as a 'divine man' derives from a particular interpretation of II Corinthians 3 and is not otherwise attested in the text. Moreover, some recent writers have questioned whether *theios anēr* ever achieved the status of a technical term or fixed concept in the ancient world. Holladay has shown that the term is rather fluid and denotes sometimes a 'divine man', sometimes an 'inspired man', sometimes a 'man related to God' and sometimes an 'extraordinary man'.[16] In other respects, however, Georgi's picture of Paul's opponents has much to commend it.

In our view, the opponents are best regarded as Hellenistic-Jewish Christians. They are itinerant preachers who boast of a special endowment with the Spirit and a special relationship to Christ, rely upon letters of recommendation and accept payment from the community, appealing to the primitive apostolic right to such payment. They have quite possibly come to Corinth from the Syrian area

[15] Cf. Furnish's cautions to this effect, p. 500.
[16] See C. H. Holladay, *Theios Aner in Hellenistic-Judaism*, esp. pp. 237–41; cf. J. D. Kingsbury, 'The "Divine Man" as the Key to Mark's Christology – The End of an Era?' *Interpretation* 35, 1981, pp. 248f.

of Peter's mission field, perhaps as 'apostles' from Antioch, in order to oppose Paul as an illegitimate apostle, and are contrasting him with Peter, whose apostolic authority is unquestioned.[17]

So far we have cited evidence only from the Letter of Four Chapters, for it is only in chapters 10–13 that explicit allusions to intruding apostles are to be found. However, there are significant correspondences between the profile of the opponents that can be drawn from the last four chapters and some polemical statements of Paul's in the first nine.

(i) In 2.17 Paul speaks of many who adulterate the word of God for profit (cf. 11. 4).

(ii) In 3.1 he implies that there are some people who, unlike himself, need letters of introduction to the Corinthians or from them (cf. 10.12, 18; 12.11).

(iii) In 5.12 Paul refers to those whose pride is all in outward show and not in inward worth (literally, 'who boast in appearance and not in heart'; cf. 11.18).

The cumulative effect of these correspondences suggests that the opponents had already begun to infiltrate the community by the time Paul wrote chapters 1–9. Therefore, when Paul declares in 4.5 that *it is not ourselves that we proclaim* but *Christ Jesus as Lord, and ourselves as your servants for Jesus's sake*, it is likely that the statement has a polemical edge and that he is alluding to opponents who are guilty precisely of proclaiming themselves.

Besides, the elaborate demonstration in chapter 3 of the superiority of the new order inaugurated by Christ over the order established by Moses is clear evidence that, in contrast to the situation he faced in I Corinthians, Paul is now confronted by Christians from a Jewish background, and aggressively Jewish-Christian at that.

However, if the opponents were already on the scene, they clearly did not yet pose the threat that Paul faced in chapters 10–13.

It is doubtful whether the opponents would have gained such a hold in Corinth so quickly, had there not been a group of people in the church who found their concept of the gospel and Christian ministry more congenial than Paul's. In our earlier volume we noted that Paul is continually contending in I Corinthians against proponents of an over-realized eschatology, that is, against people who supposed that God had given them all he had to give.[18] There are features of the portrait of Paul's opponents that emerges from

---

[17] On the likelihood that the 'sham apostles' of 11.13 are to be identified with the 'super-apostles' of 11.5 and 12.11 see our commentary on 11.5.
[18] See esp. pp. xxv–xxvii.

chapters 10–13 that strongly suggest the same error, particularly their claims to impressive personal presence, rhetorical virtuosity and the ability to perform signs and wonders (10.10; 12.12). If so, we can readily imagine the enthusiastic party in Corinth providing a base for the intruders.[19]

Besides, critics of Paul were already vocal in Corinth, even before the arrival of the new opponents, and, in part, their criticisms seem to have focused on the same aspects of Paul's ministry as the criticisms of the newcomers: his refusal to accept maintenance (I Cor. 9; cf. II Cor. 11.7–12; 12.13) and his lack of oratorical skill (I Cor. 2.1; cf. II Cor. 10.10; 11.6). What is more, attempts had already been made to compare Paul with other missionaries, particularly Apollos (I Cor. 3–4; cf. II Cor. 12.12; 13.3). Thus the intruders seem to have owed their success not only to what they had brought with them but also to what they found already in Corinth. No doubt they also accommodated themselves skilfully at this or that point to Corinthian expectations.

Light on the man and his message
In what remains of the Introduction we shall concentrate on the light that II Corinthians throws on Paul, the man, and his message.

The man
II Corinthians is often described as the most personal of all Paul's letters. It contains more biographical details about Paul's life than any other letter. For all their unscrupulous tactics, the sham apostles did serve the future unwittingly, in that they drove Paul into describing his apostolic career with a detail unmatched anywhere else, and into revealing secrets about his mystical experiences which would otherwise have remained hidden from us. He speaks of these things with the utmost reluctance. He keeps apologizing for what he is saying as boastful, foolish talk. Yet most of the hardships which he goes on to rehearse are not known to us from any other source. Acts records only a fraction of these, and it gives no hint of the profound mystical experiences which Paul alludes to in 12.1–10. And all this is torn from Paul's lips almost against his will.

Such passages are uniquely valuable for the light they throw on Paul, the man. What sort of person do they disclose to us?

[19] This is argued at length by J. Murphy-O'Connor in his article, 'Pneumatikoi and Judaizers in II Cor. 2: 14–4: 6,' *AusBR* 34, 1986, pp. 42–58.

There are certainly passages of great tenderness, such as 7.2–4 or 12.14–18. John Knox has observed that Paul is sometimes depicted as 'a fanatic incapable of feeling or eliciting affection.'[20] These passages show us what a travesty such a picture is, for in them Paul pours out his feelings towards the Corinthians, feelings of tender solicitude, pride and joy.

Nor is there any reason to doubt the sincerity of his declaration in 12.15 that he would gladly spend all he has for the sake of the Corinthians, and spend himself to the limit for their good. He is ready to do that, however meagre their response. But he would not be human, if he did not yearn for an answering love. James Denney calls this 'one of the most movingly tender passages in the whole Bible.'[21] Frances Young and David Ford also observe that it is striking how much of the language of II Corinthians expresses love, affection, intimacy and warmth, often incidentally.[22]

The letter ends with a blessing upon all the members of the Corinthian community, with all their faults, without exception (13.13).

At the same time, this letter reveals a side of Paul's personality which many find less attractive. C. H. Dodd has written concerning the Paul disclosed in II Corinthians that 'there is a touchiness about his dignity which sorts ill with the selflessness of one who has died with Christ.'[23]

In the same vein John Knox observes that 'at times Paul's indignation seems to get entirely out of hand, and he expresses himself in harsh, even brutal, terms, which he must later have regretted'; and again that he sometimes uses language which is 'about as harsh as could be imagined and comes strangely from a saint!'[24]

I do not consider either of these verdicts intemperate or unfair. On the other hand, I believe that the intense vulnerability which Paul shows in this letter is the obverse side of an intense love. I also believe that Paul was fundamentally right in his belief that in the struggle over the recognition of his apostolate more was at stake than his own personal honour. What he was fighting for was nothing less than the truth of the gospel and the salvation of his converts.

Moreover, while there are passages in which Paul seems to be primarily concerned to vindicate his apostolic status, we would be

---

[20] John Knox, *Chapters in a Life of Paul* , p. 95.
[21] James Denney, *The Second Epistle to the Corinthians* , p. 363.
[22] Frances Young and David Ford, *Meaning and Truth in 2 Corinthians*, p. 197.
[23] C. H. Dodd, *New Testament Studies*, p. 79.
[24] Knox, *Chapters*, pp. 97, 99.

doing him less than justice, were we not also to take into account his avowal in 13.7 and 9 that if only the life of the community is repaired, he will gladly renounce the use of his apostolic authority to discipline the Corinthians, even if this means that the reputation of being weak still clings to him. What matters is that they should do what is right, not that he should refute any criticisms that have been made of his apostolic style.[25]

The message

In the Introduction to our earlier volume in this series, we have set side by side what Paul perceives to be the position of the dominant party in Corinth on the various issues that have emerged in their common life and what he himself offers as a truer perception of the meaning of the gospel for belief and conduct. All this can be presumed to be part of the background of II Corinthians also. The two separate writings which make up II Corinthians represent two further attempts on Paul's part to build on what is in order in Corinth and to repair the damage done by the intruding apostles, who, as we have seen, had called Paul's character and apostleship into question. In the course of this renewed and even more intensive engagement with the situation in Corinth, Paul has to struggle harder than ever with the question, What are the marks of authentic ministry? together with the related question, What are the marks of genuine discipleship? In struggling with these questions, he is able to state even more clearly than in I Corinthians some basic convictions which are implicit in the earlier letter.[26] It is on these that we shall focus in the rest of this Introduction.

[25] A thorough-going criticism of Paul's apostolic style is offered by Graham Shaw in *The Cost of Authority*. Shaw argues that, for all his claims to preach a gospel of freedom and reconciliation, Paul is in fact constantly trying to dominate the churches to which he writes and manipulating his converts to support him against rivals. Shaw's work serves as a salutary reminder that Paul was no plaster-saint, but he is so sceptical of beliefs which were foundational to Paul, such as his belief in the resurrection of Christ or the resurrection of believers (pp. 95f., 167), that an adequate response would call for a discussion far too lengthy to be accommodated within the present commentary. For judicious critiques see the reviews by Frances Young in *Theology* LXXXVI, 1983, pp. 378–82; and I. H. Marshall in *ExpT* 94, 1982/83, p. 278.
[26] Klauck observes that 'long sections of II Corinthians belong to the theological high-points of the New Testament'; and that 'only in the Johannine literature do we find elsewhere texts of comparable density and reflective power' (*2 Kor.*, p. 5, my translation). Excellent general accounts of the thought of II Corinthians can be found in Young and Ford, *Meaning and Truth* and in Jerome Murphy-O'Connor, *The Theology of the Second Letter to the Corinthians*.

The need for congruence

At several points in the first volume, we stressed the prominence of the theme of the inescapable necessity for congruence between the messenger and the message which he or she proclaims. The conduct of Christian preachers must square with the truth of the message they bear. The style and spirit in which the gospel is proclaimed must square with its content (I Cor. 2.1–5; I Cor. 6.1–11; I Cor 9.12b–18). In II Corinthians this theme comes more and more to the forefront.

Early in the letter, Paul tries to deal with the charges of fickleness and duplicity which had been levelled at him because of his depar-ture from an earlier plan to visit Corinth in person. He had been accused of saying one thing and doing another, of saying one thing and meaning another. On the contrary, he replies, I have acted with singleheartedness and sincerity. There has been no inconsistency between my words and my deeds, between my message and my manner of life (see II Cor. 1.12–14). If I did change my travel plans, that is because I am constantly subject to the guidance of the Spirit (1.15–22; cf. 13. 5–10).

What Paul is particularly concerned to emphasize in II Corinthians is that apostolic existence is stamped with the pattern of Christ's dying and rising. As we put it at the end of our discussion of 10.12–18, 'True evangelists direct their hearers to Christ crucified and risen, and do so not only by their words but also by the example of their own lives, in which that dying and rising are re-enacted.'

That is why, when Paul reluctantly exercises the right to have his little boast in 11.16 and goes on in 11.23–33 to list the credentials which authenticate his claim to be a servant of Christ, he speaks not of the successes with which his work has been crowned by God but rather of his hardships, his sufferings and deprivations. He is facing opponents who boast of their impressive presence and rhetorical skills, their signs and wonders (10.10; 11.5f.; 12.11f.). For them, it seems, apostleship was authenticated by acts of power and glory. It is also clear that they took delight in pointing out what a poor figure Paul cut with his unimpressive presence and want of rhetorical skill, and we can imagine how they must have made capital out of the sufferings he had undergone. How could anyone who had taken such a battering be an authentic apostle? Paul's contention is that his sufferings are, on the contrary, signs of the reality of his identifica-tion with Christ crucified, and therefore signs that his life is authenti-cally apostolic. They are not a contradiction of his apostleship, as his enemies maintain; they are its most compelling vindication.

Authentic apostleship is inescapably cruciform (4.16–18; 6.3–10; 12.11–13; cf. Gal. 6.17).

Paul and his associates are all their life 'being handed over to death', continually exposed to the danger of dying, their vital energy continually being sapped (4.11), but the deepest truth about these trials of theirs is that there is in them a continual re-enactment of the death that Jesus died (4.10; cf. 1.5–7).

At the same time, this continual dying is to the end *that the life of Jesus may be revealed in this mortal body of ours* (4.10; cf. 6.8–10). There is thus a re-enactment in their lives of the rising of Jesus, as well as of his dying, not merely something analogous to his dying and rising but a sharing in the very risen life of the Crucified, and an anticipation of their participation in his final triumph over death. Yet again and again, as we point out in our comments on 4. 11, it is on the necessity for the apostle to be continually a-dying that Paul's stress falls, no doubt because of the predilection of the Corinthians for emphasizing the resurrection at the expense of the cross, a predilection which his opponents evidently shared.

Thus in 13.4 it is only in a carefully qualified sense that Paul speaks of Christ being powerfully present among believers or of himself exercising Christ's power towards them. Christ's way was marked by both weakness and power, because it was a way of cross and resurrection, which belong inescapably together. So it is for Paul also. His way too is marked by both weakness and power, dying and rising. Indeed, weakness, dying with Christ, is the dominant note, not power, living with Christ. Apostles cannot enjoy already unbroken resurrection glory but experience the divine power in the midst of suffering – a truth which is demonstrated with especial clarity in the life of Paul himself.

What is true of apostolic existence is also true of Christian existence in general. In the opening thanksgiving, Paul goes out of his way to emphasize the essential similarity between his own experience and that of his readers. He does not draw an absolute distinction between himself and the ordinary Christian who is not an apostle. Every Christian is called to die with Christ, in order to be raised with him. Nevertheless, in those who are apostles the distinctive stamp of the Christian condition can be seen with especial clarity.[27] Their loyalty is likely to prove more costly, since it is on them that the full brunt of the world's opposition to the gospel falls. They are more likely to have to literally surrender their lives for the sake of

---

[27] Cf. Ernst Käsemann, 'Die Legitimität des Apostels,' *ZNW* 41, 1942, p. 56.

the gospel, as Paul himself was to surrender his (cf. our comments on 4.7–15; 6.3–10).

It is as urgent today as it ever was that the church should heed Paul's insistence, throughout II Corinthians, on the inescapable obligation on all Christians to make their conduct square with the truth of the gospel and, more specifically, on the inescapably cruciform nature of an authentic Christian life.

There is in II Corinthians a powerful anticipation of Bonhoeffer's lifelong insistence on the costliness of discipleship. Grace, he was never tired of saying, seeks to shape the total pattern of the believer's life. It seeks to penetrate, change and rule. It demands obedience, and if a person who has received grace is not led to obedience, then they have indeed received it in vain (cf. II Cor. 6.1). His most serious charge against the Protestant churches of his day was that they had depreciated costly grace – costly, because it cost God so dear – to cheap grace. The word which is our only comfort in life and death had degenerated to a cheap bargain.[28]

The same note that was sounded a generation ago by Bonhoeffer is being sounded today by Christians whose witness to the gospel in word and deed commands the deepest respect. I think, for example, of the suggestive title of Paul Oestreicher's book, *The Double Cross*, which encapsulates so exactly the emphasis of Paul's of which I have been speaking, the necessity for the dying of Christ to be re-enacted in the believer.

I think too of a statement by Sheila Cassidy in her first book, *Audacity to Believe*, that 'the message of the gospel only has validity, if it is lived by the bearer' – a simple statement, but one that becomes acutely poignant, when it is read in the light of her own experience as a doctor in Chile, a victim of torture at the hands of the Chilean government, and the medical director of a hospice in Plymouth.[29] If the gospel is to be made credible to men and women of our time who are not believers, it will be by witness of that quality in word and deed.

Beautiful people?

To say, however, that there must be congruence between the words and the deeds of the bearers of the gospel is not to imply that Christian ministers must be 'beautiful people'. That would be to adopt a position close to that of Paul's opponents. This brings us to the second of Paul's central convictions which is stated with

[28] Dietrich Bonhoeffer, *The Cost of Discipleship* , pp. 41–47.
[29] Sheila Cassidy, *Audacity to Believe*, p. 115.

particular clarity in II Corinthians, under the pressure of controversy.

As we noted in our earlier discussion of Paul's opponents, there is reason to believe that these men boasted of their impressive presence and rhetorical expertise, as well as of their charismatic gifts and their visions and revelations, and drew damaging contrasts between themselves and Paul. The sneer of theirs which is quoted in 10.10 implies that they were able to point to a disproportion between Paul's message and his person which seemed ludicrous. They were able to claim, with some plausibility, that, while his letters were weighty and forcible, he cut a sorry figure in person and was laughably ineffective as an orator. And if, as seems quite likely, the 'thorn in the flesh' to which Paul refers in 12.7f. was some humiliating physical handicap, no doubt they made capital out of that too.

Behind all these gibes of theirs, one can detect a consistent assumption: the Christian, *a fortiori* the apostle, should be a rounded person, an accomplished person, a successful person. But in their eyes Paul looks more like a beaten and rejected person, far from being a persuasive advertisement for his message or his ministry.

'He is an embarrassment to the company of apostles,' we can hear them saying. 'He would need to look more integrated, more complete, more successful, before we could accept him as a genuine apostle.'

Faced with these allegations, Paul is inclined, in his more heated moments, to deny them and to say, in effect, 'You say that I can't talk? Just wait till we meet. Then we'll see who does the talking!' (10.11; 13.1–4). But in his more reflective moments, notably in 4.7–12, he is able to turn the taunt around and make it a means of preaching the gospel.

'Yes, indeed,' he says in effect, 'there is a vast disparity, a ludicrous disproportion, between the message I bear and myself, its bearer. The treasure of the gospel has been entrusted to a mere earthenware jar. But that is just the way it ought to be, the way it is meant to be, so that it might be made unmistakably plain that the power which is released by the preaching of the gospel does not come from us but is God's alone. The glaring disparity between the power of the message and the powerlessness of the messenger serves to protect the truth that "salvation is of the Lord"' (cf. Jonah 2.9, AV).

So Paul is not miraculously freed from the embarrassing limitations of his personality or the defectiveness of his oral communication or 'the thorn in the flesh', whatever that may have been. On the contrary, he is continually finding himself at his wits' end, at the end of his tether, and therefore driven to cast himself utterly on the grace of God, which is most fully seen in weakness, which finds its opportunity in his extremity and has full scope to work, only when his weakness makes him incapable of doing anything (12.9).[30]

The limping messenger

The great German scholar, Schlatter, gave to his commentary on Paul's letters to the Corinthians the simple title, *The Messenger of Jesus* (*Der Bote Jesu*). The Swiss scholar-preacher, Walter Lüthi, who has written a more devotional exposition of II Corinthians, comments on the simplicity of Schlatter's title and then goes on to describe how, while he was writing his own book, which has the equally simple title of *The Apostle*, there kept coming into his mind a picture from an old calendar which used to hang in his home when he was a child. It was a picture of a messenger – limping, with a wooden leg. The title? 'The Limping Messenger'. And Lüthi goes on:

'The natural man prefers to picture a messenger in the way that the ancient Greeks pictured their god, Hermes, with wings on both feet. It is the winged messenger, not the man with the wooden leg, who corresponds to our wishful thinking. But the messenger of Jesus is no winged Hermes. The apostle Paul is more like that limping messenger.'[31]

Lüthi then goes on to compare Paul with other well-known persons who have combined undoubted gifts with embarrassing limitations.

'Thus van Gogh and Rembrandt, for all their failure to live up to bourgeois ideals, are gifted painters; Calvin, with his stomach complaint, is a gifted theologian; Dostoevsky, with his epileptic attacks, is a gifted writer; Kierkegaard, who does not fit properly into any scheme, a gifted thinker; Pestalozzi, whose life was one long chain of breakdowns and failures, a gifted teacher.'[32]

Paul, the apostle of Jesus Christ, limped and stumbled, as he carried his message through the world. Yet, because the message he carried was of one who died on the cross in weakness but lives by the power of God, it reached, and continues to reach, its goal.

---

[30] Klauck (pp. 94f.) observes that 12.9 represents the secret heart of the Letter of Four Chapters.
[31] Walter Lüthi, *Der Apostel*, 1968, pp. 7f., (my translation). This is a passage which I have worked into a sermon included in my book, *Striking Home* , pp. 159f. Lüthi's reference to Hermes with wings on both feet is especially apt, since Paul himself was actually taken to be Hermes in human form, when he visited Lystra, according to Acts 14.12.
[32] Loc. cit.

COMMENTARY

The Letter of Reconciliation
1.1–7.16

1.1–7   *Constantly afflicted, constantly consoled*

1.1f.   Paul begins this letter with a greeting in the customary form, followed by a thanksgiving for the comfort which God has given him, and continues to give him, in every affliction and which has been a blessing not only to himself but also to his readers.

The essential elements of an epistolary address in the Graeco-Roman world were the name of the sender, the addressee and a word of greeting. This letter comes *from Paul, apostle of Christ Jesus by God's will, and our colleague Timothy* (literally, 'Timothy, the brother').

The question of the marks of a true apostle is one of the central questions of this letter, particularly the last four chapters. Except in one or two instances where it implies no more than that someone has been sent by a particular church, the word 'apostle' denotes one who has been called to play a unique foundational role in the church as a whole. In Luke's writings the use of the word is regularly confined to the original inner circle, the Twelve, but Paul does not support that restriction of the term, which was evidently already being advocated by some people in his own time. On the contrary, he is adamant that he himself is every inch an apostle. To be sure, this is not a title which anyone can claim for themselves. It is essential that one should not only have seen the risen Lord but also have been directly commissioned by him. Paul is utterly convinced that in his own case those criteria have been met. Hence his declaration, here as elsewhere (cf. Rom. 1.1; I Cor. 1.1; Gal. 1.1), that he is *apostle of Christ Jesus by God's will.*[1]

With himself Paul associates *our colleague Timothy* (literally, 'Timothy the brother') as a joint sender of the letter. Timothy was

[1] For a fuller discussion not only of this term but of Pauline epistolary greetings in general see my commentary on I Corinthians in this series, pp. 1f.

clearly one of Paul's most trusted assistants (see Phil. 2.19f.; I Thess. 3.2) and had not only worked with Paul in the founding of this church for well over a year (see Acts 18.5; II Cor. 1.19) but also acted as a go-between between Paul and the church after Paul's departure (see I Cor. 4.17; 16.10).

As recipients of the letter Paul names not only *God's church at Corinth* but along with them *all God's people throughout the whole of Achaia*. It is clear that, radiating out from the centre of the mission in Corinth, small house-churches have arisen in the surrounding area, which remain in close contact with the church in the provincial capital. This letter is intended for them too.

Paul concludes his greeting by invoking upon the Corinthians the same two blessings as he craves for the readers of all his letters, viz. grace and peace (cf. Rom. 1.7; I Cor. 1.3; Gal. 1.3; Phil. 1.2; I Thess. 1.1). 'Grace' in Paul carries different accents in different contexts. Thus it denotes the undeserved goodwill of God towards the world, the expression of that goodwill in God's saving acts and the particular blessings and empowerments in which that saving action becomes a reality for the believer. 'Peace' is another way of describing the effect of God's saving activity and denotes wholeness, salvation. This grace and peace flow ultimately *from God our Father* but have been made effective in human experience through *the Lord Jesus Christ*.

1.3f.   Paul now launches into what is, strictly speaking, not a thanksgiving, as is his usual practice, but rather a blessing upon God. No doubt, the particular deliverance about which he is to speak in the following paragraph is already in the forefront of his mind. Hence this deviation from the usual pattern.

In the Greek this blessing extends to the end of v. 4. It is a complex sentence but one which is illuminating in its very complexity. Reduced to its essentials, it consists of a blessing upon God, who *consoles us* (or comforts us) *in all our troubles, so that we in turn may be able to console others in any trouble of theirs* with *the consolation we ourselves receive from God*.

But Paul is not content with this bare outline. To begin with, the name of God cries out for elaboration, and so Paul speaks of *the God and Father of our Lord Jesus Christ, the all-merciful Father* (literally, 'the Father of mercies') and (to quote the NRSV) 'the God of all consolation.' The notion of consolation in affliction is indeed the central theme of the whole paragraph, and Paul seizes every opportunity to introduce an allusion to it. In all, the words 'consolation' and 'console' occur five times within these two verses, and in vv. 5–7 five times more.

Where the RSV has 'the God of all consolation', the REB reads *the God whose consolation never fails us* – a rendering which captures something spelt out in v. 4, viz. that there is no situation whatever in which the divine consolation cannot be known. Beyond that, Paul's expression also suggests that God is the only source of consolation of which this can be said. There is, in other words, no substitute for God in this matter. From God and God alone all adequate and abiding consolation comes.

Something more needs to be said, however, about the connotations of the word that the REB renders by 'consolation'. For one thing, the corresponding Hebrew word had acquired the meaning of messianic deliverance, a meaning clearly reflected, for example, in Luke 2.25 and probably also present to Paul's mind in this passage. What is more, the Greek word group in question is also capable of conveying the sense of exhortation. While the precise accent varies in different contexts, as used in the New Testament these words refer to a more invigorating activity than is suggested by the English words 'consolation' or 'comfort'. The latter rendering goes all the way back to Wiclif. 'Comfort' in modern English is a word that has gone soft, but in Wiclif's day it was closely connected with its root, the Latin *fortis*, which means brave, strong, courageous. That brings us closer to Paul's meaning. Comfort, as he conceives of it, may take the form of deliverance *from* trouble, as in v. 10, where he speaks of rescue from danger, or of deliverance *in* trouble, as in v. 7, where he speaks of empowerment to endure sufferings with fortitude. Either way, it is a 'comfort' that enables a person to stand on their feet and face life with lifted head.

It is therefore not surprising that in this very context the gift of comfort or consolation is accompanied by a challenge. The comfort which God gives to believers in trouble has a further purpose: to enable them the better to comfort others in their troubles. This takes us to the heart of the matter.

As was noted in the Introduction to our commentary on I Corinthians,[2] there is for Paul an inseparable connection between salvation and ethics, between the divine succour and the divine claim. A gift of grace, a *charisma*, is given to each believer not just for the sake of their own personal enrichment but to strengthen them to do a job. Here too Paul knows that he has to share with others what he has

[2] Nigel M. Watson, *I Corinthians*, pp. xxix–xxxii.

known of the God who consoles (cf. v. 6b). He is to make credible, not only by what he says but by what he does and is, good news of the God of all consolation, the God whose blessing can reach men and women in any situation whatever.

The universal efficacy of the consoling power of God is further emphasized by the repetition of the word 'all' in v. 4 (REB: *in all our troubles, in any trouble of theirs*).

1.5 In the preceding verses Paul has stressed the reality of our experience of both suffering and consolation. He now reaffirms that we know both suffering and consolation in abundance, and at the same time shows that both kinds of experience are intimately connected with Christ. Our experience of suffering is a sharing of the sufferings of Christ overflowing into our lives. At the same time our experience of consolation comes *through Christ*.

Two questions call for special consideration. First, what sort of suffering does Paul have in mind? Is he talking about the familiar pains, deprivations and struggles that are the lot of everyone, or about suffering for Christ's sake? Since he speaks in the next paragraph of a distressing experience he has recently undergone in the course of his ministry, it seems that it is primarily suffering for Christ's sake that he has in mind.

But what exactly does he mean by designating such suffering as *Christ's suffering?*

There are references in rabbinic texts to 'the sufferings of the Messiah' which are really references to sufferings to be endured by God's people, not by the Messiah in person. This usage is probably present to Paul's mind here but does not seem to represent the primary meaning.

It is one of Paul's most strongly held convictions, expressed particularly clearly in this letter, that Christian existence is stamped with the pattern of Christ's dying and rising. This is true not only of baptism but of the life of discipleship from start to finish. This conviction finds forceful expression, among other ways, through a whole range of compound words, about forty in fact, which all contain the prefix *syn*, a Greek preposition which means 'with' and in such words is equivalent to 'co- . . .'. Paul uses this range of compound words to describe, at one and the same time, the solidarity of believers with one another and with Christ in his dying and rising (see e.g. Rom. 6.4–6; 8.17; II Cor. 4.10; 6. 8–10; Phil. 3.10f.). In all these expressions the cross and resurrection of Christ are portrayed as events, or perhaps, better, a single event, which is not external to believers, something of which they are simply informed, but rather an event into which they enter and with which they become integrated.

This way of speaking might be taken to mean that believers undergo a dying and rising *analogous* to that of Christ, but Paul seems to have in mind a closer bond than this. We suffer not simply like him but with him, and he suffers with us. And, as we suffer with him, we also experience his consolation and begin to know the power of his risen life.

1.6   In the previous verse Paul has stressed the solidarity between himself, as a representative believer, and Christ. In this verse he stresses the solidarity between himself and his fellow believers. Whatever our lot, he says, the end result is your consolation. *If distress is our lot*, that makes for your consolation and salvation, presumably because in all our troubles we find consolation, which is given to us to be passed on. He then states explicitly what we have just presumed to be implied by the first half of the verse, viz. that *if our lot is consolation*, it is in the interests of your consolation, so that we might give you *strength to face with fortitude the same sufferings we now endure.* We do not know of any special persecution which the church in Corinth had to suffer during these years, but perhaps, as Allo suggests, Paul is referring to the atmosphere of opposition, the conflicts within families, the difficult ethical problems and the petty daily vexations which the practice of Christianity must have given rise to on all sides in a pagan city like Corinth.[3]

1.7   The paragraph ends with an expression of confidence that the hope Paul entertains for the Corinthians is well-founded, since he knows that their sharing in the sufferings of Christian discipleship is matched by their sharing in the consolation.

There is therefore in these last two verses a repeated stress on the essential similarity between Paul's own experience and that of his readers. Profoundly conscious though he is of his special apostolic vocation, he does not draw an absolute distinction between himself and the ordinary Christian who is not an apostle. As Barrett aptly observes, 'The special thing about an apostle is that a common Christian pattern comes in him to a particularly sharp focus.'[4]

[3] Allo, p.10.
[4] Barrett, pp. 62f.

The REB introduces a slightly tentative note into its rendering of this verse by translating the word *hōs*, usually translated by 'as', by 'if' – 'if you share.' There is ample evidence in I Corinthians that the Corinthians were all too prone to over-emphasize the resurrection at the expense of the cross and to think of the Christian life as a sharing here and now in Christ's resurrection glory without also sharing in his suffering, but, as Allo observes, was anything more likely to dissipate the last mistrust – which was the goal of this letter – than to express so warmly in the first lines this confidence of intimate community in pain and joy?[5]

Our only comfort in life and death
1.8–11

1.8f.   Paul has already given a hint that, in praising God as the one *whose consolation never fails us,* he has a recent experience of his own in mind. Now he tells his readers what this was. It had happened in Asia, before he went on to Macedonia, from where he is writing this letter. His allusions to the incident are tantalizingly brief, but it appears that he had been delivered from apparently certain death. As an apostle, Paul expected to face hardships, but this had quite overwhelmed him. It had been a crushing experience, *far too heavy for us to bear.*[6] He had felt in his heart that he had received a death sentence and had despaired of survival.

Throughout this paragraph Paul uses the first person plural, but there is reason to think that he is in fact referring to himself. For a discussion of Paul's various uses of the pronoun 'we', see the detached note at the end of this section.

What was this harrowing experience? There are hints that Paul suffered from a humiliating illness which attacked him from time to time. Many scholars believe, however, that he is alluding to an experience of persecution leading to imprisonment. A good case can be made for the view that Paul was in prison in Ephesus when he

[5] Allo, p. 10. Furnish (p. 121) comments that, while, formally considered, v. 7 is in the indicative mood, 'such Pauline affirmations of confidence . . . are often implicitly hortatory.'

[6] The AV renders, 'We were pressed out of measure.' Underlying the word 'measure' is the Greek word *hyperbolē*, which with its cognates occurs seven times in II Corinthians.

wrote to the Philippians.[7] Some also link this allusion to affliction with Luke's account of the riot at Ephesus in Acts 19. 23–41, but, if there is a connection, then something must have happened which was far more dangerous to Paul's life than Acts allows us to see. However, it is clear from II Cor. 11.16–33 that Acts does not give us anything like a complete record of Paul's life.

Whatever it was, Paul had survived, through what he can only describe as God's providential overruling. He speaks here like a shipwrecked man who has, against all odds, managed to get to shore and is still shivering at the thought of the peril he has just escaped.

Furthermore, he now sees that all this had happened so that he might learn, or rather relearn, a fundamental truth about his relationship with God, *to teach us to place reliance not on ourselves, but on God who raises the dead.* I say 'relearn', because this was essentially what he had discovered about God in his encounter on the Damascus road. He had discovered that he, the proud Pharisee, was in reality deeply estranged from God and yet was being called, as Christ's chosen instrument, to bear his name before the nations. Through the risen Christ God had made himself known to Paul as the one who 'makes godless people right with himself' (Rom. 4.5, Translator's New Testament). Through this recent experience in Asia, God had disclosed himself as *the God who makes the dead live* (Rom. 4.17).

To be sure, this way of speaking about God had long been familiar to Paul from Jewish liturgy, but now it had acquired an altogether new meaning.

I have argued elsewhere that this half-verse expresses as clearly as anything else in Paul's letters the meaning of faith as he understands it. It is the recognition of God as God, as the Creator and Life-Giver, powerful where human beings are weak, living where they are dead. Such faith is open-eyed towards human impotence, barrenness and sinfulness but also reckons with the reality of God, whose possibilities begin where human possibilities end, and rests its hope in God alone.[8]

1.10 Paul now states explicitly what has been implied by v. 9b, viz. that God delivered him from this mortal peril, and then moves into

---

[7] For a full statement of the case see Furnish, p. 123.

[8] See Nigel M. Watson, '. . . To make us rely not on ourselves but on God who raises the dead,' *Die Mitte des Neuen Testaments* (*Festschrift* for Eduard Schweizer) ed. Ulrich Luz and Hans Weder, pp. 384–98.

an expression of the hope that the God who has proved able to deliver him from such a desperate situation will continue to deliver him from any further perils that may befall him. As so often in the Bible, a confident hope for the future rests on what one has already experienced of the goodness of God.[9] It is not that Paul is counting on continual deliverance from physical death, whatever may happen. What he is sure of is that in every situation God's grace will prove to be all he needs (cf. II Cor. 12.9).

1.11 However, such a happy outcome also calls for the prayerful support of his friends, which he now implicitly requests, in a somewhat convoluted sentence. We might expect this request to lead into a description of Paul's deliverance from further, as yet unknown, perils. Instead, we have a picture of a veritable chorus of thanksgiving rising up to God for his gracious favour to Paul. The second half of the verse is overloaded, but the main idea seems clear: Paul is asking for their prayers; with many praying for him, God will surely bestow a gracious favour on Paul, and this will lead in turn to many prayers of thanksgiving being offered.

PAUL'S USE OF THE PRONOUN 'WE'

A striking stylistic feature of II Corinthians is the frequency with which Paul uses the pronoun 'we'. Four different uses can be distinguished:

(i) The common Christian 'we', found in statements which are true of all Christians. Examples are 3.18 and 5.10.

(ii) The missionary 'we'. Here Paul is speaking of himself and his closest fellow-workers. A clear example is 1.19.

(iii) The apostolic 'we', found in statements which are true of the circle of genuine apostles, among whom Paul counts himself. This is found in 5.18 and 20.

(iv) The authorial 'we', which refers exclusively to Paul's own person. 1.8ff seems to be an example of this use, as do 5.11 and 10.2. An authorial 'we' is common in contemporary Greek literature, where it is understood as an expression of reserve and modesty, but Paul's use of the pronoun to refer to himself seems to be due not so much to modesty as to the desire to emphasize the general validity of the things he is saying about himself. His own

[9] Cf. C. F. D. Moule, *The Meaning of Hope* , pp. 5–15, 26–38.

life is a representative existence, exhibiting characteristics which constitute what is genuinely apostolic and Christian.[10]

As we preach, we act; what we say we mean
1.12–14

Paul is now ready to address the concerns that have occasioned this letter. Between himself and the church in Corinth there has been, as we are soon to learn, a deep estrangement. Relationships have now been largely restored, thanks to the 'severe letter' and the visit of Titus, but there are still some causes of friction that need to be dealt with. Paul, it appears, has been the target of criticism in Corinth for departing from an earlier plan to visit Corinth in person, and has been accused not only of inconsistency and unreliability but of dishonesty.

1.12   As he recalls the way he has conducted himself towards others (literally, 'in the world') and particularly towards the Corinthians, Paul is aware of nothing for which he need apologize. He can claim, with genuine pride, that he has acted 'with singleheartedness and sincerity in God's sight,' to quote Knox's rendering. The word here translated 'singleheartedness' implies straightforwardness, frankness, openness.

Nor has his conduct been governed by *worldly wisdom* (literally, 'fleshly wisdom'). Similar expressions are found in I Corinthians (see 1.20f.; 2.5f.; 3.19). In these earlier passages 'wisdom' refers now to a technique of persuasion, now to a philosophy of life. The first meaning fits the present context better. Paul has not resorted to any oratorical sleight of hand but has simply relied on *the grace of God.*

This is indeed the main thrust of the opening chapters of I Corinthians, viz. that Paul's message is one of salvation by the grace of God, not by human wisdom. What he is now maintaining is that there has been no inconsistency between that message and his behaviour towards his converts. This is one of the central themes of this letter, the inescapable necessity for consistency between a

[10] Cf. Klauck, pp. 12f.; M. Carrez, 'Le "nous" en 2 Corinthiens,' *NTS* 26, 1979/80, pp. 474–86.

believer's words and their deeds and, *a fortiori*, between the words
and deeds of an apostle. Paul is being accused of inconsistency. His
contention is that there has been complete consistency between his
words and his deeds, between his message and his manner of life (cf.
also I Cor. 2.1–5).

1.13a   Nor do Paul's letters to the Corinthians carry any double
meaning. There is no need to read between the lines to get at his real
intent. There is nothing in his letters to them but what they can read
and understand.

1.13bf.   Paul now moves from the thought of them understanding
the intent of his letters to that of them understanding, and appreciat-
ing, the worth of his own person. He himself has the firm confidence
that *on the day of our Lord Jesus*, who, as he says in I Cor. 4.5, *will bring
to light what darkness hides and disclose our inward motives*, he will
have reason to be proud of the Corinthians, his children in the Lord
(cf. I Cor. 4.14f.). Do the Corinthians entertain a similar confidence
about Paul himself? In part, but only in part. It is Paul's hope that
whatever has come between them may be removed, so that they will
look forward to being as proud of Paul himself, their father in Christ,
as he expects to be proud of them.

Twice within these verses, in v. 12 and again in v. 14, Paul uses
words for pride or 'boasting', and in a positive way. Words of this
family are particularly common in II Corinthians, occurring, in all,
twenty-eight times. There is a false 'boasting', which Paul condemns, a reliance upon oneself instead of upon God (see e.g. Rom.
2.17, 23; 3.27; I Cor. 1.29; 3.21). Yet there is also a pride which
believers may rightly take in their own achievements, both now and
at the last day, so long as they remember that they are not their *own*
achievements but the achievements of the Holy Spirit working
through them.[11]

We do not need to read between the lines of what Paul has written
here to see that he is responding to criticism. The vigour of his
protestations in v. 12, together with the denial in v. 13, show that
he has been accused of duplicity, of saying one thing and doing
another, of saying one thing and meaning another. He himself
admits in v. 14 that the Corinthians do not fully appreciate his worth.

[11] Fee (p. 84) has a valuable discussion of 'boasting' in Paul. Barrett (p. 72) has a valuable
treatment of Paul's use of 'flesh' and 'grace'.

God's word is faithful, and so is ours
1.15–22

Having asserted the purity of his motives, Paul now turns to a specific criticism which has been levelled at him, viz. that he had departed from his stated plans for visiting Corinth. The details of what had happened gradually unfold as the letter is read, but, as Barrett observes, 'It is far from easy to disentangle from Paul's words in this paragraph exactly what he planned to do, failed to do, and in the end did.'[12]

1.15f. Confident that the Corinthians were gaining a deepening appreciation of his integrity, Paul had planned to give them *the benefit of a double visit*, by spending some time with them both on his way to Macedonia and on his way back. They could then have sent him on his way to Judaea. The Greek word here translated *sent on my way* is used virtually as a technical term in the New Testament for providing a person with the food, money and companions necessary to ensure their safe arrival at their destination.[13] The main purpose of this proposed journey to Judaea was to hand over the offering collected by Gentile churches for the church in Jerusalem.[14]

1.17 Such had been Paul's intention, but he had changed his mind and was now, apparently, being accused of being fickle and unreliable. It appears indeed that since writing I Corinthians he had changed his plans twice, for the plan outlined in I Cor. 16.1–9 is for him to travel from Ephesus to Macedonia, then to Corinth, and then to proceed to Jerusalem. It also seems likely that the plan to pay two visits was an outcome of the 'painful visit' referred to in II Cor. 2.1–2, and that he had later decided to send them a letter (the 'severe letter' referred to in II Cor. 2.4) instead. Titus has evidently just brought the news that this further change of plan has given rise to the criticism that he is acting irresponsibly.[15] Paul's main concern in the present paragraph is to refute this criticism. He clearly considers it vital that he should do so, since what is at stake is his credibility as an apostle.

[12] Barrett, p. 74.
[13] Cf. my notes in my earlier commentary in this series on I Cor. 16.6.
[14] Cf. the notes in my earlier commentary on I Cor. 16.1–4; also the discussion later in this volume of chapters 8 and 9.
[15] For a careful reconstruction of the most likely sequence of Paul's visits and letters to Corinth see Furnish, pp. 143f.

In framing his plans, he had not acted *as a worldly man might*. The Greek phrase which is rendered in this way by the REB literally runs 'according to the flesh'. This is a clear example of the pejorative use of the word 'flesh'.[16]

The final clause of the verse is naturally taken as clarifying this reference and thus as containing a fuller description of the 'worldly' conduct of which Paul has been accused. The REB implies that this worldly conduct consists of saying *first 'Yes, yes,' and then 'No, no.'* This is the way in which the verse has been commonly understood, but it involves the insertion of the words 'first . . . and then', which are not in the Greek text. Some versions insert the words 'at the same time'.

This interpretation also conflicts with Paul's admission in 1.23 that he did change his mind.

On these and other grounds, I prefer the interpretation proposed by Frances Young, who translates v. 17b as follows, 'Or do I make plans at the human level, so that yes being yes and no being no rests in my hands?'[17] This is the way in which the clause was understood by both Chrysostom and Theodoret.

The point of the clause could now be stated as follows:

When I make my plans, I do not act as a worldly person might, who leaves God right out of it. On the contrary, I am subject to the Spirit's direction. In other words, Paul is admitting that he did change his mind but implying that his earlier promise had been overruled by God.

1.18f. These verses can now be integrated into the argument, instead of being treated as a digression, as they commonly are. They can be understood as Paul's way of anticipating an objection to what he has just said that could be stated as follows:

'If your Yes can turn into a No, that erodes our confidence in the message that you and your colleagues have preached to us. How can we be sure that that will remain constant?'

'On the contrary,' Paul declares, 'As surely as God is faithful, so surely is *what we tell you not a mixture of Yes and No.*' A more literal rendering would run, '. . . our word to you is not Yes and No.' 'Our word' here, as v. 19 makes clear, is not Paul's promise to come to Corinth but the word of the gospel. And that word is *always Yes.*

---

[16] Cf. the notes in my earlier commentary on I Cor. 1.26; 3.1–4; and 5.5.
[17] Frances Young, 'Note on II Corinthians 1.17b,' *JTS* 37, 1986, p. 415; cf. Young and Ford, *Meaning and Truth*, pp. 101–03.

What exactly does Paul mean by that? That God has revealed himself to be constant, faithful? No doubt, but probably more as well. If God's word in Christ to humanity is Yes, that surely implies that he affirms humanity, that he commits himself to humanity, that he makes the lost cause of humanity his own cause.

What is more, this Yes which God utters in Christ is an enduring Yes. There is in the Greek a change of tense from the aorist to the perfect, indicated in the REB by the change from 'was' to 'is always'. God's affirmation of humanity is something that is continually being re-enacted, every time a believer finds his or her own life being renewed by the Holy Spirit.

But how does this truth about God as revealed in the gospel refute the charge that Paul has been fickle in his conduct? The gospel speaks of the faithfulness of God, God's commitment to the creation. True, but does that guarantee the faithfulness and commitment of the bearers of the gospel, like Paul? Paul's argument gains in force, if we can assume that he is already making implicitly the claim, which he will make more and more forcefully later in the letter, that his own character and conduct are congruent with the message he preaches. He and his colleagues had faithfully transmitted the gospel of God's faithfulness, and therefore he deserved to be trusted to have acted with integrity in the matter of his travel plans. The appeal to God's faithfulness therefore at the beginning of v. 18a is no mere formality. This is indeed the central theme of the whole paragraph.

1.20 The thought that God's word to humanity in Jesus Christ is simply Yes now catches Paul's imagination, and he develops it further, while his concern to justify his own actions recedes somewhat. Christ is God's Yes to humanity, in that he is the Yes that fulfils all of God's promises.

The Yes of God pronounced in Christ evokes the Yes of faith, and Paul now turns to the expression of that Yes by the believing community in worship, their affirmation of 'Amen', which gives *glory to God*, recognizing God as God. In the Old Testament 'Amen' often amounts to 'Yes', but a 'Yes' which recognizes the validity of what has been said, with all that that implies for the speaker. To say 'Amen' in response to a command is to bind oneself to carrying it out. Allo describes it as a formula of 'full adhesion.'[18] To say 'Amen' to God's Yes to humanity in Christ likewise implies commitment.

Not all translations bring out as clearly as they might Paul's point

[18] Allo, p. 28.

that such a response is both 'through him', that is, through Christ, and 'through us', in other words, *both* our own response *and* Christ's work in us (cf. Phil. 2.12f., where a similar balance is maintained).

1.21   The thought that even our response to God is Christ's work in us now leads Paul on to emphasize that our confidence of attaining salvation rests in God alone. If Paul and his readers find themselves belonging to Christ, as they do, *it is all God's doing*. It is he who has *guaranteed* them *as his and anointed* them. In the word translated by the REB 'guaranteed as his' there is an echo of the word 'Amen' in the preceding verse, which comes from a Hebrew root which means firm or steadfast. There are examples in the papyri of the use of Paul's word here to refer to a guarantee given by a vendor that a sale will be carried out. F. F. Bruce offers the translation, 'It is God who gives us a firm standing in Christ.'[19]

In adding that it is Christ who has *anointed* us, Paul is echoing the word 'Christ' in the previous phrase, since 'Christ' literally means 'the anointed one'.

1.22   Paul now introduces two further images, those of a seal and a down payment or first instalment, to reinforce the point that we may be confident of salvation because our confidence is in God. He never deviates from the conviction, which he affirms so repeatedly in I Corinthians, that Christians are still on the way, they have not yet arrived. Nevertheless, God *has* already *given the Spirit to dwell in our hearts*. By so doing, he *has set his seal upon us*. In commercial usage, a seal served as a mark of ownership. It also served as proof that this document had not been opened or that these goods had not been tampered with and were therefore 'the genuine article.' In the same way, the 'seal' of the Spirit certifies that this person belongs to God and represents God's handiwork; in other words, to adapt one of Luther's favourite sayings, that God has taken care of their salvation.

The Spirit therefore is *a pledge of what is to come*. The actual word Paul has used here, *arrabōn*, literally means a down payment or first instalment. It is used in the same way in II Cor. 5. 5 and Eph. 1.13f. In modern Greek an almost identical word, *arrabōna*, means an engagement ring.[20] In Rom. 8.23 Paul uses the image of firstfruits to express the same idea. The gift of the Spirit does not mean that we enjoy

---

[19] F. F. Bruce, *An Expanded Paraphrase of the Epistles of Paul*, p. 127.
[20] William Barclay cites from Moulton and Milligan's *Vocabulary of the Greek Testament* some interesting examples of the use of the word in papyri. See his *New Testament Wordbook*, pp. 24f.

already the consummation of salvation. It is but a first instalment, but an instalment that is a pledge of what is to come.

In referring to our anointing and sealing and the gift of the Spirit, Paul uses three participles, all in the past tense. It is very likely that at this point he has baptism particularly in mind. Yet in the paragraph as a whole his vision embraces the past, the present and the future. God has anointed us, set his seal upon us and given us the Spirit. He continues to maintain our firm standing in Christ. And in the gift of the Spirit we have a first instalment and guarantee of full salvation.

Your pain is my pain, your joy my joy
1.23–2.4

1.23   Paul now addresses more directly the criticism that he had shown himself to be fickle by changing his travel plans. He calls upon God to witness that his reason for not coming to Corinth as promised had been not timidity or lack of affection but consideration for their feelings. To anticipate what he says in 2.1, he had been certain that a visit at this time would prove a painful experience, for them as well as for himself, and he had wanted to spare them that pain.

It is a particularly solemn form of asseveration that Paul uses here, to which there are parallels in 11.31; 12.19; Rom. 9.1; Gal. 1.20. Not only does he call God to witness, he calls on God as witness against himself, pronouncing a sort of conditional curse upon himself, should his words prove to be untrue. As James Denney puts it, 'He stakes his life, as it were, in God's sight, upon the truth of his words.'[21]

1.24   Paul now seems to anticipate an objection to what he has just said. 'To spare us?' he hears the Corinthians saying, 'Who does he think he is that he should adopt this patronizing tone in speaking to us?'

Hence Paul's disclaimer. He has no desire to dominate them or their faith. He wants to be thought of as a partner, committed above all to helping them to find true joy.

The precise point of the last clause is not certain, owing to the

---

[21] James Denney, p. 60.

ambiguity of a dative case in the Greek. The REB translators have adopted the view that Paul is saying, 'It is by faith that you continue to stand firm, not by my coercion.' The NEB rendering reflects an alternative interpretation: 'Your hold on the faith is secure enough'; that is, 'In respect of your faith, you are standing firm.' Most commentators seem to favour the second way of reading the clause.

2.1   Paul now states explicitly what he has already hinted at in 1.23: he had chosen not to come to Corinth because he was resolved not to undergo another painful visit. Clearly Paul has paid a visit to Corinth which has proved very painful. This painful visit cannot be equated with his first visit to Corinth, which lasted, according to Acts 18. 1–18, for eighteen months and, though not without its difficulties, was overall a fruitful one. There are also later statements in II Corinthians which imply that Paul's next visit to Corinth will be his third (12.14; 13.1). The painful visit was probably occasioned by a disturbing report which Timothy had brought back to Ephesus, on his return from the visit of his to Corinth foreshadowed in I Cor. 4.17 and 16.10. Just why the subsequent visit of Paul's had proved so painful begins to emerge in 2.5–11.

2.2   There follows a slightly awkward sentence, the point of which appears to be to disavow any desire to cause the Corinthians any pain, since Paul looks to them to bring him joy. How can he expect to derive any joy from their company, if he is causing them pain?

2.3   That is *precisely the point* he had made in a letter he had sent to them, instead of paying a visit in person. This letter cannot be identical with our I Corinthians. For one thing, it had been precipitated by the painful visit (his second to Corinth). For another, as we learn from the following verse, it had been written in *great distress and anxiety*, with *many tears* – a description which hardly fits our I Corinthians. Paul refers to this letter again in 2.9 and 7.8–12. For a connected account of Paul's various visits and letters to Corinth, see pp. xviiff., xxviiff.

Before moving on to a more detailed description of the letter, Paul reiterates that his joy is their joy. The implication is that his pain is also their pain. Hence his unwillingness to inflict on them a visit which would have been painful for both himself and them.

2.4   As for the letter, while he had written it *out of great distress and anxiety* and with *many tears*, he had not meant it to cause them pain.

He had only wanted them to know the love, the more than ordinary love, in which he held them all, and holds them still. It is clear from 7.8 that Paul had been made aware of having hurt them by the letter he sent. It also appears very likely that some of his ill-wishers had been saying to the others, *à propos* of his letter, 'See, he has lost all confidence in you. He has had enough of you. He is looking for a rupture.'

There is nothing contrived about Paul's expressions of pain and hurt in this paragraph. It provides a striking illustration of what he means at 11.28, when he speaks of his daily burden of anxiety about all the churches. Here is someone who had every right to say, as he goes on to say, 'Who is weak, and I do not share his weakness? Who is led astray, and I do not burn with indignation for him?'[1] It is with fine insight that James Denney gives to this paragraph the heading, 'A Pastor's Heart.'[2]

Forgive the penitent
2.5–11

Paul has no more to say in justification of his decision not to pay the promised visit and now turns his attention to the situation in the Corinthian church at this moment. As he does so, the reason why his recent visit to Corinth had proved so painful begins to emerge.

2.5 An injury had been done to Paul by some unnamed person. It would appear that the individual in question had attacked Paul's person and apostleship in a particularly insulting and offensive way. Paul now insists, however, that *any injury that has been done* has been done not only to himself but *to some extent . . . to you all*. If he feels it is important for him to say this, it is probably because some were saying that it was all a purely personal matter between himself and the offender. But any attack on Paul's apostleship really amounts to an attack on the churches which owe their origin to him. At the time the community had failed to rally to Paul's support and reprimand the offender, which had made the experience all the more painful.

[1] F. F. Bruce's rendering of 11.29 in his *Expanded Paraphrase of the Epistles of Paul*, p. 155.
[2] Denney, p. 59.

2.9   It was largely in response to this slight, compounded by the indifference of the community, that Paul had penned the 'severe letter'. He had written, he tells the Corinthians, *to see how you stood the test, whether you faithfully accepted my authority.* Evidently Paul had demanded that they take some disciplinary action against the offender and had based this demand on the authority he possessed as an apostle and as their 'father in Christ' (cf. I Cor. 4.15).

2.6   Paul's letter had been effective. It had brought the Corinthians to their senses. In a later chapter Paul speaks of the letter giving pain which had led to a change of heart (7.8f.). They had acted to clear the matter up, by imposing some sort of penalty on the offender. The word translated 'penalty' by the REB in itself could mean nothing more serious than a reprimand, but the context implies that the action taken has had enduring consequences which, in Paul's judgment, should now be brought to an end. It seems likely that the man had at least been excluded from the central activities of the community, such as the eucharistic meal, though it appears that he is still in touch with the others.

Paul's words at this point do not necessarily imply a formal decision by a *general meeting* of the community, as the REB rendering suggests, but this is likely to have been what happened. I Cor. 5.1–5 shows that there were occasions when the community met to take disciplinary action. There is indeed a long tradition of interpretation which actually identifies the incestuous man of I Cor. 5.1–5 with the offender referred to here, but this view is now largely abandoned.[3]

Whatever the penalty was, Paul now pronounces it quite sufficient. It has lasted long enough.

2.7f.   There is no need for it to be continued any longer, because it has been fully accepted by the offender himself as something he had deserved. Indeed, there is now a real danger that he will be overwhelmed (literally, 'swallowed up') by the intensity of his distress. Paul is therefore of the opinion that *something very different is called for now.* They *must forgive the offender and put heart into him.* Paul urges them *to reassure him* of their *love for him.* The man evidently has reason to fear that he has forfeited that love.

As for Paul's own response to the slight he has received, we have already seen how he insists at the outset that it has been an injury done not only to himself but to them all.

---

[3] For a fuller discussion see Furnish, pp. 164–66. See also Martin, pp. 32–34.

2.10 He minimizes the severity of the slight to himself by means of a gracious parenthesis: (*so far as there is anything for me to forgive*). The implication is that he himself is not the party that has been primarily offended, and so his act of forgiveness is not the main thing.

Not that his own forgiveness of the offender is in doubt. Anyone who has the forgiveness of the community has Paul's forgiveness too. Indeed, he has already forgiven the offender for their sake, *as the representative of Christ*. The last five words are a rendering of a Greek phrase which runs, literally, 'in the face of Christ' and could be translated 'in the presence of Christ.' We are evidently to think of 'an act performed in the presence of Christ and under his judgement.'[4]

2.11 The paragraph ends with a further reference to the danger that may befall all concerned, if they fail to restore the offender. Satan may *get the better of us*. It is noteworthy that Paul does not speak of Satan getting the better of <u>him</u>. No doubt, that is part of what he has in mind, since he has just alerted the community to the danger of the man being overwhelmed by despair (v. 7), but such an event, if it were to occur, would also amount to a severe setback to the whole church, since it would be a demonstration of the church's failure to deal with a rupture in the community in the spirit of Christ. Since Paul and the community *know Satan's wiles all too well*, they must be constantly vigilant.

Now that the offender has been made to see the error of his ways, it is impressive to see how deeply concerned Paul is, not for himself and his injured dignity but for the other man and his need for restoration. Discipline had to be exercised, for Paul is no advocate of 'cheap grace', but, now that the offender has come to a genuine repentance, Paul's one desire is for his reinstatement and restoration.

On tenterhooks, awaiting your reaction
2.12–13

Thanks to the last paragraph, we now know something about the events in Corinth which occasioned the 'severe letter', and we also know something about its contents.

[4] Barrett, p. 93.

But how would the Corinthians react to Paul's demand that they discipline the offender? with compliance? defiance? indifference?

2.12f. We now learn that Paul had despatched Titus to Corinth to find out how his letter had been received. Shortly afterwards, he had moved from Ephesus to Troas, the seaport town from which, according to Acts 16.8–11, he had first embarked on his first crossing into Europe. His primary purpose had been *to preach the gospel of Christ* there, but he had naturally hoped that before long he would be joined by Titus with news about Corinth.

On his arrival, Paul found that a door of opportunity for serving the Lord was standing wide open, but, as the days passed without any news of Titus, he could find no peace of mind. In the end he could bear the suspense no longer, and so he decided to set out in the hope of meeting Titus at some point on his way back from Corinth. He therefore *took leave of the people* in Troas *and went off to Macedonia,* even though this meant leaving unfinished a mission which was rich with promise.

Did he meet Titus, on reaching Macedonia? For the moment Paul does not tell us, but breaks into a jubilant doxology, which suggests that he did. Five chapters later, however, at 7.5, we learn that, even when he reached Macedonia, he still found no relief, though in time Titus did arrive with encouraging news.

The sudden suspension of Paul's account of his movements in 2.14 and the equally sudden resumption of the account in 7.5 have led some scholars to the conclusion that originally 7.5 followed straight on after 2.13, and that the intervening section derives from a separate letter – or letters, if 6.14–7.1 be assigned to the 'previous letter'.

On the other hand, some scholars argue that the transition from 2.13 to 2.14 is not really difficult and might not have struck anyone as being problematic, were it not for the sudden resumption of the narrative in 7.5.

The view taken in this commentary is that the hypothesis of an insertion at this point, though certainly possible, is not necessary.

For one thing, it is a mistake to see these two verses simply as the beginning of a travel narrative which is only concluded in 7.5–16. There are clear links between 2.12–13 and the preceding paragraphs. In 1.15–2.2 Paul has maintained that his failure to pay the Corinthians the promised visit was due not to fickleness but to his desire to spare them more pain. In 2.3–11 he has assured them that his real motive in writing the 'severe letter' was to show them the more than ordinary love in which he held them all. Now he wants them to know that he gave up a promising mission in Troas in order to find out from Titus as soon as possible how they had reacted to that letter. Thus the whole section from 1.15 to 2.13 can be understood as designed to lay to rest any suggestion that he did not really care about his Corinthian converts, and not without a hint of rebuke, since the sacrifice he had made in leaving the work in Troas unfinished should not have been necessary.

Moreover, it is not quite true to say, as Johannes Weiss did, that 2.13 and 7.5 fit together 'like the fragments of a ring'.[5] The transition from 'I' in 2.13 to 'we' in 7.5, together with the transition from 'peace of the spirit' (REB: 'relief of mind') to 'peace of the flesh' (REB: 'relief') become quite awkward, if one supposes that these two verses were originally consecutive. These stylistic variations could, of course, be ascribed to a redactor, but it is hard to see why a redactor would want to make them, once he had separated the two verses by such a substantial insertion. The linguistic parallels are better explained, if one assumes that in 7.5 Paul takes up again the thread dropped in 2.13 but with slight variation of the wording. However, to recognize the possibility that 2.14–7.4 may be derived from another source or sources, we shall introduce a new paragraph heading.[6]

A whiff of God
2.14–17

2.14 For the moment Paul is overwhelmed with relief at the thought of the good news Titus has just brought – one more demonstration of the power of God to turn seeming defeat into victory (cf. 1.9f.). It is as if he were part of a great victory celebration in honour of Christ, a triumphal procession. Such processions were the prerogative of victorious Roman generals. The *triumphator* rode through the streets of Rome in a four-horse chariot to offer sacrifice to Jupiter on the Capitol, preceded by magistrates and trumpeters, the spoils of the enemy, the oxen for sacrifice and the principal captives in chains, while the army followed behind.[7] It is not clear, however, what role

[5] Quoted by Günther Bornkamm in his book, *Paul*, p. 245.
[6] For a fuller discussion of this and other problems concerning the composition of II Corinthians see the Introduction.
[7] See E. Badian's article 'Triumph', in N. G. L. Hammond and H. H. Scullard (eds), *The Oxford Classical Dictionary* (2nd ed, 1970), p. 1095.

Paul assigns to himself and his associates in the scene of triumph. The REB translators have adopted the view that they are being compared to the victorious general's captives. There is no question that the underlying Greek verb can be used in this sense, but it is a sense which does not seem to fit this context. Any suggestion that the relationship of the messengers to God is like that of conquered prisoners or that they are constantly being exposed to shame and humiliation hardly fits the setting of a thanksgiving. Some scholars who favour this interpretation cite I Cor. 4.9b as a parallel, but the overall intent of that passage is rather different, viz. to expose the shallowness of an over-realized eschatology. It would seem more in keeping with the present context for the messengers of Christ to be compared to the victorious general's soldiers rather than his captives, but there is no clear lexical support for the use of the verb in this precise sense. The reality which seems to be in Paul's mind is that he who had once fought against Christ is now one of his most trusted lieutenants.

The image of a triumphal procession now gives way to that of fragrance. The heralds of the gospel are being used by God *to spread abroad the fragrance of the knowledge of himself.* The main point of this expression seems to be that through the work of Christ's messengers a 'whiff of God', a 'rumour of God', is penetrating everywhere. A more literal translation of the word rendered 'abroad' would be 'in every place'. The image of an odour is particularly appropriate for conveying such a notion, since, as Denney observes, 'Nothing is so insuppressible, nothing so pervasive, as a fragrance.'[8]

The actual word Paul has used, however, can denote an unpleasant, as well as a pleasant, odour, and Paul exploits this ambiguity in the two verses which follow.[9]

2.15f.   Not only are Paul and his companions the bearers of a whiff or rumour of God, they embody it in their own persons. To quote the Twentieth Century New Testament, 'For we are a fragrance for God – a fragrance as of Christ himself.' Paul's words here could be taken, as they evidently have been by the REB translators, as meaning that the messengers are the incense which Christ offers to God, but the thrust of the passage seems to be horizontal rather than vertical, emphasizing the dissemination of the knowledge of God throughout

[8] Denney, p. 92.
[9] Best (p. 26) observes that 'The reference to fragrance would have meant much more in the first century world with its open drains and foul smells than it does to us.'

the world. Moreover, the messengers spread abroad this fragrance not only by what they say but by what they do and are. We have already observed more than once that the notion that the person of the messenger must conform with the message that he or she bears is fundamental to the whole epistle. As Furnish puts it in his exegesis of this verse, the apostle is 'one who is bound over in the totality of his being to the service of the gospel.'[10]

But the message which is thus disseminated by word and deed precipitates a sharp division among its hearers. Some accept, some reject. The same gospel which, in Denney's words, 'appeals to some with winning irresistible power' excites in others 'a passion of antipathy which nothing else could provoke'.[11] Consequently, some *are on the way to salvation*, some *on the way to destruction*. And yet it is the same message that has been proclaimed to each group. To the one group the message of the gospel, the 'whiff of God', proves *a deadly fume that kills*, to the other *a vital fragrance that brings life*. Paul's actual words here suggest a steady progression in each direction: on the one hand, death from beginning to end; on the other, life from beginning to end (cf. Rom. 1.17).

In these two verses Paul speaks of the preaching of the gospel having, inevitably, a double outcome. I Cor. 1.18 is another passage where he sees the gospel creating division among its hearers. Yet alongside these passages there are others, like I Cor. 15.28 or Phil. 2.10f., where he appears to entertain the hope that the entire created universe will ultimately be wholly subject to God's rule.

The thought of an inevitable double outcome seems to fill Paul for the moment with a sense of the awful responsibility carried by a preacher of the word, and hence with a sense of inadequacy. *Who is equal to such a calling?* This is a question which clearly expects the answer, 'No one. No one who relies on their own strength.'

2.17   At this point, Paul might have been expected to move to the thought expressed in v. 5 of the following chapter, that 'our sufficiency is of God' (AV). However, he is suddenly struck by the thought that his own sense of the awesome responsibility carried by the preacher of the gospel is not shared by all who exercise the same vocation, and his words take on a polemical edge. This is the first hint in the letter of the existence of people, known to the Corinthians, who are distorting the gospel. The link with v. 16b seems to

[10] Furnish, p. 188.
[11] Denney, p. 94.

be that those of whom he now speaks act as if they were equal to the calling in their own strength. But in their case the calling is not being faithfully exercised. They are *adulterating the word of God for profit*. The Greek verb which the REB renders 'adulterating . . . for profit' usually has pejorative connotations. The verb, and the corresponding noun, conjure up the figure of the unscrupulous petty tradesman or pedlar who resorts to 'every trick in the book' in order to make a profit. There are thus two distinct ideas conveyed by these terms. One is that of adulteration. An unscrupulous pedlar adulterates the wine he sells. The word is also used of teachers who corrupt learning or philosophy. The other idea conveyed by these terms is that of easy profit-making. The REB rendering suggests that both ideas are present in this context, but in the chapters which follow immediately after this it is the first idea which is more prominent.

In contrast to these hucksters, Paul claims that he and his associates *declare the word . . . in sincerity* – his actual word suggests purity of motive – *as from God*, that is, as people who know themselves to have been sent by God, *and in God's sight*, knowing themselves to be answerable to him, and *as members of Christ*, literally, 'in Christ'.

With these verses Paul has introduced the question which is to dominate the next three chapters, viz. What are the marks of a true apostle?

You are all the letter we need

3.1–3

3.1   Paul has just made a vigorous defence of the motives and behaviour of himself and his colleagues in the exercise of their ministry. But no sooner has he done so than, as happens so often in Romans, he hears in his mind someone among his readers raising an objection and anticipates it in the form of a question: *Are we beginning all over again to produce our credentials?* The verb here translated 'to produce our credentials' could be rendered, more literally, 'to recommend ourselves'.

It has been recognized for some time that letters of recommendation, such as are referred to in the second half of the verse, played an important role in the ancient world, indeed a more important role than they do in ours, with its long-distance telephones and fax machines, but the social context of recommendation terminology has not been fully appreciated until recently. The recommendation of others or oneself either by letter or in person was an accepted way of creating friendship. II Corinthians contains seven passages in which the verb 'recommend' or the related adjective (both found in v. 1) occur. Peter Marshall has argued convincingly that in all but one case (7.11) these words are being used in a technical sense to refer to the convention just described. It appears that Paul followed the convention of self-recommendation as he sought out hosts in the various communities he visited, thereby establishing a reciprocal relationship based on trust. The use of the word 'again' in v. 1 implies that the original relationship between Paul and the Corinthians has been broken and that Paul is being held personally responsible for the breach.[1]

Paul does not answer his own question but follows up with a further question introduced by the particle which signals that the answer expected is 'No'. He is not seeking to initiate the relationship of friendship all over again. Nor do he and his associates, *like some people*, *need letters* of recommendation either to the Corinthians or from them. It is not that he is opposed to the use of such letters in principle. He himself recommends colleagues of his to various churches in his own letters (see especially Rom. 16.1; cf. Acts 18.27). His point is rather that he himself has no need, as others have, of any letter of recommendation to the Corinthians – a fact which points to the uniqueness of his relationship with them. Paul had been the one who brought the church in Corinth into existence and therefore, as he reminds them in I Cor. 4.14f., had a unique right to address them as his own dear children.

'Some people', however, not named but clearly known to the Corinthians, are relying on such letters of recommendation. We are thus beginning to build up a picture of a group of people who have been working mischief in Corinth. They have come to Corinth from somewhere else and have used these letters, probably from other Hellenistic congregations,[2] to insinuate themselves into the good graces of the Corinthians, as well as seeking letters of recommendation from the Corinthian church to other communities. Furthermore,

---

[1] See Peter Marshall, *Enmity in Corinth: Social Conventions in Paul's Relations with the Corinthians*, chapters 4 and 7.
[2] If, as some have suggested, they had obtained their letters of recommendation from the Jerusalem church, they would hardly have needed letters from the Corinthian church as well.

the stricture uttered in 2.17 evidently applies to them. They are 'adulterating the word of God for profit.'

3.2   Paul and his associates have no need to resort to letters of recommendation to the Corinthians. *No, you are all the letter we need.* If any evidence is needed of the good faith of Paul and his colleagues and the authenticity of his apostleship, what more striking evidence could there be than this congregation which they have nurtured into existence, made up, for the most part, of Gentiles, not a few of whom had been fornicators, idolaters, adulterers, sexual perverts, thieves, extortioners and the like (see I Cor 6.9–11)?

There will be times, later in II Corinthians, when Paul will shrink from listing his credentials, because it sounds like boasting (see especially 12.1), but there are other passages, like II Cor. 1.14 or I Thess. 2.19f., where he speaks unashamedly of the pride that he takes in his converts and expects them to take in him. In I Cor. 9.1f. he counts on the assent of the Corinthians to his claim that they are his own handiwork in the Lord, the very seal of his apostleship.

Paul could have ended the sentence at this point, but the image of the Corinthians as a living letter catches his imagination, and he sees the possibility of developing it now in one way, now another. First, *you are . . . a letter written on our heart.* In other words, the needs and welfare of the Corinthian community are constantly on the hearts of himself and his associates.

3.2b–3   Further, the Corinthians are, in their own persons, like a letter that is plain for anyone to see and read.

But Paul hasn't finished with the metaphor. What he has said so far could be misunderstood. If the Corinthians themselves are all the letter Paul needs, does this mean that it is ultimately to them that he is appealing for confirmation of his apostleship? And is he implying that the existence of the Corinthian congregation is rooted, finally, in what he has achieved? Who, in other words, is the real author of the 'letter' represented by the Corinthian Christians? Christ, not Paul or any other apostle. What role, then, has been played by Paul and his associates? To quote the AV, 'Ye are manifestly declared to be the epistle of Christ ministered by us.' The word 'ministered' is picked up in v. 6, where Paul speaks of himself and others being *ministers of a new covenant.* The REB rendering of v. 3 implies that their task, as ministers, is simply to deliver the letter. Some versions assign to them the task of penning the letter or transcribing it. The main point, however, is clear: the role of Paul and his colleagues is strictly subordinate to that of Christ himself, the true author of the Corinthian 'letter'. As he puts it in I Cor. 3.5–7, he, like Apollos, had simply been God's agent in bringing the Corinthians to faith. The creation of faith is the work of God alone.

But Paul still hasn't finished teasing out the metaphor. Granted that the Corinthians represent a 'letter', what has it been written with? *Not with ink but with the Spirit of the living God.*

But written on what? *Not on stone tablets but on the pages of the human heart.* The living letter of which Christ is the author, through the Spirit, and which authenticates Paul and his associates as Christ's envoys consists of the changed hearts of the Corinthians themselves.

We might have expected Paul to say, 'written not on parchment,' but his mind is already moving towards another contrast which is to dominate the next three paragraphs, that between the old covenant and the new. The contrast he makes between stone tablets and the human heart involves a clear allusion to prophetic passages in both Jeremiah and Ezekiel, to Jeremiah's prophecy of a new covenant through which the law will be written upon the hearts of God's people (Jer. 31.31–34), and to Ezekiel's prophecy that God will remove the heart of stone from the bodies of his people and give them a heart of flesh (Ezek. 11.19; 36.26). Each prophet is speaking of a new God-given possibility of doing God's will, based upon a new intimacy of relationship. Paul's claim is that the Corinthians themselves are living evidence that these prophecies are now being fulfilled.

Ministers of a new covenant – by God's grace alone
3.4–6

In the preceding paragraph Paul has made bold claims. In their own persons, the Corinthians are a living witness to the good faith of Paul and his associates and the authenticity of his apostleship. Indeed, their changed lives are a sign that the prophetic promises of a new covenant and a new order are in process of fulfilment. At the same time, Paul has been careful to point out that his role and that of his colleagues is strictly subordinate to that of Christ himself. Christ is the true author of the Corinthian 'letter', while he himself is a mere amanuensis. The same concern to point to God in Christ as the true author of salvation dominates the present paragraph.

3.4f.   The claims Paul has just expressed have been made *in full reliance upon God, through Christ*. Paul and his colleagues cannot claim any credit whatever for anything they may have been able to accomplish.

To reinforce the point, Paul picks up the word 'sufficient' from 2.16 (REB: 'equal') and echoes it by using the cognate noun and verb as well. The Jerusalem Bible brings out the word-play more clearly than most versions: 'Not that we are qualified in ourselves to claim anything as our own work: all our qualifications come from God. He is the one who has given us the qualifications to be the administrators of this new covenant.'

It is very likely that this word-play was suggested to Paul by the application, in several passages in the LXX, of the title 'The Sufficient One' (the same word as is used in v. 5a) to God (Ruth 1.20f.; Job 21.15; 31.2; 40.2). In these passages it is a rendering of the Hebrew name *Shaddai*, which is of unknown origin but was widely believed at the time to mean, etymologically, 'He who suffices', i.e. 'The All-sufficient'. At the same time, the present passage undoubtedly has a polemical edge. As will become increasingly clear, Paul's adversaries, as he sees them, are guilty precisely of boasting of their own sufficiency.

This is one of the most forceful statements anywhere in Paul's letters of a conviction which is arguably the very heart of the Pauline gospel, viz. that 'Salvation is of the Lord.'[3] This conviction will be reaffirmed later in this epistle, especially in 4.7–12; 5.18–21 and 6.8–10. It also finds powerful expression in I Cor. 1.26–31, a paragraph to which, in my earlier commentary in this series, I gave the heading, 'All of grace, all of God.'

Furthermore, since, for Paul, faith gives glory to God (Rom. 4.20), recognizing God as God, it follows that faith can appropriately be described, as it is by C. H. Dodd, as a 'response to the revelation of God as the All-sufficient . . .' And again: 'For Paul, faith is that

---

[3] See my essay on II Cor. 1.9b in *Die Mitte des Neuen Testaments*, pp. 384–98.

attitude in which, acknowledging our complete insufficiency for any of the high ends of life, we rely utterly on the sufficiency of God.'[4]

3.6   It is God alone then who has empowered or qualified us to exercise the ministry which is ours, but that is nothing less than a calling to be *ministers of a new covenant*.

The concept of ministry is particularly prominent in II Corinthians. In all, the two nouns 'minister' and 'ministry', together with the verb 'to minister', occur thirty-six times in the indisputably Pauline letters. Twenty of these occurrences are found in II Corinthians.[5]

As for the new covenant, we have already had an allusion to Jeremiah's prophecy in the previous paragraph. Now this allusion becomes explicit. This new covenant is also designated as a covenant 'not of the letter but of the spirit,' to quote the AV, or, as the REB puts it, *not written but spiritual*.

In modern English usage, a contrast between letter and spirit suggests a contrast between the literal meaning and the real intent, as in the phrase, 'the spirit, not the letter, of the law,' but Paul's contrast here is controlled by the passage from Jeremiah. While the actual words 'letter' and 'spirit' do not occur in Jer. 31.31–34, they serve very well to pinpoint the contrast Jeremiah makes between two ways of knowing God's will, associated with two covenants: on the one hand, a way of knowing God's will as *letter*, as external code, as 'something coldly strange to the depths of the heart,' to use Allo's phrase;[6] and, on the other, a way of knowing God's will as *spirit*, that is, as power, in other words, a knowledge which is also an empowering to live by what one knows, a knowledge which carries the personality of the knower along with it. The use of the word 'spirit' may also have been suggested by its prominence in the passages from Ezekiel which Paul alluded to in the previous paragraph.

So long as God's will is known simply as letter, as bare external code, it leads inevitably to disobedience and death. It *condemns to death*, or, more literally, 'it kills.' *The Spirit*, on the other hand, *gives life*. There is a similar contrast between the terms 'letter' and 'spirit' in Rom. 7.5f., where 'letter' is associated with oldness, death, captivity and disobedience, and 'spirit' with newness, life, liberation and obedience (cf. also Rom. 2.29).

But is it not an over-simplification to suggest that either in the Old

---

[4] C. H. Dodd, *The Epistle to the Romans*, p. 15.
[5] Cf. Furnish, p. 199.
[6] Allo, p. 85; cf. also the passage from Calvin quoted by Barrett, p. 113.

Testament or Judaism the law is known simply as 'letter'? Is this not to isolate the law from the context of the covenant, within which obedience to the revealed will of God is motivated by gratitude to God for his goodness to Israel? Such has been the constant complaint of Jewish scholars, as well as Christian scholars with expertise in Judaism.

Indeed, this criticism is voiced as early as 1894 by James Denney. In a remarkable passage, he argues that the way Paul sets the old covenant and the new in stark opposition to each other fails to do justice to either, and he also maintains that the categories of letter and spirit both apply, in some sense, to both dispensations, so that 'it is possible to take the old and the new alike either in the letter or in the spirit.'[7]

My own judgment is that the stark antithesis that Paul draws here between the old covenant and the new, one a covenant of the letter, the other a covenant of the spirit, is an over-simplification of the relationship between them and fails to do justice to the function of the law in the Old Testament but that his strictures amount to not unfair comment on those intertestamental or post-biblical Jewish writings which are dominated by the thought of a final judgment. While aware of the risk of over-simplification, I would suggest that in works like the Psalms of Solomon or Enoch or IV Ezra the thought of the final judgment has become so central as to affect profoundly the significance of the law. Instead of being seen as the divinely given way for men and women to express their gratitude to God for his goodness, it has become rather the means by which they may make themselves fit for God's approval in the judgment. In so far as that has happened, it can not unreasonably be claimed that the letter has become deadly.

I would also add that Christians are not immune from the danger of letting their understanding of God's will become a 'letter that kills' rather than a revelation that empowers, indeed, that this is a temptation to which all religious people are exposed, and the more exposed the more seriously they are intent on doing God's will.[8]

To revert to the main thrust of this paragraph, the vigour with which Paul insists here, as elsewhere in I and II Corinthians, that 'salvation is of the Lord' suggests that the Corinthians stood in as

[7] Denney, p. 119.
[8] For a fuller discussion see my article, 'The Interpretation of Romans VII,' *AusBR* 21, 1973, pp. 27–39. For a penetrating discussion of the problems raised not only by this paragraph but by the whole section running from 3.4 to 4.6, see Gerd Theissen, *Psychological Aspects of Pauline Theology* , pp. 117–58.

much need of hearing this message as communities with a Jewish background. It seems that whereas the latter were tempted to rely on a righteousness of their own, the Corinthians were tempted to rely on a wisdom of their own. Hence Paul's insistence that our only sufficiency comes from God.[9]

Outshone by a still greater glory
3.7–11

Paul has introduced the theme of the new covenant and set it in stark opposition to the old. He now proceeds to draw out the contrast. The present paragraph is built around three *a fortiori* arguments, in vv. 7–8, 9 and 10–11. The gist of each argument is that, if the inauguration of the old covenant was attended by glory, *a fortiori* must the new covenant be glorious.

This form of argumentation is extremely common in Rabbinic literature, where it is known as 'the light and the heavy.'[10] It is also characteristic of the teaching of Jesus.[11]

The passage to which Paul is alluding all through is Exod. 34.29–35, which tells how, when Moses came down from Mount Sinai, bearing the ten commandments, *the skin of his face shone because he had been talking with the Lord,* but he himself did not know it. When Aaron and the Israelites saw how his face shone, they were afraid to approach him. Moses called them to him and gave them the commandments but, when he had finished, he put a veil over his face. Thereafter, whenever he went in before the Lord to speak with him, he would take the veil off, but whenever he came out to speak to the Israelites he would put the veil back over his face.

In vv. 7, 8 and 9 Paul uses the word 'ministry' instead of the word 'covenant'. This term will have been suggested by v. 6, where he speaks of 'ministers of a new covenant.'

3.7f. Paul begins by specifying three ways in which the old 'ministry' was inferior to the new. First, it was *engraved in written form*

---

[9] Cf. my comments on I Cor. 1.26–31 in the earlier volume.

[10] For a fuller discussion see Martin, p. 59.

[11] According to H. J. Cadbury, G. K. Chesterton once spoke of Jesus making 'furious use of *a fortiori* argument' (*The Peril of Modernizing Jesus*, p. 58).

on stone. This phrase recalls v. 3, with its allusion to Jeremiah's new covenant.

Secondly, it was a *ministry that brought death* – a statement that echoes v. 6. This way of describing the Mosaic covenant is in sharp contrast to Jewish self-understanding, which saw – and sees – the gift of the law as a gift of life, but is consistent with Paul's teaching elsewhere (see e.g. Rom. 8.2; I Cor. 15.56).

Thirdly, Paul adds to the story a feature which he will use in the allegory in vv. 12–18, viz. that under the veil the glow was fading away. There is no support for this addition either in the story in Exodus or in Jewish commentary upon it. Indeed, there are Jewish and Samaritan traditions that the glow persisted until Moses' death, and even in the grave.[12] This addition therefore very probably stems from Christian reinterpretation of the story and may well be the work of Paul himself.

The Greek word used for 'fading away' in vv. 7, 11 and 13 is of considerable importance in I Corinthians as well, where it is used eight times to refer to the supersession of the old order by the coming of Christ. It is used in this latter sense in v. 14 of the present chapter.[13] Barrett and Furnish argue that the word is also being used in this sense in the earlier verses, but the focus of Paul's attention at this point is the story of Moses coming down from the mountain. These scholars make Paul move prematurely from the story to its interpretation.

The new 'ministry', on the other hand, is engraved, we may assume, not on stone tablets but on the hearts of believers.

Further, it is a *ministry of the Spirit*, which, as we were reminded in v. 6, gives life.

Thirdly, it is implied that, whereas the glow which was seen on the face of Moses, as a result of his intercourse with God on the mountain, faded, there is nothing fading, nothing evanescent, about the effect on Christian believers of their nearness to God in Christ. Therefore, if the first covenant with all its deficiencies still had its glory, *a fortiori* must the second covenant be glorious.

Wherein the glory of the new covenant consists is not spelt out at this point. The account in Exodus does not actually speak of glory but only of how the skin of Moses' face shone because he had been talking with God. The LXX, however, introduces the word 'glorify', suggesting that what was really taking place was an assimilation of

---

[12] See Martin, p. 62, for references.
[13] See the discussion of I Cor. 1.27f. in my earlier volume.

the human to the divine. Verse 18 of the present chapter makes it clear that the glorification brought about under the new covenant also consists in an assimilation of the human to the divine but one that penetrates to the heart of the believer. In this latter verse the process of glorification is the accompaniment of the believer's transformation into the likeness of Christ (cf. Phil. 3.21).

3.9   The old covenant was a 'ministry of death' because it was a *ministry that brought condemnation.* This notion is spelt out at length in Romans, where Paul argues that the effect of the law is to bring all people, Jews and Gentiles alike, under God's condemnation. And yet the covenant which led to such an outcome was accompanied by glory. *How much richer in glory must be the ministry that brings acquittal!*

As 'the ministry that brought condemnation' sums up the thrust of Rom. 1.18–3.20, so 'the ministry that brings acquittal' sums up the thrust of Rom. 3.21–5.21. The Greek word underlying 'acquittal' is usually translated 'righteousness' and denotes now a quality of God, now the activity of God in which that quality is revealed, now the outcome of that activity of God in human lives in the form of a right standing with God and right conduct.[14] The contrast in the present verse with 'condemnation' makes the translation 'acquittal' appropriate.

Underlying the translation, 'How much richer . . .' is a verb which occurs ten times in II Corinthians and denotes abundance, overflow. Words with that meaning are to be found in each verse in vv. 8–11, and are also prominent in other passages of II Corinthians, particularly chapters 8 and 9. Frances Young and David Ford, following Bruce Malina, observe that the prominence of the theme of abundance in II Corinthians stands in sharp contrast to the material economy to which Paul was subject, which was a 'limited good' economy, in which equilibrium, not growth, was the ideal.[15]

3.10f.   Paul now underlines the incomparably greater glory of the new covenant. *The glory that once was is now no glory at all; it is outshone by a still greater glory.* The point of v. 10 is partly that, by comparison with the glory of the new, the glory of the old seems no glory at all, but v. 11 shows that Paul also has in mind the thought, already alluded to in v. 7, that while Moses had his face covered, the glory was fading away. And *if what was to fade away had its glory, how much*

---

[14] Cf. A. J. M. Wedderburn, *The Reasons for Romans,* pp. 117–22.
[15] *Meaning and Truth,* pp. 172f.

greater is the glory of what endures! Thus Paul does not deny that the old covenant had its glory, but it is a glory which fades away completely in the light of the glory of the new covenant, as the light of the moon fades away when the sun rises. This, as Barrett observes, 'even though it be a relative disparagement of Torah, is an extraordinary observation to come from the pen of a Jew.'[16]

There is nothing in the first epistle comparable to this elaborate demonstration of the superiority of the new order inaugurated by Christ over the order established by Moses. This is clear evidence that, in contrast to the situation he faced in I Corinthians, Paul is now confronted by Christians from a Jewish background, and aggressively Jewish-Christian at that.

The veil that only Christ can lift
3.12–18

3.12f.   Paul begins the new paragraph with a further contrast, this time between 'us', the ministers of the new covenant, and Moses. For our part, *we speak out boldly*, that is to say, frankly, concealing nothing and passing over nothing. The Greek noun underlying the rendering 'boldly', along with the cognate verb, can refer to boldness in the presence of God, but Paul himself consistently uses these words to refer to his frankness in dealing with other people.[17] He is well aware that he has been criticized for saying one thing and meaning another, and saying one thing and doing another (cf. 1.12–14).

Paul and his associates are enabled to speak out boldly by having *such a hope as this*. In the previous paragraph he has not spoken explicitly of hope or of the future, but he has spoken in the previous verse of 'what endures'. Moreover, his overall theme has been the glory of the new covenant, which completely outshines the glory of the old. Elsewhere, however, glorification tends to be presented as belonging to the future consummation and therefore as an object of hope (Rom. 5.2; 8.18–21; I Cor. 15.43; II Cor. 4.17; Phil. 3.21; I Thess. 2.12).

---

[16] Barrett, pp. 117f.
[17] For a fuller discussion of this word group see Furnish, pp. 206f., 230f.; Young and Ford, *Meaning and Truth* pp. 94–96. Bultmann (p. 85) aptly compares Paul's statement here with Rom. 1.16: 'I am not ashamed of the gospel.'

Emboldened by such a hope, we have no need to do as Moses did, when *he put a veil over his face to keep the Israelites from gazing at the end of what was fading away.*

We have seen how, in the previous paragraph, Paul adds to the story of the veiling of Moses' face, as told in Exod. 34.29–35, the detail that under the veil the glow faded away. He now gives to this version of the story a further twist: Moses placed the veil over his face in order to conceal from the Israelites the fading of the glow. The word here translated 'fading away' is the same word that is used in vv. 7 and 11, and also in v. 14, where the REB translates it by 'is taken away.'

What motive for this action does Paul impute to Moses? Given the contrast with acting frankly and boldly, it could be deceit or timidity. In the light of the following verse, the latter seems more likely.

3.14   Veil or no veil, however, the minds of the Israelites had become closed, so that they would not have been able to perceive the glory reflected in the face of Moses, in any case.

And now Paul takes this re-written story typologically, as a symbol of the situation of the mass of the Jewish people of his own day, vis-à-vis the revelation in Christ. In the same way as the Israelites under Moses were prevented, both by a veil and by the hardening of their own minds, from perceiving the splendour on Moses' face, so to this very day, whenever *the lesson is read from the old covenant* in the synagogue, *that same veil is there.* That is to say, the significance of the Old Testament as pointing to the time of fulfilment in Christ is veiled.

This is the first known occurrence of the phrase, 'the old covenant', which may well have been coined by Paul.

The phrase 'in Christ' is emphatic in the Greek and implies more than mere instrumentality. It is those who are united with Christ by faith who find the veil taken away.[18]

3.15   The point just made is reinforced by reiteration. *To this very day, every time the law of Moses is read, a veil lies over the mind of the hearer.*

---

[18] For a fuller discussion of the phrase 'in Christ' see my comments on I Cor. 1.30 in my earlier volume. The REB clearly understands the subject of the verb 'taken away' to be 'the veil', unlike the NEB, which took the subject to be 'the old covenant'. For a protest against the latter interpretation, which would imply that with the coming of Christ the old covenant is abrogated for the Jews, see William J. Dalton, S.J., 'Is the Old Covenant Abrogated (II Cor. 3: 14)?' *AusBR* 35, 1987, pp. 88–94.

Again, the veil over Moses' head serves as a type of the darkened, uncomprehending hearts of unbelieving Jews of Paul's day.

3.16   But Paul still has not finished exploiting the symbolical possibilities of the story in Exodus. According to Exod. 34.29–35, whenever Moses went in before the Lord (i.e. Yahweh) to speak with him, he would take the veil off. This detail is picked up by Paul (with some rewording – the word 'turn' being substituted for 'go in') as symbolizing the only way in which Jewish worshippers of Paul's time can be brought to perceive the incompleteness of the scriptures to which they attend so devoutly. For Paul's Jewish contemporary, those words in Exodus still hold good. 'Whenever he (i.e. the Jewish believer) turns to the Lord, the veil (i.e. of failure to perceive the full meaning of the Mosaic covenant) is removed.'

The word 'turns' is frequently used in biblical Greek to denote a penitent turning towards God.

'The Lord' here probably refers to God. In Paul's letters 'the Lord' usually refers to Christ, unless Paul is either quoting or paraphrasing a scriptural text. As for the reference here, the incident in Exodus 34 has been in the forefront of Paul's mind from v. 7 on. Furthermore, as Furnish shows, there is a profoundly theological orientation to Paul's argument from 2.14 right through to 4.6.[19]

3.17   If, as we have suggested, Paul is using the word 'Lord' in v. 16, so to speak, in quotation marks, meaning 'the Lord of whom Exod. 34.34 speaks,' it is likely that the term has the same reference in the following statement, viz. that *the Lord of whom this passage speaks is the Spirit.* A more literal translation runs, 'Now the Lord is the Spirit,' but the REB translators have inserted extra words to make it clear that Paul is still giving to the Old Testament story a contemporary application. Scholars who have not taken this view have sometimes thought that Paul is somehow identifying the Lord, that is, the risen Christ, with the Spirit, but that can hardly be his intention, especially since he goes on to speak of 'the Spirit of the Lord.' His point is rather that for the contemporary Jew turning to 'the Lord' means turning to the new covenant of the Spirit (cf. v. 6).[20]

And *where the Spirit of the Lord is, there is liberty.* What sort of liberty does Paul have in mind? No doubt there is an echo here of the

[19] Furnish, pp. 234f.
[20] Cf. Young and Ford, *Meaning and Truth*, p. 113. For a full discussion of Paul's conception of the relationship between the risen Christ and the Spirit see Peter Carnley, *The Structure of Resurrection Belief*, pp. 255–57.

boldness referred to in v. 12, but he is probably thinking of every-thing that restricts human life, particularly all forms of legalism.

3.18 Furthermore, we who have turned to Christ and received the Spirit are able to see what the Israelites under Moses were not able to see, *the glory of the Lord* unobscured by any veil.

A number of versions take the view that the participle translated by the REB *see as in a mirror* means rather 'reflect as a mirror does,' but the linguistic evidence clearly favours the first interpretation.[21]

If, as we have argued earlier, 'the Lord' in vv. 16 and 17 refers to God, the likelihood is that it has the same meaning here too.

While, according to Paul, our vision is not restricted by any veil, the object of our vision is not the divine glory itself, since such a direct vision of God belongs to the eschatological future, but that glory as reflected.

In the book of Wisdom (7.26) the word 'mirror' is used in parallelism with 'image', and so it is not surprising that in this verse the word 'image' (REB: 'likeness') occurs three words later. What we in fact see is Christ, who is, as Hebrews puts it, 'the radiance of God's glory, the stamp of God's very being' (Heb. 1.3).

What is more, *we are being transformed into his likeness with ever-increasing glory*. This 'seeing' that the Spirit makes possible in this present time of faith is a preliminary seeing in a mirror, not a seeing face to face, which belongs to the future, yet it has already a transforming and renewing power.

In the Hellenistic world, the idea that to behold a god or goddess has a transformative effect on the worshipper was widespread.[22] For Paul, however, this process of transformation consists in a growing conformity with the dying of Jesus, so as to live by the power of his resurrection – an idea that is to be developed in the following chapter (see 4.7–12; cf. Rom. 6.1–11; Gal. 2.19f.; Phil. 3.10f.).

And all this is the work of God. That much is clear, but the exact interpretation of Paul's last three words is not, owing to the ambiguity of the genitive case. Indeed, there are at least six different ways of translating these three words. One way of reading the phrase is the way adopted by the REB: *through the power of the Lord who is the Spirit*. This interpretation continues the close association of the Lord with the Spirit from the previous verse. The AV rendering, 'the Spirit of the Lord,' is certainly possible.

---

[21] For a fuller discussion see Furnish, p. 214.
[22] See Furnish, pp. 240f.

The use Paul makes in this passage of the story in Exodus may well strike a modern reader as ingenious but forced. However, a reader familiar with contemporary Rabbinic commentaries on the Old Testament may well have found it an exegetical *tour de force*. This passage is further evidence that in this epistle, in contrast to I Corinthians, Paul is confronted by Christians from a Jewish background.

Whether his argument is ingenious or not, however, Paul has unwittingly given impetus to a view of the Old Testament which is all too common and sees it simply as a set of prophecies pointing to Christ, and therefore as having, as David Buttrick puts it, 'the status of "mere" – mere longing or mere promise or mere preliminary revelation.'[23] Such a view fails to do justice to passages elsewhere in Paul in which he sees the gospel of the grace of God, *who acquits the wrongdoer, makes the dead live and calls into being things that are not*, fully embodied in the Old Testament (see Rom. 4.5, 17; cf. Rom. 10.6–10).

Proclaiming the message of the new creation
4.1–6

The main theme of the previous chapter has been the superiority of the ministry of the new covenant over that of the old. At the same time, there has been a strong note of polemic. In the present paragraph the same two concerns are also dominant, viz. to magnify the ministry of the gospel and to vindicate the behaviour of Paul and his associates against their rivals and detractors.

4.1f.   Paul has already spoken in 3.12 of the boldness which the hope of the gospel inspires in its faithful messengers, a hope that is fortified by the experience of continuous and progressive transformation into the likeness of Christ. Now he claims that they never lose heart. As the reason for their fortitude he cites the fact that they owe their commission as ministers of the gospel entirely to God's mercy. We are reminded of I Cor. 15.9, where Paul expresses his wonder that one so unworthy as himself, a persecutor of the church, should be called to be an apostle.

Paul then goes on to affirm, in the strongest possible terms, that

---

[23] David Buttrick, *Homiletic: Moves and Structures*, p.356.

the behaviour of himself and his associates has been not unworthy of the gospel of which they are the bearers. As we have observed several times already, this is one of the most pervasive themes of II Corinthians, the necessity for congruence between the behaviour of the bearers of the gospel and the message that they bear.

As for Paul and his associates, they have nothing to hide. They have renounced all disgraceful, underhand ways. They *do not practise cunning*. Underlying the rendering 'cunning' is a Greek word which denotes something worse than guile or malice, the behaviour of a person who stops at nothing. Nor do they *distort the word of God*.

What is the point of such a vigorous denial that their conduct has been in any way inappropriate? Has Paul himself been accused by his detractors of doing all these things? Is he implicitly accusing his opponents of doing these things? These are questions which arise constantly throughout 3.7–4.6, and it is not possible to answer them with certainty. We do well to heed the warning issued by James Denney nearly a century ago, when he wrote of Schmiedel habitually reading St. Paul 'as if (1) he had been expressly accused of everything which he says he does not do, and (2) as if he deliberately retorted on his opponents every charge he denied.'[1]

Nevertheless, it seems likely that this verse, along with v. 5, has both a defensive and an offensive thrust. The earlier chapters have afforded ample evidence that Paul has been the target of criticism (see 1.12–2.4), and we have also seen clear evidence of polemic against other teachers (see 2.17; 3.1). Paul could well have been accused of 'dirty tricks', because of his cancellation of the proposed double visit, and of distorting the word of God, because of his insistence that Gentiles need not observe the law of Moses.

In contrast to all those whose conduct does not square with the truth of the gospel, Paul and his associates have sought to commend themselves and their message to their fellow men and women *by declaring the truth openly*. The REB rendering, 'declaring', is perhaps too narrow, since, as we have seen, for Paul the gospel has to be proclaimed in deed as well as word. Conybeare renders, 'by openly setting forth the truth.'

It is also significant that Paul speaks of their efforts to commend themselves to every human *conscience in the sight of God* – an expression which suggests that anyone who is true to his or her own conscience should be able to recognize the consistency of the conduct of the messengers with their message.

[1] Denney, p. 146.

4.3f.   But now, as happens so often in Romans, Paul hears in his mind an objection from those whom he is seeking to convince. 'If you have proclaimed the gospel with the openness and integrity that you claim, why has the gospel failed to commend itself to so many hearers, particularly so many Jews? Has the truth of the message been veiled from them?' Collange has suggested that Paul is here responding to the charge that his proclamation of the gospel has been veiled by his own weaknesses – a very plausible suggestion, in the light of the direction of the next paragraph of the letter.[2]

Paul's first response is simply to say that, if there is any sense in which the gospel is veiled, *it is veiled only for those on the way to destruction*, but in the following verse he indicates that this veiling has a twofold cause: they have been *blinded by the god of this passing age*, and they have refused to believe. This is the only passage in the New Testament in which Satan is called a god, though John speaks of 'the ruler of this world' (12.31; 14.30; 16.11). It is a title in which is condensed, as Denney puts it, 'Paul's whole sense of the might and malignity of the powers of darkness.'[3]

But, while Paul sees in unbelief the work of Satan, that does not exonerate unbelievers of their responsibility. In the same way, in the letter to the Romans, the emphasis in 9.6–29 is all on divine pre-destination, but from 9.30–10.21 all on the need for the obedience of faith.

However we may account for the failure of some to believe, the outcome is that *the gospel of the glory of Christ, who is the image of God, cannot dawn upon them and bring them light*. There is an impressive accumulation here of terms for light and illumination. The verb Paul uses in the second half of the verse is probably to be understood as meaning 'see', but it can mean 'shine forth' and is cognate with the word for 'dawn' – a connection which the REB translators have managed to convey.

The description of the gospel as having for its content the glory of Christ recalls chapter 3, in which the theme of glory is so central.

To a modern reader, 'the glory of God' may well suggest God's

---

[2] See Jean-François Collange, *Énigmes de la deuxième épître aux Corinthiens. Étude exégétique de 2 Cor. 2: 14–7: 4*, pp. 132, 143.

[3] Denney, p. 149. Denney's further comments on the propriety of such language are also worth pondering: 'What St. Paul saw is that evil has a power and dominion in the world which are betrayed, by their counteracting of the Gospel, to be purely malignant – in other words, Satanic – and the dimensions of which no description can exaggerate. Call such powers Satan, or what you please, but do not imagine that they are inconsiderable.' (p. 150).

unapproachable otherness, but in the Old Testament the glory of God is frequently connected with that which reveals God and makes God known. It is thus associated with particular places, like the temple (see e.g. I Kings 8.10f.), and also with particular times and events, like the Exodus (see e.g. Exod. 24.15–18). 'The gospel of the glory of Christ' is to be understood therefore as the good news of God's self-revelation in Christ.[4]

As so used, the word 'glory' is closely related to the thought of Christ as *the image of God*. The word 'image', which has already been used in 3.18, implies a true representation, not a mere copy.[5]

4.5   His imagination fired by the thought of the gospel as divine illumination, Paul is now led to utter one of those lapidary statements which go to the heart of the matter in a way that no other writer has ever surpassed. In our admiration for the pungent brevity of Paul's formulation, however, we should not overlook the likelihood of it having a polemical edge. Why emphasize that *it is not ourselves that we proclaim* but *Christ Jesus as Lord?* Paul could well have been charged with self-praise (cf. 3.1). Moreover, he is very likely to be implying that there are others who are, in effect, preaching themselves. We have already heard of some who rely on letters of introduction to ingratiate themselves with the community (3.1). These letters may well have chronicled their deeds of spiritual power. In 5.12 Paul will speak of *those whose pride is all in outward show and not in inward worth.* Such language suggests boasting of superficially impressive achievements.

Then in 10.10 he quotes a scathing comment that is being made by his opponents about himself, to the effect that while *his letters are weighty and powerful, when he is present he is unimpressive, and as a speaker he is beneath contempt.* No doubt, in respect of the last two qualities his opponents also drew telling comparisons between Paul and their own gifted selves.

In the light of all this evidence, it is highly likely, even allowing for the possibility that 10.10 is part of a later letter, that Paul's opponents in Corinth, whose profile is steadily growing clearer, were guilty, in Paul's eyes, precisely of preaching themselves, by parading the visible evidence of their possession of the Spirit, as well as by flaunting their superiority over Paul in personal presence and eloquence.

[4] For a fuller discussion see W. D. Davies, *Invitation to the New Testament*, pp. 42–49.
[5] For a fuller discussion see Furnish, pp. 222, 248.

Paul's further statement that we proclaim *ourselves as your servants for Jesus's sake* is also to be seen as having a polemical edge. The clear implication of 11.20 is that Paul's opponents have sought, not without success, to establish themselves as the spiritual lords and masters of the community.

But within the church there is no place whatever for such a distorted understanding of leadership. On the contrary, the apostle, the leader *par excellence*, is called to be the servant of all, to spend himself or herself to the limit on behalf of others, as Paul puts it in 12.15, even as Christ did not please himself but became a servant of all (Rom. 15.3, 8).

4.6   Once again Paul has recourse to the thought of the gospel as divine illumination. With great daring he places side by side the illumination of the human heart by the light of the gospel and the creation of light itself out of the darkness of chaos by the Creator God. It is *the God who said, 'Out of darkness light shall shine,'* who *has caused his light to shine in our hearts.*

And that light, that illumination, consists in *the knowledge of the glory of God in the face of Jesus Christ*. For the connotations of 'glory' see our discussion of v. 4.

The reference to Christ's face implies a further contrast to the old order established by Moses. The Israelites with Moses may have had a partial glimpse of the glow on Moses' face that was a reflection of his intimate intercourse with God, but we Christians behold with unveiled faces the glory of God in the face of Jesus Christ, who is the image of God.[6] Cf. John 1.18: 'No one has ever seen God', not even Moses; 'God's only Son, he who is nearest to the Father's hand, has made him known.'

Treasure in earthenware jars, life in mortal bodies
4.7–12

Paul has risen to great heights in the claims he has just been making for the gospel he bears. But no sooner has he articulated these claims than he hears in his mind once more a hostile listener's objection:

---

[6] For a suggestive meditation on the face of Christ as the locus of revelation see Young and Ford, *Meaning and Truth*, pp. 248–60.

'Who is this person who is soaring to such heights and making such extraordinary claims? On the lips of one like himself, they do not ring true. Between the message and the person of the messenger there is a ludicrous disproportion.'

We have already referred, in our comments on v. 5, to 10.10, where Paul quotes the taunts which his detractors have been making about the inadequacy of his personal presence and rhetorical skills. Even if that chapter dates from a later letter, it is still evidence of the tactics that his opponents were capable of using against him.

4.7   Paul's response to this anticipated objection is, in effect, to say, 'Yes, there is indeed a disproportion, a ludicrous disproportion, between the message and its messengers. The treasure of the gospel is contained in mere *earthenware jars*.' Is Paul thinking here of the trifling value of earthenware jars or of their fragility? The word readily conveys both of these connotations, and it would be a mistake to limit his meaning to one or other of them.

Paul admits, then, the vast disparity between the treasure and its container, between the message and the messenger. But that is just the way it ought to be. In the Greek, the second half of the verse consists of a purpose clause. It is God's will that the treasure be contained in mere earthenware jars, *in order that* its unparalleled power may be seen to come from God and not be their own. No one in their senses could gainsay the power of the gospel to transform human lives, to bring men and women out of captivity to vices of every sort into freedom to walk in newness of life (II Cor. 3.1–3; cf. I Cor. 6.9–11). If the bearer of such a word of power is, in his own person, transparently powerless, without presence or eloquence, no superman but rather one who is all too human, then that simply proves that the source of the *transcendent power* does not lie in himself but in God alone. The glaring disparity between the power of the message and the powerlessness of the messenger serves to protect the truth that 'salvation is of the Lord' (Jonah 2.9, AV)[7].

4.8f.   Furthermore, the paradox that those who are in themselves transparently powerless are yet the bearers of a message of transcendent power is lived out, so to speak, in the daily lives of the apostles. Again and again, in their service of the gospel, they find themselves in desperate straits, with no way out, only to be rescued and sustained by a power outside themselves. *We are hard pressed, but*

---

[7] Cf. my comments on II Cor. 1.9.

never cornered; bewildered, but never at our wits' end; hunted, but never abandoned to our fate; struck down, but never killed.

Superficially, there are points of contact between Paul's language here and that of the Stoics, who spoke of life as a continual struggle against adversity, but, on closer examination, profound differences emerge. Central to Stoic philosophy is the ideal of *apatheia*, of freedom from emotion, but there is no trace of this in Paul. On the contrary, it is probably true to say that, as a Christian, Paul *felt* more deeply than ever. Furthermore, he knows that the source of strength lies not in himself, as the Stoics thought, but in God.[8]

4.10f.   In the next two verses these partial contrasts between human weakness and divine power are summed up and concentrated in one great contrast: death and life. Paul and his associates are all their life *being handed over to death*. In the trials that they face daily in their work for Jesus they are being continually exposed to the danger of dying. More than that: their vital energy is continually being sapped. On the other hand, their repeated escapes from seemingly hopeless situations represent a series of resurrections.

But Paul is not simply saying that there is in their own experience something *analogous* to the dying and rising of Jesus, though that is also true. Believers not only pass through 'deaths' and 'resurrections' *like* Jesus, they die and rise *with* him. Faith, for Paul, means a deep identification of the believer with Jesus in his death and resurrection. In the trials that they are continually undergoing there is a continual re-enactment in their own lives of *the death that Jesus died*, while the constant redemption of their weakness by the transcendent power of God represents a continual revelation even *in this mortal body of ours* of *the life of Jesus*, the life that Jesus lives. For Paul, the dying and rising of Jesus are not to be understood as events which are purely external to the believer, events of which one is simply informed. They are rather events into which one enters and with which one becomes integrated.

In Romans the emphasis falls more on the moral dimension of this dying and rising. In baptism we die to sin and are raised to serve God in a new way in the power of the Spirit (Rom. 6.1–11; 7.4–6; cf. Gal. 2.19f.; II Cor. 5.14f.). At the same time the believer has the hope of being raised to a new life over which death will have no power (Rom. 6.5, 8).

[8] For a fuller discussion of the contrast between Stoicism and Paulinism see Barrett, p. 139; Furnish, pp. 281f.

In contrast to Romans, this passage speaks of a kind of anticipation of the final victory over death in our mortal bodies here and now.

The thought of v. 10 is restated and intensified in v. 11, in which Paul substitutes for the word 'body' (*sōma*) the word 'flesh' (*sarx*; REB: 'mortal body'), a word which refers to present existence in all its weakness, mortality and limitations.[9]

Since Paul is acquainted with the tradition of Jesus being 'handed over' to be crucified (I Cor. 11.23; cf. Mark 9.31; 10.33), his choice of this word in v. 11 could well be intended to underline the parallel between Jesus' dying and our suffering.

His repeated use of the bare name 'Jesus' (four times in vv. 10 and 11) is probably to be explained in the same way. The name directs us to the definite historical period and the events that took place within it.

The emphasis in both these verses on the necessity for the believer to be continually a-dying, in order that the power of the resurrection might be revealed, is significant, when one remembers the predilection of the Corinthians, noted in our earlier commentary, for emphasizing the resurrection at the expense of the cross.[10] Paul now faces a similar triumphalism in opponents who claim that the power of God is revealed not in their weakness but in their strength – their charismatic presence and rhetorical skills (10.10; 11.5f.), their signs and wonders (12.11f.; cf. 11.23ff.).

4.12 Every Christian is called to die with Christ in order to be raised with him, but this pattern of identification with Christ in his dying and rising is seen particularly clearly in the life of an apostle.[11] Such identification entails loyalty to Christ, cost what it may. For apostles, however, such loyalty is likely to prove more costly, since it is on them that the full brunt of the world's opposition to the gospel falls. They are more likely to have to literally surrender their lives for the sake of the gospel, as Paul himself was to surrender his.

Furthermore, such sufferings have a vicarious side. Since apostles are servants of the church, in imitation of Christ, the Servant *par excellence*, the greater measure of suffering which their 'dying with Christ' entails leads to life for other believers. So Paul can go on to say, *Thus death is at work in us, but life in you.* All Christians can say, or

---

[9] For a fuller discussion of Paul's use of the word 'flesh' see my comments on I Cor. 3.1 in my earlier volume.
[10] See my commentary on I Corinthians, p. xxvii.
[11] Cf. Barrett, p. 141.

ought to be able to say, 'We die, so that we may live,' but apostles can also say to other Christians, 'We die, so that you too may live.' A similar thought is expressed in Col. 1.24.

What God has begun . . .
4.13–15

4.13 The previous paragraph could be described as a celebration of triumph over adversity, the triumph of life over death. It is not surprising that this celebration leads to a further expression of confidence, similar to those in 3.12 and 4.1. Paul is confident of having the same faith in God as inspired the author of Ps. 116 to declare, *I believed, and therefore I spoke out.* Paul is quoting the LXX text, which deviates somewhat from the MT.

He must surely have been aware of the words that immediately follow the words he has actually quoted, as well as of the mood of the preceding verses, which belong to a separate psalm in the LXX but are part of the same psalm in the MT. The words that immediately follow show that the speaker is one who has spoken out, in spite of being greatly afflicted. As for the mood of the preceding verses, that is one of thanksgiving for deliverance from a seemingly hopeless situation, from apparently certain death.

That has been the constant experience of Paul and his associates in the service of the gospel, but with this difference: they know that the power by which they are being continually rescued is the same power that raised Jesus from the dead, and that the life by which they are being continually sustained is the life that Jesus lives.

4.14 Such a conviction leads to certain hope. *He who raised the Lord Jesus to life,* and who is continually rescuing us even now from apparently certain death, *will with Jesus raise us too,* to share with him that life of his over which death no longer has dominion (cf. Rom. 6.9). Paul appears to be quoting a traditional formula here (cf. Rom. 8.11; I Cor. 6.14; 15.22f.), but the last words of the verse, *and bring us to his presence, and you with us,* have no exact parallel elsewhere and are probably Paul's own addition. Paul cannot contemplate his own future blessedness apart from that of his converts.

Throughout the New Testament, the resurrection of Jesus is

consistently represented not as an isolated miracle but as the beginning of God's renewal of all things.[12] In the long fifteenth chapter of I Corinthians Paul himself has insisted that there is an indivisible nexus between belief in the resurrection of Jesus Christ and belief in the final resurrection of believers. Affirm his resurrection, and you are committed to affirming their resurrection also; deny their resurrection, and you are committed to denying his resurrection too.[13]

4.15   The mention of 'us with you' now leads Paul to stress that all the efforts of himself and his colleagues, all the trials that they endure, are undertaken for the sake of the Corinthians (and, no doubt, all the other people committed to their care) and, ultimately, for the glory of God. The greater their efforts on behalf of the gospel, the greater the number of those who will share in *the abounding grace of God*, and the greater will be *the chorus of thanksgiving that rises to the glory of God*. The thought here parallels 1.11. 'Grace', like 'righteousness',[14] can denote both a quality of God, an activity of God and a gift from God to the believer. Here the word seems to be a synonym for salvation.

Living by faith in what is unseen
4.16–18

While these verses have clear links with the earlier part of the chapter, they are also closely related to the opening paragraph of chapter 5, as is implied by the REB paragraph divisions. All through these eight verses Paul keeps ringing the changes on the contrast between what is of passing and what is of permanent significance.

4.16   Paul begins by reiterating the claim made in v. 1 that *we do not*

[12] Cf. Pheme Perkins, *Resurrection: New Testament Witness and Contemporary Reflection*, pp. 125, 318.
[13] In an earlier book of mine I raised the question whether at this point Paul was simply unable to shake off a traditional belief. I went on to argue that at the root of Paul's confidence in the resurrection of believers lies the conviction that there is no way that God could be satisfied with such a partial fulfilment of his purpose for us as can be attained in this life. Indeed, God cannot be held to be content with anything less than the restoration of the whole creation. See Nigel Watson, *Easter Faith and Witness*, pp. 64–67. Cf. also my commentary on I Cor. 15.12–28 in my earlier volume in this series.
[14] Cf. my earlier comments on 3.9.

lose heart. In the verses that have followed v. 1 he has evoked an exhilarating vision of Christ as the embodiment of the glory of God, and of the gospel as good news of a new creation (vv. 4–6); of the manifestation of the life of Jesus in the fragility and mortality of present existence (vv. 8–11); and of ultimate resurrection from the dead to life with Christ in the presence of God (vv. 14f.). Given such grounds for confidence, *no wonder we do not lose heart!*

To be sure, *our outward humanity is in decay.* Paul has already acknowledged that their vital energy is continually being sapped (vv. 10f.). They are mortal, and their labours on behalf of the gospel are taking their toll on their health. Yet *day by day* they are *inwardly renewed,* and this experience of daily renewal inspires the sure and certain hope of resurrection. In the midst of present decay, they taste already the power of resurrection life (cf. vv. 10f.).

According to a more literal translation, Paul speaks in this verse of 'our outward person' and 'our inward person' – language which might suggest a dualistic view of the human person as a soul imprisoned in a body – but the first letter provides ample evidence that this is not Paul's view.[15] 'Our outward person' stands here for the person as subject to the trials listed in vv. 8–11, 'our inward person' for the person as renewed by the power of God.

4.17   *Our troubles* are real, but they are *slight and short-lived.* This may sound like a massive understatement, in the light of Paul's catalogue of hardships undergone in 11.23–33, not to mention 1.8. Nevertheless, these troubles fade into insignificance, in comparison to the 'eternal weight of glory', to quote the more literal AV rendering, which awaits us. Paul's thought here is closely paralleled in Rom. 8.18–25.

What is more, between our present troubles and the glory that awaits us there is a vital connection. Our light, momentary affliction is preparing, is winning for us, an eternal weight of glory, out of all proportion to our present suffering.

4.18   Meanwhile, we fix our eyes *not on the things that are seen but on the things that are unseen.* Paul's description of the things that are seen as *transient* or temporary, and the things that are not seen as *eternal* has quite a Platonic ring, but a distinction between an eternal world of forms and a temporal world of becoming is not what is implied. By 'the things that are seen' Paul clearly means the troubles that are his

[15] Cf. my commentary on I Corinthians, pp. xxviiif.

present lot, and by 'the things that are unseen' something like 'the things prepared by God for those who love him' (I Cor. 2.9), of which we already have a foretaste.

It is likely that 4.16–5.5, like the earlier paragraphs of chapter 4, has a more polemical edge than appears at first sight. We have already seen reason to believe that Paul is facing opponents who are boasting of their feats of spiritual power and flaunting their superiority over Paul in personal presence and eloquence (see our commentary on 4.5). For them, it seems, apostleship was authenticated by acts of power and glory. If so, we can imagine how much capital they must have made out of the sufferings Paul had undergone. How could anyone who had taken such a battering be an authentic apostle? Paul's contention, in these final verses, is that physical hardship is of negligible moment, in comparison to the glory to which it leads.

The apologetic force of the previous paragraph should also not be missed. The scars of suffering that Paul exhibits are signs of the reality of his identification with Christ crucified. They are therefore signs that his life is authentically Christian and authentically apostolic. They are not a contradiction of his apostleship, as his enemies maintain; on the contrary, they are its most compelling vindication.

Groaning, yet in hope
5.1–5

The first ten verses of chapter 5 are notorious for the difficulties they pose for the exegete. Indeed, they make up what is arguably the most difficult passage in the whole Pauline corpus. In 1973 F. G. Lang published a study of the passage in which he surveyed the interpretations of 108 scholars from Calvin on,[1] and since then the spate of writing has shown no sign of abating.

The passage has sometimes been described as a digression, but less commonly so in recent years, now that scholars are more aware how pervasively polemical this letter is. We have already found reason to think that the last verse of the previous chapter has a polemical edge, thus: We fix our eyes on the glory which endures, in contrast to those who glory in what is trivial and transient. The first five verses of

[1] F. G. Lang, *2. Korinther 5, 1–10 in der neueren Forschung*; cf. also my review article, '2 Cor. 5: 1–10 in Recent Research,' *AusBR* 23, 1975, pp. 33–36.

chapter 5 are closely linked grammatically with 4.18 by the use of the conjunction *gar* (for) in v. 1 and *kai gar* (for indeed) in vv. 2 and 4. When Paul follows up a *gar* by a *kai gar* elsewhere, he is regularly reinforcing a reason just given (see e.g. I Thess. 3.4; 4.10). This suggests that vv. 1–4 offer three parallel reasons why we fix our eyes not on the things that are seen but on the things that are unseen, and therefore do not lose heart.

5.1   Paul begins with a contrast between the earthly house, a mere tent, which houses us today, and an eternal, God-given building, not made with hands, which awaits us in heaven. If the tent is demolished, we have, we possess, the eternal building.

It is generally agreed that the demolition of the tent is an image for the death of the physical body. From the time of Pythagoras and Plato on, a tent is often used as an image for the human body in its impermanence and vulnerability.[2]

As for the eternal building, this is often, and in our judgment rightly, taken as an image for the spiritual body. It is true that the image of a building is used in Jewish apocalyptic as a comprehensive metaphor for the new age,[3] but the way Paul moves in v. 2 from the image of a building to that of a garment suggests that he is thinking of how the new age will impinge on the individual believer, hence of the spiritual body.

Many commentators argue that the present tense, *we possess*, must be taken literally, as meaning 'we possess forthwith,' in other words, that we are to receive the spiritual body at death, in contrast to I Corinthians 15 and I Thessalonians 4, where Paul envisages the spiritual body being received at the *parousia*. Others, like Barrett and Martin, argue that even here Paul is still referring to the *parousia*,[4] the present tense expressing certainty about the future.

If a choice has to be made between these two interpretations, we would choose the former. However, in view of the brevity of Paul's language and the absence of some of the key terms found in I Cor. 15.35–50, where he is undoubtedly concerned with the 'how?' of resurrection – terms like 'physical body' and 'spiritual body' – it would seem that his primary concern here is not to satisfy curiosity about the timing and nature of bodily transformation but to affirm the certainty of the consummation God has in store.

[2] See Furnish, p. 264, for a fuller discussion.
[3] See especially the passage from II Esdras 10.53–55 quoted by Furnish, p. 294.
[4] Barrett, p. 152; Martin, p. 104.

5.2   In vv. 2 and 4 Paul gives two further reasons why we do not fix our eyes on the things that are seen but on those that are unseen. *In this present body we groan.* Groaning, according to Rom. 8.22–27, afflicts the whole created order during the present age, and Christians are not exempt from it, nor is even the Spirit. But our groaning is not just a groaning under the burden of mortality but a groaning of *yearning to be covered by our heavenly habitation*, just as the groaning of which Paul speaks in Rom. 8.22f. is filled with hope and thus comparable to the pangs of childbirth. We have already argued, in our comments on v. 1, that by the 'heavenly habitation', which becomes a garment, Paul means the spiritual body.

Paul's hope is not just to put on the heavenly building or garment but to *put* it *on over this one*. In our view, he has used a double compound verb, *ependysasthai*, in order to show that the changeover from the old body to the new will be instantaneous, realized at death, with no interval of conscious nakedness. If one assumes, with Barrett and Martin and others, that 'we possess' in v. 1 refers to the *parousia*, then Paul has used the double compound verb to express the hope that he will survive until the Lord's coming.

5.3   The main problem raised by this verse is the precise meaning of the word 'naked'. In the immediate context Paul speaks of being clothed (a compound verb, v. 3), being overclothed (a double compound, vv. 2 and 4) and being stripped (v. 4) – each time, in our view, with reference to investiture with, or deprivation of, a body. If this is correct, it seems natural to take 'naked' in v. 3 as an extension of the same figure of speech and therefore as referring to existence as a naked soul without a body, the more so, since the word 'naked' is used with this meaning in Plato and other ancient authors.[5] It should be noted that this interpretation does not imply that Paul is contemplating the possibility of such an existence. Rather is he expressing relief that he will not have to endure it. The verse is introduced by a pair of particles which normally express confidence, as in the REB translation, not uncertainty.[6]

[5] See A. Feuillet, 'Demeure céleste et destinée des Chrétiens,' *RSR* 44, 1956, p. 382; Barrett, pp. 153f.

[6] It is this aspect of the matter which is overlooked by Joseph Osei-Bonsu in his article, 'Does II Cor. 5.1–10 teach the reception of the resurrection body at the moment of death?' (*JSNT* 28, 1986, pp. 81–101). He argues that 'Paul would not have dreaded the state of disembodied nakedness, if he had held the view that the resurrection body was received at the moment of death' (p. 91). Our contention is that the tone of v. 3 is not one of dread but rather of relief.

Some commentators argue that this interpretation attributes to Paul an utterance which is banal and even tautologous, but we do not find this conclusion to be justified. So far in this passage, Paul has referred to the life to come by means of images of building and clothing. The words, 'not . . . naked', are the first clear indication that the life to come will be *bodily* existence. They are therefore not tautologous. Nor are they banal. Given the distaste of the Corinthian Christians for bodily existence of any sort, Paul's words here acquire a sharp point. For them, it seems, stripping off the body and gaining a disembodied state represented the true goal. It is this view that Paul is opposing.[7]

Some scholars, however, try to resolve the problems they perceive in v. 3 by taking the word 'naked' to refer not to bodiless existence but to the state of being denuded of good works, the state of alienation from Christ, through having in some way denied one's baptism.[8] However, this view seems less likely than the commoner interpretation, given Paul's repeated use of the image of clothing to refer to the reception of the resurrection body. It would certainly have required a real leap of understanding on the part of the Corinthians to catch a reference to judgment at this point.[9]

5.4   The next verse takes up v. 2 and spells it out in more detail. Life *within this earthly frame* is burdensome, and Paul groans under it, yet this groaning is ultimately one of longing, not of despair. It is not that he wants to have the old garment stripped off, that is, to escape into a state of permanent disembodiment. Rather does he long to be clothed afresh with the new garment, in other words, for a new and lasting embodiment and, what is more, if our understanding of v. 2 is correct, at death, so that, to adopt a literal translation, the mortal, that is, our present physical existence, may be swallowed up, that is, instantly succeeded, by eternal life.

[7] Cf. T. Francis Glasson, '2 Corinthians v. 1–10 *versus* Platonism,' *SJT* 43, 1990, pp. 145–55. For a discussion of the rather desperate remedy adopted by the majority of editors of the United Bible Societies' Greek New Testament, see Furnish, pp. 267f.
[8] For a list of scholars who take this view, see Furnish, pp. 268, 298f. This is also the view preferred by Furnish himself and by Lang (2. *Korinther 5, 1–10*, p. 188).
[9] The view I am advocating involves taking *endysamenoi* in v. 3 as repeating the sense of the double compound verb of the previous verse, but the possibility of this construction has been shown by J. H. Moulton in *A Grammar of New Testament Greek: Prolegomena*, p. 115. Some argue that Paul intends a distinction between the double compound in vv. 2 and 4 and the single compound in v. 3, and interpret the latter as a reference to the putting on of Christ in baptism, and the former as a reference to the fulfilment of salvation. See Furnish, pp. 267, 296f.

5.5 This verse rounds off the thought of the paragraph. The consummation of which Paul has been speaking is sure, because it rests ultimately on the purpose of God, who has given us, in the Spirit, a pledge or advance payment of the salvation for which we yearn. For a discussion of the Greek word, *arrabōn*, which is used here, see our comments on 1.22.

The movement of Paul's thought here is very similar to that of Rom. 8.18–25. In both passages there is a contrast between our present affliction and the coming glory, which far surpasses it. In both passages we long, indeed groan, for the consummation. And in both, in the midst of our longing, we yet have the Spirit.

Living in chastened hope
5.6–10

5.6 Paul now picks up once again from 4.1 and 16 the theme of confidence. *We never cease to be confident.* We are always of good courage, come what may.

This confidence rests on hope and is therefore inseparable from a longing for fulfilment. In the previous paragraph Paul has twice spoken of how we groan in our yearning to be clothed with resurrection life. Now he speaks of our present life as a kind of exile. The body, that is, our present physical body, is our present home, but, so long as life lasts, *we are exiles from the Lord.*

This may seem a strange expression from the lips of one who speaks so often of living in Christ, and Christ living in him. Indeed, Lang argues that the usual interpretation of the words here translated 'we are at home' and 'we are exiles' as referring to two kinds of existence, viz. existence in this life and existence in the life beyond, is mistaken. These terms are more naturally taken as denoting two opposing attitudes, the attitudes contrasted in 4.18, viz. aiming at what can be seen and aiming at what cannot be seen.[10]

This view, however, is hard to maintain in the light of v. 9, where Paul puts being at home and being in exile side by side, as if the distinction between them were of no ultimate importance.

Lang is probably right, though, in suggesting that Paul has

[10] Lang, *2. Korinther 5, 1–10*, pp. 189–91.

borrowed the word for 'being at home' from his opponents, in order
to contradict their position, since neither this term nor its converse is
used anywhere else by Paul or elsewhere in the New Testament or
the LXX. They may well have spoken of being at home in the earthly
body, in line with their over-realized eschatology and claims to
present glory, thus prompting Paul to create the contrast between
being at home and being an exile, in order to assert the incompleteness of life in the body.

With this verse we may compare Rom. 8.23, where, using all the
devices for emphasis available to him in the Greek language, Paul
declares that it is precisely we Christians to whom the Spirit has been
given as firstfruits who groan within ourselves, as we eagerly await
our adoption and liberation from mortality. The gift of the Spirit does
not diminish that longing for fulfilment which we share with the
whole creation, it intensifies it.

5.7   The previous verse could give the impression that in this life we
are entirely separated from Christ. That may be one reason why Paul
now introduces the contrast between faith and sight. Though exiles
from the Lord, we are still linked with him by faith.

At the same time, the polemical thrust is maintained. Paul's
opponents pride themselves on what can be *seen* of the Spirit's
presence in their lives, but Paul will shortly dismiss this as outward
show (5.12).

5.8   Once again, as in v. 6, Paul expresses in the same breath
confidence and longing. We are in good heart, but this is because of
our hope, and therefore we would really prefer death to life, since it
would bring us into a closer union with the Lord. Better by far to be at
home with him and exiled from the body.

Indeed, if our interpretation of v. 1 is correct, exile from the
present body would mean the assumption of a new and glorious
body and therefore, in a sense, no 'exile', no deprivation at all. Yet it
would still mean, for Paul, severing links which are dear to him and
leaving work unfinished.

There is in this passage something of the oscillation of mood that
we find in Phil. 1.21–26.

5.9   Paul's longing for closer union with Christ now recedes before
one overwhelming desire, that of being *acceptable* to the Lord,
wherever we are, at home or in exile, that is, whether remaining in the

body or being in the nearer presence of Christ beyond death. In the light of that supreme ambition, whether Paul lives or dies becomes ultimately irrelevant. This verse qualifies the clear preference for death which Paul has expressed in v. 8, just as Phil. 1.24ff. qualifies 1.23.

Once again his words are likely to have a polemical edge. Let the Corinthians take note that he and those associated with his apostolate are intent on pleasing the Lord, not on winning honour from men.

5.10 What gives urgency to Paul's overriding desire to be acceptable, or well-pleasing, to the Lord is his conviction that we must all appear before him as our judge and *have our lives laid open* before him.

Underlying the rendering 'laid open' is a word often translated 'manifested'. Its prominence in this letter (nine times in all) is probably due to the predilection of Paul's opponents for pointing to the manifestation of the power of God in their ecstasy, their rhetorical skills and impressive presence (cf. 10.10; 11.5; 12.11). If so, Paul is saying that the only manifestation that really matters is the manifestation of the true worth of who we are and what we have done *before the tribunal of Christ.*

The prominence of the theme of judgment in the Corinthian correspondence, and in I Corinthians particularly, is something to which we have drawn attention elsewhere.[11]

Some scholars have argued that the belief in a last judgment represents a relic of Paul's Jewish past, but there is good reason to maintain that it has been thoroughly assimilated and Christianized. One way in which the traditional Jewish belief is modified in Paul's letters, and in the New Testament generally, is that the role of the supreme judge is sometimes, as here, fulfilled by Christ rather than by God.

In I Cor. 3.10–17 we can see another way in which some current Jewish beliefs have been modified. In contrast to the judgment scene in the Testament of Abraham, chapters 12 and 13, where salvation depends on a preponderance of good deeds over bad, Paul in this chapter envisages even the Christian jerrybuilder, whose contribution to the building of the church has been unworthy of the foundation, yet being saved, 'though only by passing through the fire.' In other words, we will be judged not by our works but by our

---

[11] See my commentary on I Corinthians, pp. xxvif.; cf. also my article, 'Justified by faith; judged by works – an antinomy?' *NTS* 29, 1983 pp. 213–15.

faith, by whether we have said a fundamental Yes or No to God in Christ.

At the same time, our works will be judged, that is, the true worth of the work we have done for God will be exposed for what it is. In the same way, the kind of judgment Paul has in mind in II Cor. 5.10 appears to be an exposure of the worth of believers' works rather than a testing of their fitness to be admitted to the presence of the Lord at all. The judgment of which he speaks here is evidently occasioned not by the sins of Christians but by their efforts to be well-pleasing to their Lord (v. 9). Note also the recurrence of the note of confidence in vv. 5, 6 and 8.

The syntax of v. 10 is difficult, which may be due to Paul's having added a reference to the body. It may well have occurred to him that his negative remarks about the body in vv. 6 and 8 could be misunderstood, and this may have prompted the reference to conduct in the body.

Paul's primary concern at this point is what judgment will mean for Christians. What it may mean for non-believers is a question he does not really address.

Constrained by the love of Christ
5.11–17

5.11   Here Paul returns to the theme of the apostolic ministry of proclamation, before going on to expound in greater detail the content of the message of the cross. He has just held before his readers the ineluctable fact of final judgment. All believers will appear, stripped of all disguises, before the judgment seat of Christ. Paul now declares that his ministry is controlled by that sobering prospect. It is *with this fear of the Lord* ever before his eyes that he *addresses* his *appeal to men and women*.

A more literal rendering of v. 11 would run, 'we seek to persuade men and women.' 'Persuade' is not a word we would expect Paul to use for proclamation, since it was often associated with clever but deceptive rhetoric. He is probably responding to the charge that he was unscrupulously adept at persuasion, at talking people round (cf. Gal. 1.10). The truth of the matter, however, is that he sees himself as a steward of the gospel, accountable to the Lord, who will disclose all the secrets of his heart, all his inward motives (cf. I Cor. 4.1–5). Indeed, he knows that to God his life lies open all the time. Behind the rendering 'lie open' stands the same Greek verb that is translated 'laid open' in v. 10. For the reasons for its prominence in this epistle see our comments on that verse. For Paul's frequent use of the pronoun 'we' to refer to himself, see our note following 1.8–11.

It is, moreover, Paul's hope that the truth of what sort of person he is is also plain to the Corinthians. Not that the Corinthians could ever know him with the depth with which he is known by God. What Paul does hope for is that the Corinthians will recognize in their *heart of hearts* (more literally, in their 'consciences') the fundamental integrity of his actions, the fact that he is a person with nothing to hide.

5.12   As happens so often in this letter, Paul now anticipates a reaction that some of his hearers and readers are likely to make to what he has just said: 'There he goes, recommending himself to us all over again.' For the probable social context of the word 'recommend' and the implications of Paul's repudiation of the suggestion that he is beginning to recommend himself all over again, see our comments on 3.1.

If Paul is not recommending himself all over again, what then is he doing? He is giving the main body of Corinthian Christians, who, he hopes, are still loyal to him, a reason to take pride in him. If they truly understand the message of the cross, then they will recognize that it is precisely Paul's sufferings that mark him out as a legitimate apostle of the crucified one. Not only so, it is also Paul's hope that they will express publicly the pride they feel in the Pauline apostolate and make public their support for Paul, and thus *have something to say to those whose pride is all in outward show and not in inward worth*, more literally, 'who boast in appearance and not in heart.' For a discussion of the prominence of words denoting boasting in this epistle see our comments on II Cor. 1.12–14. In 11.18 Paul speaks of those who *brag of their earthly distinctions*, literally 'boast according to the flesh,' and seems to mean the same thing. Goodspeed's rendering of 5.12 runs, 'who pride themselves on external advantages and not on sincerity of heart.' As noted already in connection with 5.7 and 10, the external advantages on which these opponents prided themselves appear to have included signs of the power of the Spirit in their lives in the form of ecstatic speech, rhetorical skills and impressive presence (cf. 10. 10; 11.5; 12.1 and 11). To these we should probably add their commendation from official sources (cf. 3.1), their Jewish descent (cf. 11.22) and a direct contact with the historical Jesus (cf. 5.16). The next verse suggests that it may well be ecstatic speech that Paul particularly has in mind at this point.[12] All these, he contends, are external things, matters of outward show. What really matters is sincerity of heart, a heartfelt devotion to those to whom one has been sent, and to that Paul lays claim without apology.

5.13   The next verse is probably not a comment on what Paul has just said, as is implied by the REB, but a defence of the motives undergirding all his ministry, in response to his critics. We can readily imagine them finding fault with his apostleship on the grounds that it was not supported, as theirs was, by public displays of ecstasy. Paul could, in fact, cite ecstatic experiences of his own (cf. I Cor. 14.18; II Cor. 12.1–4), but ecstasy is of no benefit for others (cf. I Cor. 14.6). Ecstatic speech is addressed to God.

The natural foil to ecstatic speech is sober, rational speech, and this contrast had already been made by Plato.[13] Paul's sober speech (REB: *sound sense*) is motivated by concern for his converts. In neither case is his speech motivated by self-interest. In the verses which follow, Paul lets us into the secret of his freedom from self-regarding motives.

5.14f.   Paul has spoken in v. 11 of having the fear of the Lord before his eyes, but fear, whether for oneself or for others, is not the deepest motive of the true evangelist. It is rather *the love of Christ*. Since Paul goes straight on to speak of the death of Christ *for all,* 'the love of Christ' should almost certainly be taken as referring to Christ's love for us rather than to our love for him (cf. Rom. 5.6, 8 and 10). But Christ's love is poured out for the whole of humanity. Really to accept such a love, to expose oneself to it and allow it to become the spring of one's actions, is to be caught up in its outreach towards the world.

In the latter part of v. 14 and v. 15 Paul spells out more precisely what it means to be controlled by the love of Christ. Christ died in order to bring about in us too a kind of dying, the death of the old, self-centred self and the coming to life of a new self that lives not for

---

[12] While explicit references to hostile intruders are confined to II Corinthians 10–13, there are, in our judgment, sufficiently close correspondences between the portrait of Paul's opponents which emerges from those chapters and certain polemical statements which Paul makes in the first nine to make it likely that they were already making their presence felt when Paul wrote chapters 1–9. For a fuller discussion see the Introduction, pp.xxxiif.

[13] For fuller discussions see Furnish, p. 325; Martin, p. 127.

itself but *for him who* for our sake *died and was raised to life.* Thus our response to his dying for us is to live for him. The best commentary on v. 15 is probably provided by Gal. 2.19f.

Verse 15 is one of those pellucid statements of Paul's which take us to the heart of his gospel. The last clause of v. 14, *and therefore all mankind has died,* can be interpreted in more than one way, but makes good sense, if interpreted along the lines of v. 15, that is, as meaning that through the death of Christ the way has been opened up for all to die to themselves that they might live for him.

This interpretation becomes more plausible in the light of the understanding of expiation that appears to inform the regulations for sacrifice in Leviticus 16 and 17. What happens in the act of atonement is not adequately described as an unloading of the sin of the people on to the sacrificial animal, which then pays the penalty they have incurred, through being put to death in their place. There is rather an identification of the representative sinful person with the sacrificial animal, in such a way that through its death the sinner offers his own life to God. The sprinkling of the blood on the altar, as in Lev. 17.11, signifies the surrender of life to God.

It is in this inward sense that there is an identification of the people, through the priest, with the animal offered in sacrifice, and it is in this inward sense, I suggest, that Christ's death entails the death of humanity also. His sacrificial self-offering enables us to offer our lives too.[14]

Scholars have often found in v. 14b a statement that could be used to support the penal substitutionary theory of the atonement, according to which Christ, in his dying, suffered in our place the penalty required of sinful humanity by the righteousness of God. On this view of the clause, 'all mankind has died' in the sense that the death which all were required to undergo has been undergone in their place by Christ. The penalty has been paid by him. Scholars who have interpreted the verse in this way have usually found further support for their interpretation in v. 20.

However, it is hard to believe that any such idea is in Paul's mind in vv. 14 and 15. According to the penal substitutionary view, Christ dies so that we might not need to die, but in v. 15 Paul goes on to say that Christ died precisely so that we too might die, in the sense of dying to ourselves.

In speaking of the intent of Christ's death, Paul speaks in universal

---

[14] For a fuller discussion see Lang, *An die Korinther*, pp. 295f. Leviticus 16 and 17 also throw light on Romans 6.

terms: *He died for all*. But, in speaking of the appropriation of the benefits of his dying, he speaks of *those who live*, thereby focussing attention on those who respond to his dying by a deliberate act of faith and thus find new life.

Paul does not emphasize at this point that living for Christ means living for others, but that this is so has been made abundantly clear in his first epistle, not only in chapter 13 but also in chapter 8, where, as we have tried to show in our earlier commentary, the concept of love determines the argument of the whole chapter.

5.16   Many versions make v. 16 the beginning of a new paragraph, but both v. 16 and v. 17 are statements of consequences which follow from what has been said in vv. 14 and 15. Paul has declared that the perception that one died for all leads to a redirection of one's life so radical and far-reaching that 'death and resurrection' is not too strong an expression to use for it. He now points to a particular area of a believer's life where change ought to be apparent, their estimate, their appreciation, of other people. We see other people through new eyes. *With us worldly standards have ceased to count in our estimate of anyone*. In the light of the repetition of 'all' in the two preceding verses, 'us' and 'our' in this verse should be taken as including the whole community of believers.

The more literal RV reads, 'Wherefore we henceforth know no man after the flesh.' The Greek word underlying 'flesh' here seems to denote what is external or superficial – a use comparable to that found in Rom. 2.28 and I Cor. 1.26. One's estimate of the worth of another person can be based on superficial things, like their appearance or race. One can mistake an acquaintance with such superficial aspects of a person for the knowledge of who they really are.

All this is also true, Paul adds, of our understanding of Christ. Even if worldly standards *counted* once *in our understanding of Christ, they do so now no longer*.

To what is Paul referring here? Is he thinking of his former Pharisaic estimate of Jesus, of how he was led by Jesus' lowly life and shameful death to make a disastrous misjudgment? That is quite possible, but it is also possible that once again his words have a polemical edge. Only four verses earlier, he has alluded disparagingly to the pride taken by his opponents in external advantages. These opponents, we later discover, were Jewish Christians who evidently came from Jerusalem (see 11.22f.). There is one respect in which these opponents are likely to have had a clear advantage over

Paul which they would have exploited to the full: a direct acquaintance with the historical Jesus.[15]

Whether this is so or not, it is highly likely that in the verse as a whole Paul is alluding to the superficial judgments that his opponents passed upon himself.

The main thrust of v. 16b is that a superficial acquaintance with Jesus fades into insignificance compared to knowing him as Saviour and Lord, the knowledge of the person who, through union with Christ, has died to sin and risen to new life.

It is noteworthy that Paul does not speak of 'knowing Christ after the Spirit', though the context would seem to suggest it. Probably, as J. Louis Martyn has argued, he has avoided such an expression because it was the sort of thing that his opponents, with their claims to have arrived, would have said only too readily. For Paul himself, however, who sees believers living not entirely in the new age but at the juncture between the old age and the new, the implied opposite of 'knowing after the flesh' is 'knowing after the cross.'[16]

Scholars have sometimes read v. 16b as if Paul were belittling all knowledge of the historical Jesus in comparison to the knowledge of the risen Lord, but this reading of the clause rests on the dubious assumption that the phrase 'after the flesh' goes with 'Christ', thus implying a contrast between a 'Christ after the flesh' and some other Christ.[17] It is 'fleshly' (i.e. superficial) knowledge of Christ that Paul is repudiating, not a 'fleshly' Christ in contrast to a 'spiritual' Christ.

5.17 Paul's thought now focusses once again on the transformation in which the believer participates. He has spoken of it in terms of dying and rising. Now he declares that *for anyone united to Christ* (more literally, 'if anyone is in Christ'), *there is a new creation: the old order has gone; a new order has already begun.*

---

[15] Furnish considers that 'the evidence for the beliefs and particularly for the christology of Paul's rivals is too indirect, fragmentary and ambiguous' to support the view that Paul is responding to the criticism that he had not known Jesus in the flesh, though he allows that Paul's remarks in 10.7ff.; 11.23; and I Cor. 9.1 could have been prompted by some such complaint (p. 331).

As for the question whether Paul had been acquainted with Jesus before the crucifixion, this text alone does not give us any clue, but if he had known Jesus, we would expect a clear allusion to the fact somewhere.

[16] J. Louis Martyn, 'Epistemology at the Turn of the Ages: 2 Corinthians 5: 16,' in W. R. Farmer and others (eds), *Christian History and Interpretation*, pp. 283, 285.

[17] The same phrase, 'after the flesh', is also used in v. 16a, where it is clearly adverbial, qualifying the verb 'we know'. This makes it likely that it is also used adverbially in 16b, qualifying the verb 'we have known', not the noun 'Christ'. For a fuller discussion see Furnish, pp. 312f., 330.

The REB rendering, *There is a new creation*, is certainly preferable to 'he is a new creature,' as in the AV. The context, along with the background of the expression in Jewish apocalyptic,[18] shows that Paul has in mind something more inclusive than the transformation of individual believers.

In the last clause Paul uses a perfect tense, so that an even more emphatic rendering would be in order, like 'everything has become new' (NRSV).

In their rendering of this clause the REB translators have also left untranslated the Greek word traditionally rendered 'behold' or 'lo', a word which again and again throughout the Bible introduces something extraordinary and marvellous (see e.g. Dan. 3.25; Matt. 2.9; 28.7; Luke 2.7). The use of the word here lends to the verse a triumphant note.

Such an emphatic statement of the radical change brought about by union with Christ as we find in this verse is the more remarkable, when one recalls Paul's constant concern throughout the first letter to qualify the 'now already' of the Corinthian enthusiasts by 'not yet', a concern which we have also found expressed in II Cor. 4.7–12 and 5.1–10. That Paul should now permit himself such an unqualified statement suggests that, while the errors of his opponents are never forgotten, they are not always in the forefront of his mind. Sometimes, as here, he is content simply to celebrate the gospel.

Messengers and ministers of reconciliation
5.18–6.2

5.18f.   Paul has just affirmed, without any qualification whatever, the fullness of salvation available now in Christ. But behind Christ he sees God the Father. Christ is the mediator in both creation and new creation, but God is the ultimate source both of the original gift of life and of its renewal (cf. I Cor. 8.6). Hence, *All this has been the work of God.*

In the same breath Paul points to two decisive acts in the past by which God has both brought us salvation and given us a part in his saving outreach to the world. The concept he uses to describe

---

[18] Parallels to Paul's language here are found not only in apocalyptic literature but as far back as Second Isaiah. See Furnish, pp. 314f.

salvation at this point is that of reconciliation. In all, the verb and the noun are used no fewer than five times in vv. 18–21. The only other passages where Paul speaks of reconciliation between God and humanity are Rom. 5.10 and 11 and Rom. 11.15. In the light of the relative infrequency of this terminology in his letters, the thought lies to hand that in these verses Paul may be using traditional material. This idea is strengthened by the degree of parallelism between v. 18 and v. 19. In each verse Paul speaks of God's act of reconciliation accomplished in Christ and his appointment of us as ministers or messengers of reconciliation. Since the 'us' of v. 18 follows on naturally from the 'us' of v. 16 ('we' in the Greek), it seems likely that v. 18 is Paul's own composition, designed to introduce v. 19, which represents, or at least includes, a traditional theological formulation. On this view, v. 18 is Paul's statement in advance of the essence of v. 19.

Some such view of the composition of vv. 18 and 19 is quite widely held. Furnish locates the original formula in v. 19ab and cites five arguments in support of this conclusion, one being that v. 19 is introduced in the Greek by a pair of conjunctions which is best explained as a citation formula, meaning, 'as it is said.'[19] 19c could very well come from Paul's own hand, given the uniquely high claim that he makes in v. 20 for the authority of the Christian ministry.[20]

If this view of the composition of vv. 18 and 19 is correct, it is significant that in v. 18 Paul has recast the traditional formula to give it a personal dimension: *He has reconciled us to himself . . . and has enlisted us.*

We have already noted that the term 'reconcile' is not central to Paul's vocabulary, not like the term 'justify'. Rom. 5.9 and 10 suggest, however, that for him these two terms are essentially synonymous. These two verses stand in clear synonymous parallelism to each other, each following the pattern, 'If, as is the case, we have been . . ., *a fortiori* we shall be . . .' Within this framework 'we have been justified' in v. 9a corresponds to 'we were reconciled' in v. 10a.

Another feature of Paul's use of the language of reconciliation to which all commentators rightly draw attention is that for Paul God is always the subject of reconciliation, never its object. There are

---

[19] Furnish, pp. 320, 334.
[20] Martin assigns clauses a and c to the traditional formula, together with 20ab, and regards 19b as Paul's own elucidation of the meaning of reconciliation (pp. 138–40), but the non-Pauline use of the plural, 'misdeeds', in 19b counts against this view (cf. Furnish, p. 319).

several passages in II Maccabees where we read of God being reconciled to his people (II Mac. 1.5; 5.20; 7.33; 8.29), but in Paul the work of reconciliation is one in which the initiative is taken by God. Men and women are reconciled or allow themselves to be reconciled.

5.19   In contrast to v. 18, where Paul has used verbal forms which point to actions completed in the past, in v. 19 the decisive divine act of reconciliation is represented as a process rather than a completed act – *God was reconciling*. The use of the imperfect tense suggests that, while the initiative in the work of reconciliation belongs to God, men and women still need to appropriate it and enter into it – a notion that is clarified by the following verse.

It is equally possible to translate v. 19a by 'In Christ God was reconciling the world to himself.' Indeed, this construction seems to be favoured by most recent commentators, on the grounds that an emphasis on the incarnation is not apparent in the rest of the paragraph.[21]

The one element of v. 19 which has no counterpart in v. 18 is the phrase, *no longer holding people's misdeeds against them*. This expression is similar to the expressions 'counting as righteous' and 'not counting sin' which Paul uses in Rom. 4.6 and 8 as synonyms of the word 'justify', which, in turn, as we have noted above, is evidently considered by Paul to be essentially synonymous with 'reconcile'.

5.20   Paul now focusses on the task of the ministers or messengers of reconciliation, and also brings into focus the response which such ministers are seeking. To this end, he introduces a new image, that of an ambassador. *We are therefore Christ's ambassadors* (more literally, 'We are ambassadors for Christ'). An ambassador is commissioned by a king or emperor and comes with his authority to further his cause. That seems to be the point of the metaphor here, that the ministers of the gospel are Christ's accredited representatives and spokespersons in the world.

In our judgment, the words which follow should not be introduced by 'as if', as in the REB. The actual Greek word Paul has used here (*hōs*) does not, strictly speaking, mean 'as if' but 'as', and its use with a participle, as here, implies that the words it introduces represent part of the thought of the subject of the main verb (here 'we are ambassadors'). The force of the construction here therefore is that Paul and his fellow evangelists act as Christ's ambassadors <u>in</u>

---

[21] This is the view taken by Furnish (p. 318), Martin (p. 153) and Best (p. 56).

the conviction that God is appealing to men and women through them. There is no suggestion of any doubt whether God is actually speaking through them.[22]

Ambassadors in the secular world may be content to present a formal message but not the ambassadors of Christ. *We implore*, we *entreat, we beg*. The king whom Paul and his associates represent does not force peace upon his rebellious creatures. He respects their freedom to choose and meets them in Christ as a suppliant.

On the face of it, the expressions Paul has used in vv. 18 and 19 might suggest that the work of reconciliation is entirely God's doing and that human beings are simply its passive objects. This would amount to a mechanization of the process of salvation. The truth is that reconciliation is incomplete until men and women respond. The particular expression Paul has used to describe that response, however, is highly significant. The burden of the apostolic entreaty to men and women is a passive imperative, *be reconciled to God!* In other words, what is required of them is not that they *do* anything at all but rather that they allow something to be done to them.

In the present context, however, this appeal is addressed not to unbelievers but precisely to the Corinthians. Perhaps it is Paul's hope that a renewal of their relationship with God will lead to full reconciliation with himself.

5.21   Verse 19 introduced the concept of the forgiveness of sins, but simply as a fact, with no attempt to explain how it was effected. Verse 21 throws some light on that mystery. What has been effected in the death of Christ is a kind of exchange. *Christ was innocent of sin, and yet for our sake God made him one with human sinfulness, so that in him we* (who, it is implied, are sinners) *might be made one with the righteousness of God.*

There is good reason to think that here once again Paul is quoting a traditional formulation. For one thing, the form of words he has used in v. 21b, which literally runs, 'that we might become the righteous-ness of God in him' (RV), is without parallel elsewhere. Elsewhere men and women are declared righteous or made righteous (see e.g. Rom. 3.24, 28; 5.19); they do not *become* the righteousness of God.[23]

In the more literal rendering of the NRSV the main clause reads,

---

[22] For a fuller discussion see my book, *Striking Home*, p. 118. Furnish (p. 339) and Martin (p. 156) take a similar view.

[23] For a fuller discussion of the reasons for thinking that Paul is quoting a traditional formula here see Furnish, p. 351; Martin, pp. 140, 144.

'For our sake he made him to be sin who knew no sin.' This clause is often cited as affording support for the penal substitutionary theory of the atonement, referred to in our commentary on v. 14. We cite James Denney as representative of this view: 'The sin is laid by God on the sinless One; its doom is laid on Him; His death is the execution of the divine sentence upon it.'[24]

Such an understanding of the verse is certainly possible, and becomes more plausible if one interprets the last clause in a strictly forensic sense, as equivalent to, 'that we might be declared righteous.' If this clause refers to a judgment *for* us, sinners though we be, then the preceding clause is naturally taken, given the antithetical parallelism of the verse, as referring to a judgment *against* Christ, sinless though he was.[25] But it is by no means assured that the final clause of the verse denotes a judicial declaration. Recent studies of the righteousness word group have emphasized the creative overtones of the word 'justify' in Paul, as well as the connotations of fidelity and power attaching to the word 'righteousness', as applied to God.[26] In the light of this evidence, an interpretation of v. 21b in strictly forensic or declaratory terms seems arbitrary, and there is much to be said for understanding 'righteousness' here in a more inclusive sense, comprehending both right relationship with God and transformation of life. If v. 21b is understood in this inclusive way, it becomes natural to understand v. 21a also in a more general way, as denoting Christ's total identification with sinful humanity.

There is also the possibility, dismissed too readily, in our judgment, by some scholars, that Paul is dependent here on a Jewish-Christian faith formula in which the death of Jesus was described as a sin-offering. 'Sin' is used with that meaning in the LXX in Lev. 4.21, 24; 5.12; and 6.18, and, furthermore, the death of the Servant is compared to a sin-offering in Isa. 53.10. If sacrificial ideas are in the background, we may refer to what was said in connection with v. 15 about the rationale of expiatory sacrifices in the Old Testament. What the act of sacrifice was believed, we suggested, to involve was an identification of the representative sinful person with the sacrificial animal in such a way that through its death he offered his own life in the name of the people to God. Hebrews understands this whole ritual to be in itself ineffective but nevertheless a God-given

---

[24] Denney, p. 220; cf. Martin, pp. 144f.; Kruse, pp. 129f.
[25] So especially Kruse, loc. cit.
[26] I am thinking especially of the work of Käsemann, Stuhlmacher and Ziesler. For a useful recent survey of the question see Wedderburn, *Reasons for Romans*, pp. 117–21.

pointer to the perfect self-offering of the Son of God once and for all (Heb. 10.5–10). It is, we believe, not fanciful to understand II Cor. 5.21 in a similar way. In his dying Christ made that perfect offering of himself to God which the sacrifices of the Old Testament could point to but never fully embody.

6.1 The first verse of chapter 6 reinforces the appeal of 5.20, so that vv. 1 and 2 are quite properly linked with the last paragraph of chapter 5, as in the REB. In 5.20 Paul has spoken of himself and his associates as Christ's ambassadors, whose words are used by God himself to address his appeal to men and women. The opening phrase of v. 1 in the REB, *Sharing in God's work,* which is a rendering of a single word in the Greek, recalls this earlier statement. Paul is now about to make a fresh appeal. Let it be clearly understood that it is in Christ's name and with his authority that the appeal is being made.

In 5.20 Paul addressed to the Corinthians the sort of appeal that one would expect to find in a call to unbelievers, as a reminder of the constant need for their faith and life to be renewed by the gospel. This verse is a further reminder that salvation is not accomplished in an instant. The Corinthians *have received the grace of God.* If they have any inkling of what this gift means, they cannot do other than allow it to reshape their lives. As recipients of grace, they can be expected to reflect something of that gift in the graciousness of their own conduct towards others. If not, God's grace will *come to nothing.*

This exhortation is couched in very general terms, but we may assume that Paul has in mind the delicate situation between the Corinthians and himself. If they allow themselves to be swayed by those opponents whose influence is already being felt in the community, with the result that they reject both him and the message which he has not only preached but sought to embody, then the grace of God will have been wasted on them.

6.2 Paul reinforces this appeal with a quotation from Isa. 49.8, with the aim of impressing upon his readers the decisive nature of this present time. In the context of Isaiah 49, the Lord hears the lament of Israel, his servant, that his work has brought no fruit or reward and comes to Israel's aid in *the hour* of his *favour, on the day of deliverance.* In the long history of God's people there have been many hours of God's favour, many days of deliverance. But, to adapt the words of Heb. 1.1f., whereas in times past God acted through his servants in fragmentary and varied fashion, in this the final age he has acted decisively in his Son. Therefore the hour of God's favour *par excellence*, the day of deliverance *par excellence*, is now. Let the Corinthians take this to heart and allow the grace of God, which they have received, to renew their being and control their actions.

In addressing such an urgent appeal to the Corinthians, Paul no doubt has painfully before his mind all the contemporaries of Jesus who had the opportunity to hear what ear had never heard and yet did not perceive the gracious visitation of God but let the acceptable year of the Lord pass by.

The pauper millionaires
6.3–10

Paul now concludes his defence of his apostolic ministry with a passage which builds up to a climax as moving as anything in all his writings. Since v. 3 is, grammatically, linked quite closely with v. 1, some versions do not begin a new paragraph at this point.

6.3   In v. 1 Paul has urged the Corinthians not to allow the grace of God, which they have received, to come to nothing. For their own part, he and his colleagues leave nothing undone to make sure that, if any of their hearers do reject the offer of the grace of God or, having accepted it, misuse it, it will not be because of obstacles that they have put in the way. The word translated 'offence' in the REB literally means something that makes another stumble, hence an obstacle, something that 'puts another off'. If the gospel is rejected or misused, let it be because of the inherent offence of the gospel itself; let it not be said that it was never given a fair hearing because the failings of Paul and his colleagues had brought the ministry, and thereby the gospel itself, into discredit.

6.4f.   As recently as 5.12 Paul has disclaimed any intention to recommend himself again to the Corinthians, but here he declares that it is the constant aim of himself and his colleagues, *as God's ministers*, to recommend themselves *in all circumstances* by their *steadfast endurance* of all the troubles and difficulties that come their way. Yet there is a world of difference between the kind of self-recommendation which he is describing here and that for which he has criticized his rivals. They boast of superficially impressive things, like ecstatic experiences. The credentials which Paul and his colleagues claim to exhibit are rather signs of a total commitment to the gospel, whatever suffering it may cost them, the signs, in other words, of a cruciform discipleship.

In vv. 4 and 5 Paul enumerates nine different kinds of suffering, which fall into three groups of three. The first three words in the list are all general terms. The word translated 'affliction' occurs nine times in II Corinthians. The word translated 'distress' suggests someone shut up in a narrow place from which no escape is possible. The corresponding verb is found in 4.8b and is there translated 'cornered'.

In the second triad of terms for trouble Paul specifies particular sufferings that have been inflicted upon himself and his colleagues by other people, and in the third triad he lists various hardships that they have willingly undergone in the service of the gospel. Thus they have been beaten, put in jail and faced angry mobs. They have worked to the point of exhaustion, stayed awake through sleepless nights of watching and gone without food.

As for being mobbed, the Corinthians themselves must have been well aware that this had happened to Paul in Corinth, as well as in many other places (see Acts 18.12–17; cf. 13.50; 14.5f., 19; 16.22; 17.5–9, 13; 19.23–41).

The words *overworked, sleepless, starving* are taken by some scholars to refer to the physical labour Paul underwent in working at his trade as a tent-maker, so as not to be a burden to newly-founded congregations. This view is certainly possible, but, in the light of the similar list of trials in 11.27f., it seems more likely that the reference is to the toils, anxieties and privations entailed by actual missionary work.

6.6   Here Paul extends the list of the credentials which authenticate the ministry of himself and his colleagues, by listing qualities they seek to exhibit in the exercise of that ministry.

The third item in the list, which is translated by 'patience' in the REB and by 'long-suffering' in the AV, is attributed in Rom. 2.4 and 9.22 to God. Here it evidently denotes a patience with the obstinacy and stupidity of other people that reflects the nature of God. The fourth item, 'kindliness', denotes an active generosity and goodwill.

The fifth item literally runs 'by Holy (or holy) Spirit". Since the other items in the verse all denote personal qualities, it is probable that Paul is thinking either of the gifts of the Holy Spirit (the view taken by the REB), the capacities for service which the Spirit bestows, or (what is perhaps more likely) of the graces which are the fruit of the Spirit, as in Gal. 5.22f.

The sixth item literally means 'love without hypocrisy'. The same expression is used in Rom. 12.9.

6.7   In v. 7 Paul turns more to the resources on which he and his colleagues rely in their efforts to commend the gospel. Thus there is the 'word of truth' (REB: *by declaring the truth*), that is, the gospel, and *the power of God*.

As for *the weapons of righteousness in right hand and left*, these could be understood as moral qualities which the apostolic messengers exhibit, but the context suggests rather a resource on which they draw, so that it seems more natural to think of righteousness as divine power active in the believer (cf. our commentary on 5.21).

The significance of the references to the right hand and the left is likely to be that in combat the right hand was used for attack and the left hand for defence.

It is highly probable that Paul has included some, at least, of the items listed in vv. 6 and 7 with an eye to his opponents. Thus we, unlike them, declare nothing but the truth (cf. 2.17; 4.2). Further, they may claim that their apostleship is validated by miraculous powers and ecstatic experiences, but we can point to a truer manifestation of the power of God than that. We have experienced a power that sustains us in our suffering for the gospel, a power that (as we will learn from 12.9) is most fully seen in weakness.

6.8–10   Apostles therefore have to learn to sit lightly to what is said about them. Their lot includes the highs and the lows of human experience – *honour and dishonour, praise and blame*.

Paul's correspondence as a whole shows that he provoked enthusiastic devotion from some, passionate hostility from others. In the decades following his death, this polarization of opinion was, if anything, accentuated, some even identifying him with the advocate promised by Christ in the Fourth Gospel, others seeing him as the arch-deceiver and corrupter of the original gospel.[1]

With v. 8b the construction changes, and we have a series of antithetical pairs each introduced by 'as'. In the RV the first pair is rendered, 'as deceivers, and yet true'. The first half of this phrase is

[1] See Henry Chadwick, *The Enigma of St Paul* , pp. 3f.

surely a description of what Paul and his co-workers appear to be in the eyes of the unbelieving world, the second half a description of what they are in the eyes of God.

However, the contrasts which follow in vv. 9 and 10 do not lend themselves to being interpreted as consisting of a false perception followed each time by a true one. Each characterization appears to be a valid one; the difference is rather that the second characterization represents each time a profounder truth than the first, a truth apparent only to believers. If we must have a formula which covers every one of the seven contrasting pairs, then Allo's suggestion commends itself. In his view, the first member of each pair represents the reputation which Paul and his helpers have been given, whether this is true or false, that is, the things that men believe about them or would like to believe about them, whereas the second member of each pair represents what the apostles really are, whether or not that is recognized by others.[2]

Paul's overall intention, however, in contrasting, seven times over, a mistaken, or at least partial, perception of his apostolate with a truer one is surely clear. He is appealing to the Corinthians to abandon the shallow judgments they have passed upon him under the persuasion of his opponents and instead to see him as God sees him, as a faithful servant of Jesus Christ by whose ministry they themselves, along with many others, have been incalculably enriched.

To turn to the second pair of contrasting perceptions, it is true that Paul and his co-workers are *unknown* men and women, mere nobodies, in the eyes of the world. It is also true that Paul's apostolic credentials are not recognized everywhere as authentic. Yet in a profound sense he and his co-workers are well-known. The REB suggests that they are known to all men, but it is likely that Paul also means that they are known to God (cf. 5.11).

Again it is true that Paul and his co-workers are *dying*, in the sense that they are continually exposed to the risk of being killed, and that their vital energy is continually being sapped. Yet again the more profound truth is that their lives are continually being renewed. Indeed, in the light of that renewal, the continual wasting of their energy can be seen as a dying in a deeper sense, a dying to self, a dying with Christ, in order to be raised with him.

In the same way, Paul and his co-workers are being *disciplined by suffering*, and yet they are not *done to death*. Once again, as in the

[2] Allo, p. 177.

previous pair of contrasts, the second item in the pair suggests a deeper level of meaning in the first. The word rendered 'disciplined' could equally be translated 'punished'. It is quite likely that Paul is exploiting this ambiguity. 'Punishment' could well have been the verdict of his opponents on his sufferings – well-merited punishment due to him as an erstwhile persecutor. But what others may see as punishment is, in Paul's eyes, proof of God's fatherly discipline.[3]

Again it is true that Paul and his co-workers have sorrows, occasioned in no small measure by the Corinthians themselves.[4] And yet in their sorrows they *have always cause for joy*, a joy which nothing can destroy, because it is inspired by the Spirit (cf. Rom. 14.17; Gal. 5.22; Phil. 4.4).

It is true that Paul and his co-workers are *poor* in worldly goods, and yet they *bring wealth*, spiritual wealth, *to many*.[5]

It is also true that Paul and his co-workers are *penniless*, and yet in a profound sense they *own the world*. They look like dispossessed men and women, and yet in their Christian faith, their Christian calling, the Christian fellowship, in a word, in Christ they have everything that is most worth having (cf. I Cor. 3.21f.).

This passage is of a piece with 4.7–12, where Paul speaks first of all of the treasure of the gospel being lodged in the frail earthen vessels of the apostles, and then goes on to contrast the misery of their outward circumstances with the divine power by which they are continually being sustained. There is ample reason to believe that Paul's apostleship was continually belittled by his opponents on the grounds that it bore so much the marks of privation and suffering. Paul does not for a moment deny the reality of the suffering. In 4.10–12 he contends that these marks, far from being a contradiction of the genuineness of his apostleship, are in fact its most compelling vindication, since they are a sign that his life is being conformed to the dying and rising of Christ. The attentive reader is likely to be reminded of this earlier passage, in reading vv. 4–5 and 9 of the present chapter. The main thrust of the last three verses of the present paragraph, however, is that privation and suffering do not

---

[3] In this pair of contrasts and the preceding one Paul seems to be reformulating the language of LXX Ps. 117.17 and 18. See Furnish, p. 347.

[4] Sorrow is a keynote of II Corinthians. In all, the verb and the noun occur eighteen times out of a total Pauline usage of twenty-three occurrences.

[5] Furnish (p. 359) observes that, while there are parallels in the literature of Cynic and Stoic philosophy to the idea of a person being poor in material goods but rich in the things that matter, there are no clear parallels to the idea of being rich through bringing enrichment to others.

represent the last word that can be said about his apostleship. The last word, the deeper truth, is that, in the midst of ignominy, he and his co-workers are known to God; that, though always at the point of dying, they yet live; that, though they are grieved, they rejoice continually; and, though they are penniless, in reality they own the world.

An open mind and an open heart
6.11–13

6.11   Paul is about to draw to a close the apologia for his ministry which has occupied him since 2.14, but, before he does so, he draws the attention of his readers to the full and frank way in which he has opened his mind and heart to them. Not only does he address them directly, he addresses them as 'Corinthians' – the only time he does so in this letter – and with unmistakable affection.

In the RV v. 11a reads, 'Our mouth is open to you, O Corinthians.' In other words, he has hidden nothing from them, kept nothing back. He has indeed *opened* his *heart* to them. The fears, the hopes, the struggles, the joys of apostolic ministry and of his ministry to them, in particular, are all plain for them to see.

6.12   In that heart of his which he has opened so wide they can surely see that there is room for them. Any constraint, any stiffness, any coldness that there is in the relationship lies on their side.

Underlying the rendering 'constraint' is a verb (also used in 4.8b) which is cognate with the final noun of v. 4. The basic idea conveyed by this word group is that of restricted space, not having enough room. Here the thought is of a heart that is not big enough to have room for another.

6.13   In return for the frankness and openness that Paul has shown to them, cannot the Corinthians *open* their *hearts* to him? That would be no more than a *fair exchange*, and he, after all, has the right to appeal to them as a father to his children. The claim made in 4.14f. of the first epistle still holds good: they may have thousands of tutors in Christ, but they have only one father. Paul, and Paul alone, can claim to have 'fathered' their life in Christ.

The vigour with which Paul protests his own frankness and cordiality in these verses suggests that he is responding to criticisms to the effect that his own behaviour towards the Corinthians has been less than perfectly frank and cordial.[6] While he does not use the language of reconciliation at this point, in appealing to them to open their minds and hearts to him, he is, in effect, appealing for complete reconciliation with himself and his fellow workers, just as he had earlier appealed to them to be reconciled to God (5.20).

Have no truck with unbelievers
6.14–7.1

The transition from v. 13 to v. 14 is very harsh, the latter verse having no apparent connection with the former. Verse 13 ends with an appeal from Paul to the Corinthians to open their hearts to him. Verse 14 introduces a stern injunction to have nothing to do with unbelievers. Nor does 7.1 lead easily into 7.2.

It is also difficult to see what relevance the new paragraph has to the principal task to which Paul is addressing himself throughout these chapters, that of repairing a relationship which has been strained and fractured.

It would be easier to relate this new paragraph to its context, if one could understand the word 'unbelievers' in v. 14 as referring to Paul's opponents. Some interpreters do take this view, but it is one which runs quite counter to Paul's usage elsewhere. Elsewhere in Paul the word regularly refers to people outside the community of faith.

Not only is the transition to the new paragraph harsh; if it is omitted and one reads 7.2 straight after 6.13, one gets excellent sense and connection.

In noting how difficult it is to establish a connection between 6.14–7.1 and its context, we have already encountered one of the arguments advanced by many scholars for regarding this whole paragraph either as a non-Pauline interpolation or as a fragment of an earlier Pauline letter which has been wrongly inserted at this point. This is a question to which we shall return. First we need to

[6] Cf. 1.17f., 24; 2.4; and the commentary on these passages.

form some impression of the structure and main thrust of the passage.

6.14a As already noted, the paragraph begins with an abrupt summons to Paul's readers not to *team up with unbelievers*. There is a clear allusion here to Deut. 22.10, which prohibits ploughing with an ox and a donkey yoked together. At first sight, it might seem that Paul (if Paul is indeed the author) is forbidding mixed marriages, but, as one reads on, it becomes apparent that the prohibition has a wider application.

6.14b–16a The opening imperative is now reinforced by a series of five rhetorical questions which highlight the incongruity of forming close ties with pagans. Five times over, the question is asked, 'What fellowship (or equivalent term) can there be between A and B?'

Each time A and B stand for entities which are completely opposite, totally incompatible – *righteousness* and *wickedness*, *light* and *darkness*, *Christ* and *Belial*, and so on. The implication is that believers are to have nothing whatever to do with unbelievers.

A notable stylistic feature of this series of rhetorical questions is the way Paul rings the changes on terms for partnership or fellowship, a different word being used each time.

The word 'Belial' or 'Beliar' was originally a common noun meaning worthlessness, evil, but in the intertestamental literature it came to signify Satan. The word is used nowhere else in the New Testament, but is a common term for the devil both in the Qumran texts and the Testaments of the Twelve Patriarchs.

The fifth rhetorical question, *Can there be a compact between the temple of God and idols?* leads into a confessional statement that *we*, that is, the Christian community, are *the temple of the living God*.

6.16b This declaration is then reinforced by a catena of scriptural quotations and allusions. The first quotation, in 16b, is a combination of Lev. 26.12 and Ezek. 37.27. This is not exactly a declaration that the people of God are God's temple – such a statement is never actually made in the Old Testament – but rather a promise of God's continuing presence with his people.

6.17 The presence of the holy God requires that God's people also be holy, and so the next quotation is a summons to the people to separate themselves and *touch nothing unclean*. The principal text here is Isa. 52.11. In their original setting the words of this verse are a summons to the people in exile in Babylon to leave Babylon and its idols behind. This quotation reinforces the admonition of v. 14a to have nothing to do with unbelievers.

6.18   In the final quotation in v. 18 there are echoes of the promise of God to David in II Sam. 7.14, linked with an echo in v. 17c of Ezek. 20.41. These two promises are evidently understood as contingent upon obedience to the commands which have just been stated.

Elsewhere in the New Testament, II Sam. 7.14 is interpreted messianically, but here it is quoted as a promise that those who are loyal to God's will will know God as a father. The wording of the original promise, 'and he will be my son,' has been changed to 'and you shall be my sons and daughters.'

7.1   Seeing these promises of the presence of God fulfilled in the Christian community, Paul deduces from them the duty of believers to *complete* their *consecration in the fear of God*, by cleansing themselves *from all that can defile flesh or spirit*.

This is an extraordinary statement to come from Paul's pen, for in it believers are addressed as the agents of their own cleansing and as capable of completing or perfecting their consecration or holiness. It is difficult to imagine the author of Galatians and Romans conceiving of anyone but God as the agent of cleansing or the perfecter of holiness.

THE QUESTION OF AUTHENTICITY – AGAIN

At the beginning of our discussion of this paragraph we observed that many scholars consider it to be either a non-Pauline interpolation or a fragment of an earlier Pauline letter. The expressions we have just noted in 7.1 as coming strangely from the pen of Paul provide proponents of the first of these two theories with a further argument for their position. Our own judgment is that this theory is most likely to be correct.

At the same time, the theory that the paragraph is a fragment of an earlier Pauline letter, more specifically, a fragment of the so-called Previous Letter referred to in I Cor. 5.9, also merits a mention. The reader is referred to our comments on that verse in our earlier volume in this series for a fuller discussion of the question. As we observed at that point, this theory is no longer as popular as it once was. A major argument against it is that the Previous Letter urged the Corinthians to have nothing to do with those who are *sexually* immoral, whereas there is no specific reference to sexual immorality in the paragraph in question.

Besides, while this theory does provide an explanation of the harshness of the transition between 6.13 and 14, it does not account for the many non-Pauline features of the paragraph.

As for the view that the paragraph is not the work of Paul, we have already noted that proponents of this view point to the harshness of the transition between 6.13 and 6.14, as well as the occurrence of unusual expressions in 7.1.

Other features of the paragraph which have already been noted can also be taken as supporting the same conclusion. Thus the series of five rhetorical questions implying that believers ought to have nothing whatever to do with unbelievers is hard to reconcile with much of the teaching of I Corinthians. According to I Cor. 7.12–16, for example, a Christian married to a non-Christian partner must not seek a divorce, unless the other party wants it.

Again, if Christians are invited to a meal by an unbeliever, they are to eat whatever is put before them, without raising questions of conscience (I Cor. 10.27). Such passages evince a readiness for reasonable compromise which seems to be totally lacking from the paragraph we are considering.

The paragraph also contains a quite remarkable concentration of *hapax legomena*, that is, of words which occur here and here only in Paul's letters or even in the entire New Testament or the entire Greek Bible. There are, in fact, nine such words in 6.14–7.1.[1]

The paragraph also contains several un-Pauline expressions which have not yet been noted. The formula used to introduce the Old Testament quotation in v. 16, 'As God said,' is found nowhere else in Paul. Nor is the Greek word *pistos*, found in v. 15, used by Paul anywhere else in an absolute way to denote a believer. Elsewhere the word functions as an adjective, with the meaning 'worthy of belief', or 'faithful'.

Furthermore, nowhere else in the certainly Pauline epistles is there any citation of, or even allusion to, any of the scriptural passages reflected in 6.16c–18.

---

[1] Eight of them are listed by Sakae Kubo in *A Reader's Greek-English Lexicon of the New Testament* , p. 167. The ninth is the name Belial.

In our judgment, the cumulative effect of all these arguments, as well as others which could be mentioned and are set out in larger commentaries,[2] is so strong as to tip the scales not only against the hypothesis of Pauline authorship but also against the mediating view favoured, with some hesitation, by both Furnish and Martin, to the effect that Paul has here incorporated, with minimal changes, non-Pauline material.[3]

Anyone who adopts the position that this paragraph is not the work of Paul, however, is confronted by the problem of finding a plausible explanation of how the insertion came to be made. Why would anyone want to insert such a sizable block of material in such a disruptive way?

Furnish observes that the proponents of such theories have generally despaired of finding an explanation.[4] It seems unlikely that a consensus will ever be reached on this problem, but, in our view, the explanation offered by Friedrich Lang is at least worthy of serious consideration. Lang writes that anyone who read Paul's summons to the Corinthians to open their hearts wide in isolation from the concrete situation in Corinth and understood it as a fundamental apostolic direction for the Christian conduct of life could easily sense in it the danger of unlimited openness on the part of Christians towards the heathen world and therefore consider a restriction to be necessary.

Hence one can understand a later writer wanting to qualify Paul's appeal for openness with the proviso that the heart must not be opened so wide that the boundary between the church and the world completely disappears. It would be a fundamental misunderstanding of the openness in love which Paul has in mind, if the church were thereby to lose its Christian identity. It is with this intent, Lang surmises, that a later writer has inserted this paragraph as a warning to the church against relapsing into heathen vices and as an urgent summons to sanctity.[5] However,

[2] See Furnish, pp. 376–83; Martin, pp. 190–95.

[3] Furnish, p. 383. He adds that 'this passage remains an enigma within II Cor,' and observes that while 'it may be integral to the context,' 'it remains only marginally Pauline.' Martin inclines to the view of Rensberger that 'Paul has used a piece of tradition put together previously by a Christian of Essene background' (p. 193). Affinities between this paragraph and the Qumran texts have often been noted. For a full discussion see Furnish, pp. 377f; Martin, p. 193. One scholar who has consistently advocated Pauline authorship is J. Murphy-O'Connor. See his articles, 'Relating II Corinthians 6.14 – 7.1 to its Context,' *NTS* 33, 1987, pp. 272–75; and 'Philo and II Cor 6: 14–7: 1,' *RevBib* 95, 1988, pp. 55–69.

[4] Furnish, p. 380.

[5] Lang, *An die Korinther*, pp. 310f.

such an insertion as Lang suggests for II Cor. 6.14–7.1 would have to have been made at a very early stage of the process of manuscript transmission. Otherwise, there would be some evidence somewhere of a shorter text.

Your place in our hearts is secure
7.2–4

7.2   The new paragraph begins with a renewed call to the Corinthians to make room in their hearts for Paul and his associates. This was the note on which 6.13 ended, though the actual verb used here is different.

Paul follows up this appeal with a protestation that he and his associates have *wronged no one, ruined no one, exploited no one*. The first of these verbs is used in 7.12, where it refers to the wrong done to Paul by a member of the Corinthian community. The word 'ruined' could refer to ruining someone financially or ruining their inner life by erroneous teaching or immorality. The former meaning is more likely here, in the light of the verb which follows. This verb means to exploit or defraud or take advantage of someone and is used in 12.17–18, where Paul appears to be responding to the charge of having derived some benefit for himself from the collection for Jerusalem.

Paul would hardly have made such a denial as this without good reason. In all probability, these things are being said about him. However, the fact that he is content with a bare denial suggests that he is responding to unpleasant rumours rather than to an open attack.

7.3   For the moment, Paul's main concern is not to refute insinuations but to express his unbroken love for the church. If, as he says, his words are not meant as a reflection on the Corinthians, it would seem that, whoever has been accusing him of taking advantage of his converts, it is not the Corinthians themselves.

He then reiterates an earlier assurance that there is plenty of room in his heart for them. The reference is probably to 6.11–13. What is more, the place of the Corinthians in the hearts of Paul and his associates is secure, *come death, come life*. Paul holds the Corinthians so close in his heart that nothing in life or death can part him from them, and, in saying that, he is speaking also for his colleagues.

7.4   So great is Paul's confidence in his relationship with the Corinthians that he feels free to speak to them *with great frankness*,[6] holding nothing back.

Equally great is his *pride* in them. This is a remarkable statement, given all the heartaches they had caused him, and were yet to cause him, but even more exuberant expressions are to follow.

In all his many troubles Paul's *cup is full of consolation*. These words recall his outpouring of praise in 1.3–4 to 'the God whose consolation never fails us,' who 'consoles us in all our troubles.'

What is more, Paul's cup *overflows with joy*. The actual verb he has used here suggests overflowing abundance. The same verb is used in Rom. 5.20 of grace immeasurably exceeding sin.

What is the reason for this extravagant expression of joy and confidence? The most obvious explanation is that Paul's mind is already running ahead to the incident related in vv. 6–13, the arrival of Titus bringing good news from Corinth. If so, this counts as an argument against the view, already noted in our commentary on 2.12–13, that 2.14–7.4 represents all or part of a separate letter.

This passage illustrates a side of Paul's character which is often ignored. As John Knox has observed, Paul is sometimes depicted as 'a fanatic incapable of feeling or eliciting affection.'[7] Passages like this show what a travesty such a picture is, for these verses are largely taken up with the expression of Paul's feelings towards the Corinthians, feelings of tender solicitude, pride and joy.

A double comfort
7.5–7

7.5   Paul here resumes his account of recent events which he broke off in 2.13. In response to the painful visit, he had written to Corinth the letter of tears. Half regretting that he had sent it and desperate to

---

[6] For a discussion of the connotations of the word here translated 'frankness', see the commentary on 3.12.
[7] Knox, *Chapters*, p. 95.

know the reaction of the Corinthians to its contents, he had then despatched Titus to find out their reaction in person. Not finding Titus in Troas, he had then gone off to Macedonia. The present passage picks up the story at that point.

As was noted in our discussion of 2.12–13, the sudden suspension of Paul's account of his movements in 2.14 and the equally sudden resumption of the account in 7.5 have led some scholars to the conclusion that originally 7.5 followed straight on after 2.13, 2.14–7.4 being an insertion. The position adopted in this commentary is that this hypothesis, though possible, is not necessary. We noted in our discussion of the previous passage that the exuberance of Paul's gratitude in 7.4 for the consolation he has received in all his many troubles becomes more understandable, if his mind is now turning back to the thought of the meeting with Titus. This counts as an argument in support of the position we have adopted.

When Paul reached Macedonia, there was no Titus, and therefore no relief for Paul. Instead *trouble* met them *at every turn*. As for the *fears within*, we can readily imagine what they were all about: Paul must have been sick with anxiety about the response of the Corinthians to his letter. As for the *fights without*, these were presumably disputes with adversaries of some sort.

7.6f.   Eventually Titus did arrive, and with the welcome news that the Corinthian church was once again loyal to its foundation apostle, but the first hint the reader has of this happy outcome is a reference to the one *who brings comfort to the downcast*, even God. As early as 1.3, Paul celebrated 'the God whose consolation never fails us,' and his reference in v. 4 of the present chapter to his cup being full of consolation also prepares us for this further demonstration of the mercy of God.

The mere arrival of Titus was itself uplifting to Paul's spirits. Even more encouraging was Titus's report that he had been greatly encouraged about the Corinthians. The REB has here obscured Paul's repeated use of the same root. Behind the renderings 'brings comfort', 'comforted' and 'encouraged' there stands the same Greek verb. Indeed, the verb and the corresponding noun are used four times, in all, in vv. 6 and 7, in a manner reminiscent of Paul's use of words of this family ten times over in 1.3–7.

What had been so encouraging for Titus, and is now so encouraging for Paul, was the strong reaction among the Corinthians in Paul's favour. They were longing for him, no longer reproaching him for failing to make the promised visit but missing him, longing to see him. They were also grieving, were in mourning, over the hurt that he had suffered and that had led him to cancel the promised visit. And they were eager to take his side, were showing zeal on his behalf. There is little wonder that such news made Paul happier still.

In all this, Titus had carried a heavy responsibility, but in one respect he had been uniquely qualified to do so, for, unlike Timothy or Silvanus, he had been present at the Jerusalem conference (Gal. 2.1) and was therefore able, in the face of Judaizing opponents, to report authoritatively on the recognition accorded to Paul's gospel and his mission to the Gentiles by the pillar apostles in Jerusalem (Gal. 2.6–10).

Godly sorrow
7.8–13a

7.8f.   Having expressed his relief at the news brought by Titus that the Corinthians were once again loyal to him, Paul now reflects on the effects on the Corinthians of a letter he had sent to them which had caused them pain and which is clearly to be identified with the 'severe letter' referred to in 2.4 and 9. The grammar of the first two sentences is quite convoluted, perhaps because Paul is still embarrassed about the tone of this letter.[8] The general sense, however, is fairly clear. Even if he did hurt the Corinthians by sending them this letter, Paul does not now regret it. At the same time, he did, at one time, regret having sent it. He had written it in the hope of winning them back to himself, but then he had been tormented by the thought that it might drive them away from him completely. He now sees that the letter did give them pain, *though only for a time.* Nevertheless, he is actually glad that he sent it, *not because of the pain but because the pain led to a change of heart,* to repentance. They had borne the pain as God would have them bear it. As a result, they have come to no harm from what Paul did. They would have come to harm, had they not taken Paul's painful rebuke in the way God meant them to.

7.10   If, as Paul has just said, there is a way of bearing pain that

---

[8] For a skilful analysis of the different thoughts Paul seems to be trying to express at this point see Barrett, pp. 209f.

accords with God's will, there are also other ways which do not. Paul now elaborates the contrast between these two types of reaction to pain, one of which brings blessing and the other destruction. Those who bear pain in God's way are led to *a change of heart*. When rebuked, as the Corinthians have been rebuked by Paul, they are 'big enough' to acknowledge that they have deserved it and to repent of what they have done. Such a change of heart leads to salvation and therefore *brings no regrets*.[9]

On the other hand, there are those who bear pain *in the world's way*. When rebuked, they are not 'big enough' to admit that they may have deserved it but are consumed with self-pity. Their hurt is 'the sorrow of the world' (RV), which *brings death.*

The contrast Paul draws here between two kinds of sorrow could be described as a contrast between mere remorse, a state of mortification at having been found out, and true penitence, which involves the acknowledgement that one has sinned against God, along with a genuine concern for the injured party.[10]

7.11 The response of the Corinthians to Paul's letter of rebuke has been one of true penitence. They have borne the pain that the letter caused them *in God's way;* their sorrow has been a godly sorrow.

Paul is certain that this is so, for *just look at the results!* First of all, their sorrow has made them *take the matter seriously* and vindicate themselves. They have been eager to clear themselves of complicity in the wrong, by taking Paul's part.

Furthermore, their sorrow has made them indignant and apprehensive. Their indignation was, no doubt, aroused by the thought of the hurt that had been done to Paul. Their apprehension could have been a fear of God's displeasure or of Paul's, but perhaps the latter is more likely. They may well have been afraid that he would break off fellowship with them.

What is more, their sorrow has *aroused* their *longing* for Paul's presence in person, their *devotion* to him, and their *eagerness to see justice done.* In all these ways they have demonstrated that the hurt

[9] It may seem that the latter statement goes without saying, but Paul is probably using here the rhetorical figure of oxymoron, in which contradictory terms are conjoined in order to arrest attention, thus, 'regret which brings no regrets.' For a fuller discussion see Furnish, p. 388.

[10] See Denney, pp. 255f., for a full discussion. Tasker (p. 106) draws a link between the 'sorrow of the world' and the state of listless depression which mediaeval Christian moralists called *accidia*. For a full discussion of *accidia* from a psychiatric and theological perspective see Frank Lake, *Clinical Theology*, pp. 111–13.

which was done by the wrongdoer does not reflect their own attitude to the apostle, and so *at every point* they have *cleared* themselves *of blame*.

7.12–13a   Paul now picks up the first of the words he has just used to describe their response and declares that his main concern in writing the letter had not been for *the offender or* for *his victim*, that is, in all probability, himself, but to let the Corinthians see for themselves, in the sight of God, how devoted to Paul and his fellow-workers they really were. In other words, his letter had forced them to ask themselves, in the sight of God, whether they were really committed to Paul, his apostolate and gospel, or not. The answer to that question had been a resounding affirmative. *That is why* Paul and his associates *have been so encouraged*.

This is the first time in the paragraph that Paul uses a verb in the first person plural. Between vv. 8 and 12 he consistently uses verbs in the first person singular, perhaps because he wants to take full responsibility for the 'severe letter'.

As for the identity of the wrongdoer, it is not necessary to conclude, as Barrett does, that he was not himself a Corinthian.[11] But to say that is not to exclude the possibility that his actions had been influenced by the agitators who had come in from outside. It is likely that the incident was connected with the intrigues of Paul's opponents.

As for the nature of the injury done, the most likely scenario is that the offender had insulted Paul in a particularly hurtful way and contested his apostolic authority in the presence of the assembled community.

A double cause for joy
7.13b–16

7.13b   Over and above the encouragement that Paul and his associates had derived from the news that the Corinthians were once again loyal to him, they had been made far happier still by the evident happiness of Titus himself. Paul uses a double comparative in the Greek to convey the delight it had given them to see how

---

[11] Barrett, pp. 212f. Contrast Furnish, p. 396; Martin, p. 238.

happy Titus was about the outcome of his visit. The Corinthians had *all helped to set his mind completely at rest*. Just as the encouragement which Titus received in Corinth was a further encouragement for Paul (vv. 6f.), so the joy of Titus has been a further reason for joy.

The extravagance of Paul's language at this point is an indication of just how apprehensive he and his colleagues must have been about the sort of reception Titus might be given, but the support Titus had received had been total. Some form of the word 'all' occurs in every verse of the paragraph, which indicates that, at least as Paul perceives the situation at the moment, the entire church has come round and is now loyal to him.

7.14   Whatever apprehension he may have felt about the outcome of Titus's visit, Paul had dared to express his pride in the Corinthians in Titus's presence, in other words, to predict that all would yet be well. It is easy to imagine Titus listening to such a prediction with some scepticism, but now Paul's confidence has been fully justified. To quote the more literal rendering of the RV, 'I was not put to shame.' The same expression is used in the Old Testament to express the confidence that one's hope in God will not prove misplaced. One will not be let down, not made to look foolish (see e.g. Ps. 119.31; Isa. 54.4; cf. Rom. 1.16).

This happy issue now emboldens Paul to claim that truth is a mark of everything he says. Every word that he and his colleagues had addressed to the Corinthians *bore the mark of truth*, and now his confident prediction has proved to be as true as the message they had delivered to them in the first place.

It is critically important for Paul that he be recognized as telling the truth. Just as in 1.17–20 he appeals to the faithfulness of God, of which his gospel speaks, as creating a presumption in favour of his own integrity in the matter of his travel plans, so now he takes delight in observing that his daring prediction about the Corinthians has also proved to be true.

7.15   Titus's heart *warms all the more* to the Corinthians, as he recalls *how ready* they all were *to do what he asked* (more literally: 'as he remembers the obedience of all of you').

The REB rendering here suggests that Titus had made specific demands with which the Corinthians had complied, but the primary reference is probably to their compliance with the demand for disciplinary action against the offender conveyed by the Severe Letter.

Titus had come to Corinth in fear and trembling, but in the event it was the Corinthians who had met him *in fear and trembling*. This statement suggests that the Corinthians had received the Severe Letter before Titus met them, and therefore makes it unlikely that he had been the bearer of the letter, as some scholars suppose.

7.16   Four times over in this chapter, in vv. 4, 7, 9 and 13, Paul has spoken of his joy, and joy is the note on which the chapter ends, joy at being able *to have complete confidence* in the Corinthians.

On this positive note the first main section of the letter ends, but one cannot help asking whether Paul's complete confidence in the Corinthians was not prematurely optimistic. If one takes the view, as many scholars now do, that chapters 10–13 are part of a later letter and not part of the 'severe letter', as many used to think, then the answer has to be that his confidence was indeed premature.

The Collection for the Church in Jerusalem
8.1–9.15

Paul now turns to a new topic. He has said all he has to say, for the time being, about the strained relationships between himself and the members of the church in Corinth. He is now seeking their co-operation in the collection he is in process of raising among the Gentile churches for the relief of impoverished Christians in Jerusalem. This was a project which was very dear to Paul's heart, and he devotes the whole of the next two chapters to it, though the relationship of these two chapters to each other and to the earlier part of the letter is, as we shall see, problematic.

This is not the first time that the Corinthians have heard about this project. Paul has already given instructions for the organization of the collection in Corinth in the opening verses of I Corinthians 16, and it is clear from v. 10 of the present chapter that the Corinthians had initially shown some interest in the project.

In our commentary on I Corinthians 16.1–4, we have already considered some of the reasons why this project was so important to Paul. To begin with, it was a response to a genuine need. More than that, however, it was a tangible sign of the unity of Jewish and Gentile Christians within the one church. It is also quite possible that Paul hoped that, when he arrived in Jerusalem accompanied by a number of representatives of the Gentile churches, bearing their gifts, they would be seen, by Christians at least, as the firstfruits of that influx of Gentiles into the church which, as he dares to hope in Rom. 11.11–27, would eventually stir unbelieving Jews to envy and win them over to the Christian gospel.[1]

The grace of generosity
8.1–9

What Paul is now urging the Corinthians to do is to complete the scheme with the same eagerness with which they adopted it. Moreover, he has already asked Titus to return to Corinth with two

---

[1] In addition to the literature concerning the collection cited in our commentary on I Cor. 16.1–4, see also Furnish, pp. 409–13; Martin, pp. 251–58.

companions to receive their contributions, in preparation for the final visit to Jerusalem which he is planning to make, along with representatives of the Gentile churches. His main aim in the present chapter is to inform the Corinthians of these plans and secure their full co-operation.

8.1   To spur on their generosity, Paul begins by telling the Corinthians about the miracle of generosity which has occurred in Macedonia – almost without Paul's help, it would appear. The churches of Macedonia will have included the congregations Paul had established in Philippi, Thessalonica and Beroea.

It is particularly striking that, in presenting the appeal, Paul does not dwell at any length on the need of the Christians of Jerusalem. Indeed, he does not mention the name of Jerusalem at all.

He does touch on their need at one point, in vv. 13–15, and puts it to his readers that it is a reasonable thing to ask them to meet that need out of their own surplus. The dominant concept of these two chapters, however, is that of grace. The word is used, with a variety of shades of meaning, no fewer than ten times.

At the heart of the first chapter stands the moving reminder of the grace of our Lord Jesus Christ, who 'beggared himself' for us, so that we, by his poverty, might become rich. Such divine generosity towards us constrains us to make us a generous response and to show something of Christ's loving, self-giving spirit in our dealings with one another. In vv. 6 and 7 the word 'grace' is used to denote such a generous act in response to the love of God. In v. 1, however, the response itself is described as the gift of the grace of God. The generosity of the churches of Macedonia is not just their doing, not simply their response to the grace of God, it is God's doing, a sign of God's grace at work in them.

8.2   In the following verses Paul spells out in greater detail just how remarkable the response of the churches of Macedonia has been. *The troubles they have been through have tried them hard*, but they have stood the test. Indeed, their troubles have served to reveal their true worth. Even in the midst of their severe troubles, they have been *exuberantly happy*. This is the first of several striking contrasts in this verse, between trouble and happiness, affliction and joy.

The other main contrast is between poverty and abundant generosity. *From the depths of their poverty they have shown themselves lavishly open-handed.* There is in the original a play on two cognate words which links their joy with their generosity. The RV indicates clearly which words are cognate: 'The abundance of their joy and their deep poverty abounded unto the riches of their liberality.' Something of the effect of Paul's word play has also been captured by the Twentieth Century New Testament, which reads, 'Tried though they were by many a trouble, their overflowing happiness, and even their deep poverty, resulted in a flood of generosity.' The Greek word rendered 'liberality' by the RV and 'generosity' by the TCNT usually denotes simplicity, sincerity, uprightness. Here it appears to denote the generosity which gives without second thoughts or any trace of pride or condescension.[2]

8.3f.   Paul can testify that the churches in Macedonia have gone *to the limit of their resources, and even beyond that limit.* Furthermore, *they begged us most insistently, and on their own initiative, to be allowed to share in this generous service to their fellow-Christians.* Paul had evidently not felt justified in seeking any contribution from the Macedonians, since they were so impoverished, but they had begged to be allowed to participate in the privilege of helping to meet the needs of the saints.

8.5   Once again Paul emphasizes the generosity of the churches in Macedonia, but what he particularly stresses this time is not the amount of their contribution but rather its spiritual dimension. He had hoped for a gift of money, but they had turned 'a gesture of economic relief' into 'an act of Christian devotion.'[3] *First of all*, they had given themselves to God. By that same act of dedication, they had also given themselves to Paul and his fellow-workers. Paul does not say that 'they gave themselves first of all to the Lord and then to us,' as if these were two distinct acts, but, by inserting the word 'first' before the phrase 'to the Lord', he emphasizes the priority of the Godward aspect of their commitment. However, since Paul has committed himself completely to the collection project, their commitment to it is at the same time a commitment to him and his fellow workers.

8.6   Encouraged not only by the extraordinary response of the

[2] For a discussion of the significance of the theme of abundance in II Corinthians, see our note on 3.9.
[3] Barrett, p. 221.

churches of Macedonia but also by the success of Titus's recent visit to Corinth, Paul now informs the Corinthians, albeit somewhat indirectly, that he has asked Titus to return to Corinth to receive their contribution. It is only in vv. 17ff. that he speaks explicitly of Titus paying them a visit. At this point he speaks of Titus bringing their *share in this further work of generosity to completion*, as he is also the one who *has already made a beginning*. Paul can hardly mean that Titus was the one who had introduced the project to the Corinthians, since it is clear from I Cor. 16.1–4 that their support for it had been obtained before Paul wrote I Corinthians, and II Cor. 7.14 seems to imply that the visit from which Titus had just returned was his first. However, the Corinthians appear to have failed to follow through their original commitment, so that it fell to Titus to revive their interest.[4] Underlying the rendering 'work of generosity' is, once again, the word 'grace', which here seems to refer primarily to the gift which the Corinthians are in process of making. At the same time there is the suggestion that Titus will be building not only on whatever actions the Corinthians have already taken to gather together a sum of money but also on the good relationship that he has established with them by his recent visit.

8.7   Paul has already spoken in v. 2 of the abundance of joy and the deep poverty of the churches of Macedonia 'abounding' or overflowing in a wealth of generosity. Now he uses the same verb of the Corinthians themselves. You, he says, 'abound' or excel in everything – *in faith, speech, knowledge, and diligence of every kind, as well as in the love you have for us*. Only at the beginning of the first epistle, in I Cor. 1.5–7, does Paul make such complimentary remarks about the Corinthians. The words 'speech' and 'knowledge' are indeed common to both lists. As for the fifth item in the list, it is not certain from which side the love is being shown, owing to an uncertainty about the original text. The reading adopted by the REB makes good sense in the context, but two of the best manuscripts, p46 and B, contain a reading according to which the love is being shown to the Corinthians by Paul and his companions. This is certainly the more difficult reading, but it is arguable that it is difficult to the point of improbability. The main point is clear: charismatic endowments demand to be expressed in action. For this, the collection for Jerusalem offers the best possible opportunity.

---

[4] For the likelihood that Titus himself raised the issue of the collection on his own initiative, see the Introduction, pp. xxviii.

Underlying the rendering 'generous service' is, once again, the word 'grace'. Essentially, the word has the same sense here as in v. 6, but at the same time it forms an *inclusio* or bracket with its use in v. 1, where it refers to the work of God. There is thus the suggestion that this act of service on the part of the Corinthians will also be a sign of God's grace at work in them.

8.8   The gift Paul is seeking is not to be wrung out of the Corinthians but is to be given willingly and from the heart; only in this way will it be a response to grace. That is why Paul does not simply give a command but appeals to the faith and love of the church. In the light of the zeal shown by others, particularly the Macedonians, he wants to give the Corinthians the opportunity to show that their love too is genuine.

8.9   Paul now goes to the heart of the matter, the heart of all Christian giving, all Christian service. Whatever we give to others, whatever we do for others, is given and done as a response to the self-giving of our Lord Jesus Christ; and an act of self-giving, of grace, was the heart of the mystery of his being. Behind the rendering 'generosity' stands once again the word *charis*, grace.

Writing to the Philippians, Paul speaks of Christ emptying himself, making himself nothing, by becoming truly human; here he speaks of him impoverishing himself, becoming poor for our sake, and the sake of the Corinthians, in particular, and all so that through his poverty we *might become rich* (cf. also I Tim. 3.16). He does not specify wherein the wealth of the Lord consisted, but the parallel from Philippians suggests that he is thinking of the wealth of one who enjoyed a heavenly existence with God. But he surrendered all that, becoming one with us in our poverty, to the point of ending his life in 'the absolute, naked poverty of crucifixion.'[5]

Wherein, then, does Christ make us rich? There is a clear implication in the passage that Christ became like us so that we might become like him, but not in the sense of acquiring divine status but rather of finding salvation (cf. Rom. 10.12; 11.12) and, more specifically, of being filled with his generous, self-giving spirit. If the Corinthians have already been made rich in love, as well as in every kind of spiritual gift, as Paul has already acknowledged (v. 7), then let them demonstrate their spiritual wealth by the generosity of their response.

[5] Barrett, p. 223.

A question of equality

8.10–15

8.10f.   Once again Paul is careful to avoid any suggestion that he is giving the Corinthians an order. What he is offering is rather advice, albeit the advice of one who believes himself to be guided by God's Spirit (I Cor. 7.40), and advice which has their interests at heart. They made a good beginning the previous year. They were 'the first not merely to do anything but to want to do anything'.[6] Now let them *go on and finish it*. Let them *be as eager to complete the scheme* as they were *to adopt it*. As was noted in our commentary on v. 6, the Corinthians had evidently failed to follow through their original commitment, until their interest was revived by Titus. The word 'complete', used in v. 11, is the only explicitly imperatival form found in chapters 8 and 9, though both chapters amount to sustained exhortation.

8.12   But Paul is not asking the impossible. He is only asking that they give in proportion to their means. Where there is a genuine willingness to do that, one's gift is acceptable to God. No one is asked to give what they do not have.

8.13f.   Nor is it Paul's intention that they should relieve the needs of others at the cost of causing hardship to themselves. *It is a question of equality*, of ensuring that at the present time what they can spare meets the need of the Christians of Jerusalem. Who knows? At another time the need of the Christians of Corinth may be met by the Christians of Jerusalem out of what they can spare. *The aim is equality.*

8.15   To clinch his point that the redressing of imbalance is in fundamental harmony with the biblical revelation, Paul quotes from the Exodus account of the gift of manna. According to that account, those who harvested the manna gathered different quantities, yet the whole process was divinely ordered so that there was neither superfluity nor want. *'Those who gathered more did not have too much, and those who gathered less did not have too little.'*

Paul's advice is directed to a specific community at a specific point in time, yet his insistence on the right of all to a fair share was never more timely than today, when in every respect – economically, socially, culturally and educationally – the rich are getting richer and the poor poorer.

[6] Moffatt's translation.

An operation beyond reproach
8.16–21

8.16f. Paul has already indicated that he has asked Titus, who had evidently revived the interest of the Corinthians in the collection, to return to Corinth to receive their contributions (v. 6). Titus is by no means reluctant to perform this service. On the contrary, Paul thanks God for inspiring Titus with the same keen interest in the welfare of the Corinthians as he has himself. Not only has Titus responded to Paul's request, his keenness is such that he is setting out for Corinth on his own initiative.

We noted in our commentary on v. 7 that the dominant concept of chapters 8 and 9 is that of grace. The concept of keenness, zeal, enthusiasm (Greek *spoudē*) is also prominent, being found in vv. 16 and 17, as well as in vv. 7, 8 and 22.

8.18 Along with Titus, Paul and his associates are sending two other brethren whom he does not name directly. It is important to remember, however, that this letter was not being delivered by a postman but, in all probability, by Titus himself, who would have named the brethren when he introduced them in person.

Each of Titus's companions is described (literally) as 'the (i.e. the well-known) brother who . . .'

The first companion is one whose reputation is described as being high among all the churches for his services to the gospel. There is an ancient tradition that this person was Luke the evangelist, but this is unlikely, and we can only conjecture who may have been meant. As good a case as any can be made out for one of the trio of Sopater, Aristarchus and Secundus – three Macedonians listed among Paul's entourage in Acts 20.4, as he sets out from Greece for Syria.

8.19 What is more, this same person has been duly appointed by the Macedonian churches to travel with Paul and his companions and help them in the *beneficent work* which Paul is superintending. Behind the rendering 'beneficent work' stands once again the word 'grace'. Paul has a particular interest in the collection but he is anxious to make it clear that it is a project of all the Gentile churches and is being implemented by people who are not only entirely trustworthy but duly accredited representatives of the churches.

In anticipation of the protestation of the purity of his motives which he is about to make in vv. 20 and 21, Paul adds that the project, or possibly the appointment of this brother, is motivated by the desire to *do honour to the Lord and show our own eagerness to serve.* 'Eagerness' is another key concept of this chapter, along with 'grace' and 'keenness', being also found in vv. 11 and 12.

8.20f.   Paul is clearly taking great pains to ensure that the collection is not only administered honestly but is also seen to be administered honestly. He is quite confident that their *aims are entirely honourable, not only in the Lord's eyes, but also in the eyes of men and women,* but he is determined that no one should have any opportunity to find fault with their administration of such *large sums.* The whole operation is to be completely above board. It is clear, however, from II Cor. 12.16ff. that, in spite of his precautions, he was accused by his opponents of appropriating contributions to the collection.

Trustworthy delegates
8.22–24

8.22   Paul now introduces Titus's second travelling companion, whom once again he does not name directly. As was the case with the person introduced in vv. 18f., we can only conjecture who he may have been. This person too is highly recommended, in terms similar to those used to commend Titus in vv. 16f. He is introduced as one of whose devotion Paul and his associates have had ample proof, in many ways and on many occasions. Underlying the REB renderings 'enthusiasm' and 'all the more keen' are Greek words which are related to those translated 'keen' in vv. 16f. Like Titus also, this brother is now more eager than ever to promote the collection among the Corinthians, probably because of the confidence inspired by the success of Titus's recent visit.

8.23   Paul now sums up in a few succinct words what he has been saying over the previous seven verses in commendation of Titus and his two companions. *If there is any question about Titus,* he is Paul's *partner and fellow-worker,* where the Corinthians are concerned. The word here translated 'fellow-worker' is the same word as Paul uses to describe his relationship with Apollos in I Cor. 3.9. Titus was clearly an associate whom Paul esteemed very highly. *As for the others, they are delegates of the churches and bring honour to Christ.* The word here translated 'delegates' is usually rendered by the word 'apostle'. Here it is clearly not being used to describe those witnesses of the risen Lord, commissioned by him, who played a unique foundational role in the establishment of the church. It denotes rather people who have been sent by a community to perform a specific task (cf. Phil. 2.25 for a similar use).[7]

The last phrase literally reads 'the glory of Christ'. This implies somewhat more than that they bring honour to Christ or are a credit to him. As was noted in our exegesis of I Cor 2. 7f.; I Cor 15. 40f.; and II Cor 3. 7ff., the word 'glory' in the Bible frequently has connotations of revelation. The glory of God is that which makes the invisible God visible, that which makes God known. Hence when Paul describes these delegates as 'the glory of Christ', it is probably being implied that they are people through whom Christ is being made known.

8.24   These three persons are now on their way to Corinth for the specific purpose of receiving the contribution of the Corinthians to the collection for Jerusalem. Paul has already indicated in v. 8 that the collection affords the Corinthians the opportunity to demonstrate the genuineness of their love. He now implies that he has ventured to predict that they will rise to the occasion, such is his confidence in them.

Let them therefore give the delegates, *and through them the churches, clear evidence* of their *love;* let them show that the confidence Paul has expressed in them is no empty boast.

---

[7] For a summary of the range of meanings conveyed in the New Testament by the word *apostolos* see C. K. Barrett, *The Signs of an Apostle*, pp. 70–73.

The collection – again?

9.1–5

9.1   It may well seem, at first sight, incongruous that, after spending the whole of the previous chapter commending the collection for the saints in Jerusalem, Paul should now say, *About this aid for God's people, it is superfluous for me to write to you*. On this and other grounds, many scholars take the view that chapters 8 and 9 cannot have been written at the same time. Among those who separate these two chapters, however, there is no consensus. At least five different views have been advocated by different scholars about the relationship between the two chapters. One view which has received support from several recent scholars, including Friedrich Lang and Ralph Martin, is that chapter 8 represents the conclusion of the letter of reconciliation, whereas chapter 9 was sent at the same time or shortly afterwards, and addressed to the other communities of Achaia. For our part, however, we do not find any of the arguments for separation entirely convincing and have no difficulty in reading chapter 9 as a continuation of the argument of chapter 8.

To revert to the argument for separation alluded to at the beginning of this discussion, it may seem equally incongruous for Paul to say that it is superfluous for him to write to the Corinthians about the collection and then continue to commend it for the next fourteen verses, but the fact remains that he has done so. If he himself saw no incongruity in thus continuing the commendation, then perhaps we are mistaken to attach too much weight to any incongruity we may feel between 9.1 and the preceding chapter.

Besides, in v. 1 Paul may well be using the classical stylistic device of the *praeteritio*, by which an author speaks as if he were at most touching upon a subject but thereby creates the basis for a detailed discussion.[1]

9.2   Paul now explains why commendation of the appeal is superfluous. He has no doubt of the genuine interest of the Corinthians in the project. Indeed, he has spoken about their enthusiasm for it to the Macedonians, and with some pride, and thereby stimulated so effectively the eagerness of the Macedonian churches to help, that in 8.1–6 he has been able to hold them up as an example to the

---

[1] Cf. Klauck, p. 71. For fuller treatments of the relationship between chapters 8 and 9 see the Introduction, pp. xxvif.; also the larger commentaries, especially that of Furnish, pp. 429–33.

Corinthians, who, in the meantime, have failed to follow up their initial enthusiasm with appropriate action.

9.3f.   Paul's real intent in the present paragraph is to explain why he has decided to send to Corinth the brothers mentioned in 8.16–24. Why has he decided to send them? Why not wait until he comes to Corinth in person, as he is clearly planning to do (v. 4), to finalize the organisation of the Corinthian contribution? The truth is that once again his credibility as an apostle, as well as the credibility of the Corinthians as believers, are at stake. If he were to come to Corinth to receive the contribution of the Corinthians, bringing men from Macedonia with him, and were to find that nothing was happening, he, to say nothing of the Corinthians, would be shamed. He would be seen as having given other churches a false impression of the commitment of the Corinthian church, in order to coax money out of their purses. Indeed, the Corinthians might have grown indifferent to the whole project, and then his confident reports about their commitment would certainly prove to be an empty boast. As he states clearly in v. 5, it is essential that the Corinthian contribution should both be, and be seen to be, a free offering, a *genuine bounty*, not something extorted from them against their will.[2] If, on the other hand, the Corinthians have their contribution ready by the time Paul reaches Corinth, accompanied by the Macedonian representatives, their commitment will then be clear beyond all doubt. That is why Paul has sent the three friends mentioned in the previous chapter. Everything has been done with a view to the eventual handing over of the Corinthian contribution to the official collection delegation to be led by Paul himself.

9.5   In v. 5 a new term is used to describe the collection, not 'grace' or 'gift of grace' as in chapter 8, but 'blessing' or 'gift of blessing'. The gift of the Corinthians is to be a means by which God bestows blessing on the recipients. But, if their gift is to have this spiritual dimension, a generous, whole–hearted response is called for. By introducing the notion of blessing, Paul effects a transition to the main idea of the next section (vv. 6–15).

---

[2] For reasons for taking the word *pleonexia* here as meaning 'extortion' see Barrett, p. 235; Furnish, pp. 428, 439.

Bountiful sowing – bountiful reaping

9.6–11a

9.6   Paul now reinforces the appeal for a generous contribution to the collection for Jerusalem with a further argument. The scantier the seed sown, the scantier the harvest; the more plentiful the seed sown, the more plentiful the harvest. With its epigrammatic, symmetrical form – two statements of synonymous parallelism in antithesis to each other – the verse has something of the ring of a proverb.

We noted above that in v. 5 Paul introduces a new term to describe the collection, the word 'blessing'. His hope is that the response of the Corinthians will be sufficiently generous to be a means of blessing to the recipients. The same word is picked up in v. 6b. The point Paul is now making is that those who give so generously that their gift becomes a means of bringing God's blessing to the recipients will themselves be blest by God through their giving. The precise form of the blessing, however, has yet to be made clear.

9.7   Paul now appears to draw back for a moment, as if sensing that he has brought too heavy a battery of arguments to bear on his readers. *Each person should give as he has decided for himself; there should be no reluctance, no sense of compulsion.* The Greek word here translated 'reluctance' essentially means pain. They are not to think of the collection as a painful or compulsory due that they have to pay (cf. Deut. 15.10). God loves a giver who gives freely and joyfully (cf. Prov. 22.8a, LXX).

This verse, with its exhortation to free, spontaneous generosity, might be thought to stand in some tension with the previous verse, which seems to encourage giving with an ulterior motive, giving for the sake of a reward. Some rewards, however, are so intimately bound up with the activity with which they are connected as to have no appeal to anyone without a genuine desire to perform the activity for its own sake. The following verses make it clear that this is the kind of reward Paul has in mind. God rewards generosity by granting the opportunity for further generosity.

9.8f.   There is no need for us to fear that through generous giving we will be reduced to a state of destitution. God is able to see to it not only that *every need* of our own is *always met to the full* but also that we *have something to spare for every good cause.* The word *charis*, grace, is used here once more. This is the eighth time it has been used since the beginning of chapter 8 (cf. our introductory comments on that chapter). The notion of abundance is another of the key concepts of these two chapters which is picked up again in this verse, and in both halves of the verse.

Behind the REB rendering, *with every need always met to the full*, stands the Greek word *autarkeia*, a technical term of Stoic philosophy. *Autarkeia*, for the Stoics, meant inner freedom from care about outward things – possessions and the means of livelihood. Paul uses the word to describe God's provision of believers with what they need, thus setting them free to overflow with every kind of good work. He is thinking of something much more comprehensive than the provision of money. He speaks of an abundant flow of grace of every kind, which must include the fullness of the *charismata*, the central theme of I Corinthians 12. Some form of the word 'all' occurs five times in this verse.

Paul reinforces the point with a quotation from Ps. 112.9 – in its context, a description of the ideally righteous person, the person whose beneficence is lavish and unending. The image conveyed by the first Greek verb he has used is that of a farmer scattering seed broadcast. Behind the rendering 'benevolence' stands a Greek word traditionally translated 'righteousness'. 'Righteousness', however, is often, as here, a rather cool and colourless translation of the underlying Hebrew concept, which denotes a readiness to do right by everyone with whom one has to do, a positive energy on the side of the needy. The implication here is that God provides the righteous person with the resources to be lavishly generous to the needy and never stop doing deeds of charity.

There is no explicit indication of the subject of the verbs in the quotation, and some scholars have argued that there is at least the suggestion that the agent of the scattering is God, and that it is God's righteousness that lasts for ever. The usual interpretation, however, fits the context admirably.[3] Nevertheless, it is a central thought of the whole paragraph that spontaneous giving places the giver within the movement of grace which flows from God to humanity.

9.10–11a   Paul now states explicitly what is implied by the previous verse. Picking up again the image of sowing from vv. 6 and 9, he declares that God, *who provides seed for sowing and bread for food*, as Isaiah says (Isa. 55.10), will provide in abundance the 'seed' they

---

[3] For a fuller discussion see Furnish, pp. 448f.

need, and thus enable them to live out the picture of the lavish sower of deeds of charity sketched in v. 9. God will thus *swell the harvest* of their *benevolence*, so that they *will always be rich enough to be generous*.

Grace upon grace
9.11b–15

9.11b–12   Paul has spoken of grace flowing forth from God like a wave and energizing God's people for generous giving. He now pictures that grace producing a counter-wave of thanksgiving. The generosity that he is sure the Corinthians will exercise, under the stimulus of his ministry and that of his colleagues, will lead many to thank God. It will thus have a twofold effect. On the one hand, it will be *a contribution towards the needs of God's people*. At this point Paul introduces yet another Greek word to describe the collection, the word *leitourgia*, from which is derived the English word 'liturgy'. In the Athenian democracy this word was used to denote a public service undertaken by private citizens at their own expense. It might, for example, take the form of equipping a trireme, financing a theatrical performance or sending an embassy. Wealthy citizens might be elected to perform such services, but they were considered as honours, not impositions. By their participation in the collection, the Corinthians will be performing a comparable service for the people of God. At the same time, their generosity will result in *a flood of thanksgiving* flowing back to God.

9.13   Not only will those who receive the aid give thanks to God for it, they will glorify God for this sign that fellow-believers have been tested and not found wanting. The gift will be recognized as a confession of faith in deeds as well as words, as the sign of a *faith expressing itself through love* (Gal. 5.6).

The recipients of the aid will also, Paul trusts, praise God for the *liberal contribution* of the Corinthians *to their need and to the general good*. Underlying the rendering 'liberal' is a word that has already been used in v. 11 (REB: 'generous'). As in v. 11, so here it denotes a generosity that holds nothing back.

The action in which this generosity will be expressed will do more than relieve the needs of fellow-Christians; it will be a demonstration of *koinonia*, of the common participation of givers and receivers in the one gospel of the grace of God in Christ.

9.14 Thus the generous action of the Corinthians will strengthen the ecumenical community of the body of Christ. The members of the original Christian community in Jerusalem, seeing how richly the grace of God has been at work in the Corinthians, will *join in prayer* on their behalf, and *their hearts will go out* to them.

Once more Paul uses the word 'grace' – the ninth occurrence of the word in chapters 8 and 9. At the beginning of chapter 8 he pointed to the signs of God's grace at work among the Macedonian churches. Now, as he draws his appeal to a close, he expresses the hope that grace will have its way among the Corinthians as well. Once more he speaks of the divine abundance or overflowing.

9.15 God's gift beggars all description. It is *beyond all praise*. For the tenth time in these two chapters Paul uses the word 'grace', this time in the sense of thanks. Thus *charis* in the sense of divine grace evokes *charis* in the sense of human thanksgiving.

This expression of thanksgiving which rounds off the chapter is no doubt evoked by the whole movement of grace from God to humanity and back again, but Paul probably has in mind particularly the effect of that grace in bonding Jewish and Gentile believers into one, through bonds of mutual generosity and gratitude.

Retrospect
The words Paul has used in these two chapters to describe the collection – 'work of grace' (*charis*): 8.6, 7, 19; 'ministry' (*diakonia*): 8.4; 9.1, 12, 13; 'blessing' (*eulogia*): 9.5; and 'community service' (*leitourgia*): 9.12 – all show clearly that it represents for him much more than a response to human need and has profound theological significance. As grateful response to the grace of God, it is both an expression of, and a means of strengthening, the unity of the church, made up of both Jewish and Gentile believers.

Prospect
Throughout his entire appeal on behalf of the collection Paul exhibits a remarkable optimism. He seems to be fully confident that the response of the Corinthians will be generous, and that the believers in Jerusalem will accept the gift not only as a welcome sign of

brotherly and sisterly solidarity but as convincing evidence of the Christian faith of the giving communities. Were these hopes realized? The evidence is tantalizingly incomplete.

As for the Corinthian response, Paul's statement in Rom. 15.26 that Achaia, as well as Macedonia, has contributed to the relief fund probably implies that the Corinthians did respond in some degree. On the other hand, according to Acts 20.2–5, no Corinthian is found among the delegates accompanying Paul on his final visit to Jerusalem.

As for the willingness of the church in Jerusalem to accept the gift, Rom. 15.31 shows that within a matter of months from the date of II Corinthians 8 and 9 this had become for Paul a matter of acute concern.

In Acts 21.17–20 Luke reports that the Christians of Jerusalem received Paul's party gladly, yet there is no mention of the relief fund, even though this would have been the moment for its presentation. The strange silence of Acts at this point may well mean that the money was simply accepted, without being in any way acknowledged as a sign of solidarity and Christian maturity, as Paul had hoped. Indeed, the possibility cannot be excluded that the Jerusalem church actually declined to accept the gift.[4]

---

[4] For a fuller discussion see our comments on I Cor. 16.1–4 in our earlier volume; cf. also Furnish, pp. 452f.

The Letter of Four Chapters
10.1–13.14

A different situation

The contrast between the opening verses of chapter 10 and the preceding chapters is abrupt to the point of being extraordinary. No more word of the collection. Moreover, the relationship between Paul and the Corinthians seems to be on an entirely different footing from what it has been over the last nine chapters. The situation reflected in these later chapters is not one of reconciliation after estrangement but of acute tension and the threat of apostasy. Paul is desperately anxious that he may lose the loyalty of the Corinthians for good. They have been brainwashed by intruders from outside, who have been waging a smear campaign against him. While there are some verses in the first nine chapters, like 2.17; 3.1; and 5.12, which suggest that these intruders were already present in Corinth at that stage, there is no suggestion of a conflict as sharp as this. In the face of this threat, Paul finds it necessary to defend his authority with great vigour and at considerable length. The conclusion seems irresistible that chapters 10–13 did not originally belong to the same letter as chapters 1–9. Whether they were written later or earlier is a question which we have discussed in the Introduction to this volume. We consider a later date more likely.

Structure

The broad structure of the argument in chapters 10–13 is fairly clear.

In 10.1–18 Paul rejects certain charges which are being made against him by his opponents, to the effect that he is weak in personal presence and that he seeks self-praise.

The central section, 11.1–12.13, contains the apostle's reluctant self-commendation in response to the smear campaign being conducted by his rivals.

In the third section, 12.14–13.10, Paul prepares for an imminent visit.

What is at stake

No reader of these four chapters can fail to be struck, if not actually offended, by the sharpness of Paul's strictures on his opponents. It must be remembered, however, that what is reflected in chapters 10–13 is more than a struggle between competing missionaries. This is a struggle in which Paul's person, Paul's apostleship and his message of reconciliation in Christ are inextricably intertwined. If the Corinthians reject Paul's person, they will at the same time be rejecting his God-given insight into the gospel. What is at stake, therefore, is nothing less than their salvation. This accounts for the sharpness of Paul's tone.

It must also be noted that in these chapters Paul has recourse to a number of rhetorical devices which had already been used by philosophers, from Socrates on, in debates with their opponents, the sophists. Some of the strategies common to this philosophical tradition and Paul's argumentation here are the following:

the attempt to defend not only the person of the speaker but the truth to which he witnesses (*passim*);

a declaration that the speaker will make no use of rhetorical methods, which nevertheless slip in through the back door (11.6, 18; 12.11);

the use of irony and bitter sarcasm (11.1–6; 12.15, 21) and paradox (12.10);

the citation of the opponents' charges at climactic points of the argument (10.2, 10; 11.6);

an admission of the truth of those charges but in such a way as to place their substance in a fundamentally different light (11.16; 12.5).[1]

Ready to fight but not with the weapons of this world
10.1–6

10.1   Paul begins by appealing to his readers *by the gentleness and magnanimity of Christ*. What he is contending for by means of this appeal is a renewal of the loyalty of the Corinthian community, a loyalty which has been subverted by the calumnies of his opponents.

---

[1] For a fuller discussion of Paul's use of rhetorical devices in these chapters see especially Christopher Forbes, 'Comparison, Self-Praise and Irony: Paul's Boasting and the Conventions of Hellenistic Rhetoric,' *NTS* 32, 1986, pp. 1–30; also Martin, pp. 300f. The identity of the opponents is discussed in the Introduction, pp. xxix–xxxiii.

The 'I' is especially emphatic. An emphatic 'I' (expressed by the pronoun *egō* in the Greek and not simply by the verbal termination) is characteristic of chapters 10–13. Out of 239 instances of an emphatic 'I' in II Corinthians, 147 are found in the last four chapters.[2]

Paul follows up his appeal by describing himself as being *so timid when face to face with you, so courageous when I am away from you.* It is hard to see how these words could express Paul's own assessment of himself. Most commentators and many versions, therefore, including the REB, assume that he is quoting things that are being said about him in Corinth. The word which is here translated 'timid', when used elsewhere in the New Testament, carries the positive meaning, 'humble', 'lowly'. On the lips of Paul's opponents, it will have meant something like 'servile', 'cringing'.[3]

In appealing to 'the gentleness and magnanimity of Christ', to counter the calumnies that are being spread about him, Paul is implicitly appealing to the cross, since it is in the cross that these qualities of Christ are definitively revealed. In his own face-to-face dealings with the Corinthians, Paul has shown a true humility, which his opponents have dismissed as a servile timidity, but such 'timidity', far from being a sign that he lacks the credentials of an apostle, is rather a sign of his conformity to Christ crucified.

10.2   It now transpires that Paul has decided to pay a visit to Corinth to deal with the disaffection. There is a clear allusion to disparaging things that are being said about him. There are *those who assume my behaviour to be dictated by human weakness.* A more literal rendering would be, 'some people who consider us to be walking according to the flesh.' In the reference to 'some people' Paul's opponents come into view. For Paul's use of the pronoun 'we' to refer to himself, see our note on 1.8–11.

Only the context can clarify the precise sort of deficiency that is meant by the term 'flesh'. Here there is a suggestion of timidity and cowardice. It is clear from v. 10 that Paul's opponents are saying that he is feeble in face-to-face encounter.

In the present verse Paul is probably quoting a catchword of his rivals which throws light on their own self-understanding. They are evidently claiming that in their missionary activity the Spirit of God is at work in a particularly striking way. They are boasting of their miraculous deeds and ecstatic manifestations of the Spirit. Paul,

---

[2] See M. Carrez, 'Le "nous" en II Corinthiens,' *NTS* 26, 1979–80, p. 475.
[3] For a fuller discussion see Marshall, *Enmity in Corinth*, pp. 323–5.

however, is no true pneumatic person. He is all too human. He lacks the signs of an apostle (cf. 12.12).

Paul's decision to continue working at his craft was probably also used against him (cf. 11.7–11), and his opponents no doubt exploited to the full any criticisms of him that they found already circulating in the community, like the criticisms that he was guilty of insincerity (1.12f.), unreliability (1.14ff.), incompetence (2.16), and unintelligibility (4.3). For his part, Paul is of a mind to show these disparagers the full force of the intrepidity of which he knows himself to be capable – the verse contains no fewer than three words denoting confidence, assurance, boldness – but he asks his readers to spare him the need to do so.

10.3f. Paul has just repudiated the suggestion that he and his associates 'walk according to the flesh.' This remark prompts him to further reflection on the way in which his life is, and is not, determined by 'the flesh'. As we noted in our earlier volume, in our comments on I Cor. 3.1–4, Paul uses the term 'flesh' in a bewildering variety of ways. He can use it to refer to humanity without any pejorative nuance. He can also use it, with more emphasis on the creatureliness of humanity, to refer to human beings as weak, finite and vulnerable. He can also use the term to refer to humanity in its alienation from God. The word is used twice in this verse, the first time in a sense that corresponds to the first or the second of the usages just noted, the second time in a clearly pejorative sense. A more literal translation would be, 'For while we walk in the flesh, we do not wage war according to the flesh.'

'We walk in the flesh,' that is to say, we live in this world, we are creatures of this world, with all the weakness that attaches to creatures, to those who are merely human. Yet 'we do not wage war according to the flesh.' That is, though we live in this world, we do not fight with the weapons of this world in its alienation from God. On the contrary, *the weapons we wield are not merely human.* In more literal translations the Greek word rendered as 'merely human' in the REB is translated 'fleshly'. This is an adjectival form with connotations corresponding to the pejorative use of the word 'flesh' noted above. We wield weapons which God supplies, weapons which *are strong enough with God's help to demolish strongholds.*

10.5 The precise nature of the strongholds against which Paul does battle is now made a little clearer. *We demolish sophistries.* The Greek word rendered 'sophistries' is often used in a neutral sense to describe human reasoning, but here, in the light of the next phrase, it must refer to any sort of reasoning which rejects God's revelation, every thought *that rears its proud head against the knowledge of God.*

For his part, Paul's aim is to *compel every human thought to surrender in obedience to Christ.* This is not a declaration of war on the use of human reason. For Paul, the exercise of the powers of understanding is part of God's mandate to humanity. The mind must not lie fallow, if worship is truly to glorify God (I Cor. 14.6–19). What Paul is attacking is 'the wisdom of this world' (cf. I Cor. 1.18–25), the wisdom which is used to fortify the self against the revelation of God.

10.6   The last few verses have been expressed in entirely general terms, but Paul now makes it clear that this vigorous opposition of his to all proud sophistry touches the Corinthian church. Changing the metaphor from warfare to law enforcement, he affirms his determination *to punish any disobedience once your own obedience is complete.*

Paul can hardly mean that as soon as the Corinthians have become truly obedient he will resort to punishing them. Even though their obedience falls short of what he would wish, he must be making a distinction between the church as a whole and those who represent the really disobedient party – those who, as we are to learn from 10.12–18, have intruded upon his mission field, flouting the division of apostolic work agreed upon at the Jerusalem conference, and sought to undermine his authority.

The Corinthians themselves, however, will need to give full recognition to Paul's authority once more, before he feels free to take disciplinary action. Without this precondition, attempted punitive measures could drive the church completely to the side of his opponents. It is already clear that in these four chapters Paul is by no means as sure of the congregation as he is in 7.16.

Concerning the form of punishment nothing is said. Whatever else Paul has in mind, he probably envisages the expulsion of the 'false apostles' once and for all from the Corinthian community.

A person to reckon with in word and deed
10.7–11

10.7 The opening words of v. 7 can be taken as a command, a statement or a question. If they are taken as a command, as in the REB, they have the force of an exhortation to the Corinthians to look at facts that are plain before their eyes. If they are taken as a statement or a question, they have the force of a reproach to the Corinthians for looking only at appearances. The first interpretation seems to be slightly more appropriate to the context, and is in line with 3.1–3.

Paul goes on to urge anyone who is *convinced that he belongs to Christ* to *think again and reflect that we belong to Christ as much as he does*. He would hardly have said this, had he not had a particular person or group in mind. Both here and in vv. 10 and 11 he refers to the opposing party by means of a verb in the third person singular. He could be referring to 'anyone' of the group of opponents referred to in the previous paragraph, but it seems more likely that he has the ringleader of the opposition in view.

This opponent and those associated with him were evidently claiming to belong to Christ, and to belong to him in a sense which disparaged, and was meant to disparage, Paul. It is therefore unlikely that they were simply claiming to be Christians; they must have been laying claim to a particularly close bond with Christ, to being Christ's servants and apostles in a way that Paul was not. A similar claim is echoed in 11.23.

It is possible that they based this claim partly on their having been, unlike Paul, personally acquainted with the earthly Jesus, or at least authorized by those who were.[4]

It is also possible that these opponents claimed that their apostleship, unlike Paul's, was authenticated by their complete dependence on the generosity of others. When the disciples are sent out by Jesus in the synoptic gospels, they are bidden to take neither money nor pack but to depend on such hospitality as may be offered them. As Theissen has shown, there is reason to believe that these instructions were still being followed by itinerant missionaries in Paul's time and for decades to come; indeed, that in some quarters a lifestyle of homeless itinerancy and poverty was seen as a mark of a true apostle. Paul, however, by working to support himself,

---

[4] Cf. our discussion of II Cor. 5.11–17, especially note 15.

was laying himself open to the charge of not being an authentic apostle.[5]

For his part, Paul does not, at this point, deny the right of his opponents to belong to Christ; what he does contest is their claim to have a monopoly of Christ.

10.8f. Paul would be perfectly entitled to claim with pride not only that he belongs to Christ but that he is Christ's authorized apostle. He has no doubt of his ability to make good such a claim. There is no danger of him being put to shame by being exposed as an impostor. Nevertheless, he is not going to dwell on that authority, which has been given to him by the Lord to build up the faith of his converts, not to pull it down. The latter statement probably contains a pointed allusion to the damage being done by his opponents to the fellowship and faith of the church.

The Corinthians must not think of Paul, therefore, as *one who tries to scare you by the letters he writes*. Paul already has in mind the disparaging comment that he is about to quote in the following verse.[6]

10.10 Paul now cites *verbatim* the taunt that has been in his mind from the beginning of the paragraph.

'His letters are weighty and forcible enough,' so it is said, 'but his personal presence is feeble, and as a speaker he excites contempt.'

According to the best-attested reading, this taunt is attributed to one person, who, however, as stated earlier in connection with v. 7, seems to be acting as the ringleader of a group.

Few present-day readers of the New Testament would find the positive comment on Paul's letters surprising, but the disparaging comment on his personal presence and his effectiveness as a speaker is hard to reconcile with the picture of Paul that emerges from Acts. Such a disparaging remark, however, would have been totally ineffective, had there been no grounds for it. It is hard to avoid the conclusion that Luke's account of the orator on Mars Hill and elsewhere gives us a somewhat idealized picture.

Paul's opponents were able to claim then, with some plausibility,

---

[5] See Gerd Theissen, *The Social Setting of Pauline Christianity*, pp. 41–48, 66f.; cf. also our discussion of I Cor. 9.1–12a in our earlier volume.
[6] The precise connection of thought between vv. 8 and 9 is not clear. In our judgment, it makes best sense to suppose, with Lietzmann, that Paul has left out the statement that he will not appeal to his authority. For fuller discussions of the problem see the commentaries by Barrett (pp. 258f.), Furnish (p. 467) and Martin (pp. 310f.).

that he was laughably ineffective as an orator. This does not necessarily imply a lack of rhetorical schooling and Hellenistic education; it is the actual presentation of his message that is being held up to ridicule.

But not only Paul's performance as a speaker but his entire personal presence is being derided as feeble. No doubt, the outcome of his intermediate visit to Corinth, ending, as it had, in a humiliating rebuff to him, lent plausibility to this taunt. Some sort of sickness may also have contributed to the impression of feebleness, but the main grounds for the charge seem to have been that he lacked the ability to speak in ecstasy and work deeds of power. He was, in short, not a truly spiritual person. We seem to hear echoes of the same taunt in 12.9, 12; 13.3–4. Paul's opponents, on the other hand, prided themselves on being strong precisely where he appeared to be weak – in charismatic gifts, in personal presence and rhetorical virtuosity. In fact, Paul possessed a fullness of charismatic gifts, including the gift of tongues, but deliberately refrained from using the latter in public, because it had to do with the one-to-one relationship of the believer with God.

10.11   Whoever uttered the remark that Paul has just cited was no doubt making light of any warnings of disciplinary action that he might carry out. 'He may threaten disciplinary action at a safe distance, but, when he appears in person, he will prove utterly ineffective.' Let that sort of person take note that, when Paul visits Corinth in person, his actions will not belie the impression which his letters make, when he is at a distance. He will do just what he has said he will do in his letters and discipline the offenders.

Labouring within our proper sphere
10.12–18

In this, the final paragraph of the chapter, the real opponents of Paul in Corinth, the intruders who have infiltrated from outside, come into sharper focus, and we begin to see more clearly what it is about their bearing and their actions to which he takes exception.

10.12   In the opening words of the paragraph the tone changes from solemn warning to irony. In fact, Paul considers that he has every bit as much right as his opponents to be considered Christ's servant and apostle, yet here he makes the ironical observation that *we should not dare to class ourselves or compare ourselves* with them.

Paul then states one of the things about his opponents to which he takes exception: they *commend themselves*. There are hints in 3. 11 and 5.12 that Paul himself has been accused of self-commendation; here he turns the charge around.

Furthermore, these opponents *measure themselves on their own* - one could translate, 'they measure themselves by themselves.' They *find in themselves their standard of comparison!* Paul is objecting here not only to them being a 'mutual admiration society' but also to them being a law to themselves, acknowledging no authority outside themselves, instead of being in all things subject to the gospel. By such conduct they only show their folly.

Christopher Forbes has argued persuasively that an understanding of contemporary rhetorical conventions provides a convincing background against which to interpret not only this verse but Paul's exercise in boasting as a whole. He shows, by means of a wealth of examples, that popular teachers of rhetoric made extensive use of the technique of comparison in the interests of self-advertisement, as well as teaching it to their pupils. Wherever they came from, Paul's opponents were evidently conversant with these conventions.

As for Paul's response, in repudiating such methods, as he does here, and in engaging in a forceful parody of them, as he does in 11. 23ff., he is aligning himself with a long tradition of anti-sophistic polemic that reaches back to Socrates.[7]

10.13 Not for us, Paul continues, such immoderate self-satisfaction. *Our boasting will not go beyond the proper limits.* Nor indeed is it our way to acknowledge no authority outside ourselves. On the contrary, we work within the limits God has laid down for us. Here Paul passes from the thought of the boastful bearing of his opponents to what he considers to be their invasion of his God-given sphere of service.

To make sense of this passage, we need to take into account Paul's conviction of having been commissioned by Christ to carry the gospel to the Gentiles, a conviction recognized as valid by the leaders of the church in Jerusalem – James, Peter and John – when they met with Paul and Barnabas in Jerusalem at the conference referred to in Gal. 2.1–10. The three Jerusalem leaders acknowledged that Paul

---

[7] See Forbes, 'Comparison, Self-Praise and Irony,' *NTS* 32, 1986, pp. 1–10.

had been 'entrusted to take the gospel to the Gentiles, as surely as Peter had been entrusted to take it to the Jews' (Gal. 2.7). The trouble-makers in Corinth are evidently Jewish Christians who, in Paul's view, have invaded his mission field, flouting the agreement reached in Jerusalem. They had no right to 'barge in', so to speak, whereas Paul himself had every right to be in Corinth. It fell within his God-given sphere of service.

10.14 The exact translation of the next verse is difficult. What is clear, however, is that Paul is affirming his right to come to Corinth, since it fell unquestionably within the sphere of operation assigned to him by God.

Furthermore, no one can deny that he had been the first to bring the gospel to that city. The verb translated in the REB as 'reach' frequently carries the meaning in classical Greek of anticipating, being beforehand with. Paul's decision to preach in Corinth, therefore, had been consistent with a further fundamental conviction of his, viz. that he had a particular calling to take the gospel to places where the name of Christ had not been heard (cf. Rom. 15.20).

10.15f. Making another pointed allusion to the intruders in Corinth, Paul declares that he and his associates do not boast beyond their due limits (the REB fails to do justice to a phrase in the Greek at this point), by taking the credit for work that has been done by others. Nor do we *work beyond our proper sphere.*

The rest of the verse is again difficult, but it is clear that Paul sees a close connection between the growth of the faith of the Corinthians, the increasing recognition of his own ministry and his release for further missionary work. Before he can move on, the faith of the Corinthians, which is now at risk because of the conflict, must be brought to greater maturity. When that happens, and Christ is manifestly present in their community (cf. 13.5f.), it will not only be a sign that they have passed the test but also a vindication of Paul's ministry, so that he will be free to sail for new shores. And all the time he will be continuing to work within the limits set for him by God, since, paradoxically, those limits lie beyond the borders of the existing church. As we learn from Rom. 15.23f., one place to which Paul has been longing to take the gospel for many years is Spain.

Wherever he goes, however, it is a point of honour with him never to encroach on anyone else's sphere of influence or to take the credit for work already done by someone else. He is here reiterating the criticism of his opponents that is implicit in each of the last three verses.

10.17   The verb translated as 'priding' in the REB rendering of the previous verse could be translated as 'boasting'. In some older versions the verb 'glory' is used. The Greek word is one which Paul uses both in the Corinthian epistles and in Romans as a description of sin. 'Boasting' lies at the root of sin. The besetting temptation of Jews is to boast of their righteousness, while the besetting temptation of Greeks is to boast of their wisdom. To become a Christian, in Paul's understanding, means to renounce all boasting of one's own achievements and to boast only of what God has done through Christ. 'God forbid that I should boast of anything but the cross of our Lord Jesus Christ' (Gal. 6.14). This attitude, however, does not exclude a legitimate pride in what one has been able to accomplish with God's help. Thus Paul can refer, without any sense of involving himself in contradiction, to the communities of his converts being his boast on the day of Jesus Christ (II Cor. 1.14; Phil. 2.16; I Thess. 2.19). The text which Paul quotes here in v. 17 (from Jer. 9.24) is also quoted in I Cor. 1.31.

10.18   Paul ends the chapter with another thrust at his opponents. *It is not the one who recommends himself*, as his opponents have been doing, *who is to be accepted* but *the one whom the Lord recommends*. There is thus a return to the theme of the opening verse of the paragraph, in which Paul takes exception to the way in which his opponents recommend themselves and acknowledge no authority outside themselves. Here, however, he states clearly where the true source of authority lies: with the Lord.

If one should ask, 'How is one to know who it is whom the Lord recommends?' Paul's only answer would be that true evangelists direct their hearers to Christ crucified and risen, and do so not only by their words but also by the example of their own lives, in which that dying and rising are re-enacted.

Paul reluctantly plays the fool
11.1–6

11.1   Paul now asks his readers to bear with him in what he describes as 'a little foolishness'. Several times in this and the following chapter – at 11.16f., 21; 12.1, 11 – he reiterates this apology for speaking as a fool. Why the contents of these two chapters amount to 'foolishness' will become clearer, as we review their main thrust.

Throughout chapter 11 and most of chapter 12 as well, Paul is seeking to vindicate his apostleship, both by defending himself against criticisms that have been made of him and by describing the hardships he has undergone in the service of the gospel, as well as the weakness that has led him to a fuller experience of the power of God. At the same time he engages in fierce polemic against the intruders into the church in Corinth. Verses 12–15 of this chapter contain the harshest words against opponents that we have from his pen. Several times – in 11.16ff., 30; 12.1, 5f., 9 – he implies that what he is saying amounts to a kind of boasting. It is probably this aspect of what he has to say that he primarily has in mind, when he describes what he is doing as 'foolishness'.

Several times – in 11.18, 21, 30; 12.1, 11 – he expresses his reluctance at speaking so foolishly and boastfully. He dislikes boasting – he dislikes speaking of himself at all – but the Corinthians themselves have driven him to it by their gullibility in succumbing to the tactics of his enemies (12.11).

The latter part of v. 1 could equally well be construed as a statement rather than as a command, as it is in the REB. Most commentators and modern versions, however, take it as a command.

11.2f.   Paul freely admits that he is *jealous* for the Corinthians. The Greek word that he has used denotes a zeal on their behalf against anyone who would harm them or lead them astray.[1] Paul is confident that the 'jealousy' he feels on behalf of the Corinthians is one with the 'jealousy' with which God watches over the faithfulness of his people (Exod. 20.5f.).

---

[1] Cf. N. H. Snaith, 'Jealous, zealous,' in A. Richardson (ed), *A Theological Word Book of the Bible*, pp. 115f.

And indeed Paul has grounds for serious concern, which he proceeds to express by means of a marital metaphor derived from the Old Testament. Behind v. 2b stands the image of the marriage of Yahweh to Israel (cf. Isa. 50.1; 54.1–6; 62.5; Hos. 1–3). The role Paul has played in Corinth has been like that of a father who has betrothed his daughter to a suitor, thinking to present her to her husband *as a chaste virgin*, but who now fears that she is about to lose her innocence. Paul is afraid that, as the serpent in his cunning seduced Eve, so the *thoughts* of the Corinthians *may be corrupted*, with the result that they will lose their *single-hearted devotion to Christ*. Christ is their *true and only husband*, to whom alone their devotion is due.

11.4   Paul now spells out the reasons for these fears of his. Although the form of expression he uses is hypothetical, *For if some newcomer proclaims . . .*, he is clearly not talking about a remote possibility but about something that has actually been happening. *Some newcomer* has been proclaiming *another Jesus, not the Jesus* whom Paul preached. He has brought *a spirit different from the Spirit* they received from Paul, *a gospel different from the gospel* they had already accepted, and what has been their reaction? With cutting sarcasm Paul declares, *You put up with that well enough*.

Who is it whom he has in mind? It will soon become apparent that he is referring to a group rather than an individual, though it seems to have had a ringleader.

On the basis of Paul's brief remarks here and elsewhere, some scholars have attempted quite elaborate reconstructions of the theology of Paul's opponents. The diversity of reconstructions proposed, however, should serve as a warning against the danger of outrunning the evidence.[2] Nevertheless, some conclusions can be drawn.

First of all, it is no accident that Paul speaks of a 'newcomer', literally 'one who comes', not, that is, 'one who is sent'. Unlike Paul, this man and those he represents have no mandate from Christ to come to Corinth.

In charging the intruders with preaching 'another Jesus', Paul cannot mean that they have been preaching a different person; his point must be that they have been presenting a radically different conception of the same person. In the light of the evidence of the

---

[2] Furnish's cautions to this effect, p. 500, are timely. For a survey of different reconstructions of the theology of Paul's opponents see Martin, pp. 336–38.

epistle as a whole, we may surmise that the nub of Paul's objection to their message is their failure to put Christ crucified at the heart of it.[3]

As their conception of Christ differs from Paul's, so does the spirit which accompanies their preaching and informs their conduct. The upshot is that they preach a different gospel. Paul could have said that their message was not a gospel at all but a 'badspel'.[4]

We are reminded of Paul's passionate outburst against a gospel which is no gospel in Gal. 1.6–9. Like his opponents in Galatia, these opponents in Corinth are evidently Jewish Christians (see 11.22), but, unlike those in Galatia, they do not appear to have been pressing upon the Corinthians the demand to be circumcised and keep the law. The question of circumcision and the law plays no part in chapters 10–13 (contrast Gal. 2.1–5; Acts 15.1). A good case can be made for regarding them as wandering preachers from a Jewish-Christian background who had come to Corinth from Peter's mission field in Syria. The possibility that they claimed to be literally putting into practice the command of Jesus to his disciples to depend wholly on the hospitality of others has already been mentioned in our commentary on 10.7–11.

Paul's exclamation at the end of v. 4 that the Corinthians *put up with* it *well enough* when false teachers come among them links up with v. 1, where the same verb, 'put up with', is used twice. If they 'put up with' false teaching, they surely ought to be able to 'put up with' a little foolishness from Paul.

11.5   Paul now makes a sarcastic reference to *super-apostles*, to whom he believes himself to be in no way *inferior*. It is of considerable importance to determine as precisely as possible who it is whom he has in mind in all the polemical statements he makes in this and the following paragraphs.

First of all, the preachers of 'another Jesus' of v. 4 must be identical with the 'sham apostles' of vv. 12–15.

Furthermore, the sham apostles of vv. 12–15 can hardly be the Jerusalem apostles, though such an identification has at times been suggested, notably by F. C. Baur and the Tübingen School. Paul, after all, is in the process of raising a collection on behalf of the Jerusalem church.

What then about the 'super-apostles' of v. 5? On the face of it, they

---

[3] Note the admirable statement by Fallon quoted by Martin, p. 341.
[4] Cf. Martin's suggestion (p. 336) that Paul could appropriately have called his opponents' message 'a dysangelion, i.e. bad news'.

would appear to be the same people as the false teachers referred to in v. 4. To this identification the objection is sometimes made that Paul would hardly have described himself as being 'in no way inferior' to the bearers of a false gospel but would have used some more damning expression, but that argument fails to give sufficient weight to the sarcasm of Paul's statement. The expression 'super-apostles' can readily be understood as a sarcastic castigation of the extravagant self-praise of the intruding missionaries.

Those who, like Käsemann or Martin, or Barrett in some of his publications, distinguish the 'super-apostles' of v. 5 from the false teachers of v. 4 identify the former with the Twelve or with the three whom Paul calls 'pillars of the community' in Gal. 2.9, James, Peter and John, to whose authority the intruders in Corinth may have appealed, with or (more probably) without their consent. Against this view it can be argued that there is no hint in the text that Paul is referring to a different group in v. 5 from those referred to in v. 4. It is, however, probably correct to suppose that the intruders did have some connection with the Jerusalem church, at least to the extent of claiming to be authorized by them, though not (one hopes) with their consent.[5]

11.6 Paul now alludes once again to the taunt that he has already quoted in 10.10. 'Yes,' he concedes, 'I may be no speaker.' The Greek word he has used suggests someone untrained, a mere layman. Furnish points out, however, following Norden and Judge, that the rhetoric which Paul is here disavowing would not have been that of the great Attic orators like Demosthenes but rather the highly flamboyant style known as 'Asianism', which was immensely popular among the sophists of Paul's day.[6]

Nevertheless, Paul continues, *knowledge I do have*. 'Knowledge' here must refer to knowledge of Christian truth. In this area Paul can confidently claim that he is no layman. Moreover, *at all times* he has *made known the full truth* to the Corinthians. No opportunity for teaching has been missed, and nothing has been held back.

---

[5] For fuller discussions of the problem see Furnish, pp. 502–05, and Martin, pp. 336–41. As for Barrett, on p. 277 he writes that 'it is impossible to identify the *super-apostles* with the Jerusalem apostles, Peter and his colleagues,' but on the following page he concludes that there is very probably at least some connection between the *super-apostles* and Jerusalem. In his article on 'Christianity at Corinth' he does identify the two groups. See *BJRL* 46, 1964, pp. 294f.

[6] See Furnish, p. 490.

Your humble, loving servant
11.7–11

11.7   Paul now turns to another complaint that is being made against him, viz. that he had declined to allow himself to be supported by the Corinthian congregation while working among them. It is clear from I Corinthians 9 that this decision of his to remain financially independent of the church in Corinth had rankled from the start. Now it appears that his opponents in Corinth have been exploiting this dissatisfaction.

Why this matter should have been such a sore point in Corinth becomes more intelligible, when we take into account certain social conventions of the time. We noted in our commentary on I Cor. 9.1–12a that, by remaining financially independent of the Corinthians, Paul was flying in the face of Graeco-Roman conventions of friendship and patronage. In Graeco-Roman society friendship between equals was initiated and sustained by certain recognized conventions, particularly the exchange of gifts. People from higher and lower levels of society could become bonded together as patron and client. This relationship also entailed certain recognized obligations and benefits. Other apostles, including perhaps Apollos and Peter, had evidently accepted patronage, and Paul had been expected to do the same. Potential patrons in Corinth are likely to have felt slighted by his refusal to do so, and the whole community is likely to have perceived Paul's stubbornness in maintaining his independence as a repudiation of friendship.[7]

Not only was Paul supporting himself, he was doing so by working as a tentmaker or leatherworker (cf. Acts 18.1–4) and was thus aligning himself with the artisan class, who are often stigmatized in Graeco-Roman literature as uneducated, useless and catering to extravagant luxury.[8]

In the form of an indignant rhetorical question, Paul asks the Corinthians whether he had committed an offence (RV: 'Did I commit a sin?'), in preaching the gospel of God to them at no charge to themselves. In I Cor. 9. 18 he argues that his determination to preach the gospel free of charge had been a paradigm of the content

[7] For a full and well-documented discussion of these conventions see Marshall, *Enmity in Corinth*, especially chapters 1, 5 and 6. For a useful summary see Furnish, pp. 507f.; cf. also our references, in connection with I Cor. 9.1–12a and II Cor. 10.7–11, to the work of Theissen.

[8] See Ronald F. Hock, *The Social Context of Paul's Ministry: Tentmaking and Apostleship*, chapters 3 and 4.

118

of the gospel, the message of God's free grace. Here he speaks of humbling himself in order to exalt them. In using the word 'humbling', he may well be picking up the actual words of his critics. The words 'humble' and 'humbled', which are noble words for Paul, are likely to have meant for his critics something like 'base' and 'demeaned'.[9]

It is clear what Paul means by humbling himself. In what ways does he think of the Corinthians being exalted? No doubt, through being relieved of a burden, in the first instance, but also, probably, through being enabled to obtain salvation.

There is in this verse a hint of a christological allusion. Christ for our sake became poor so that through his poverty we might become rich (8.9). One could equally say that he humbled himself so that we might be exalted. Rightly seen, therefore, Paul's self-humiliation is a sign of the conformity of his life with the pattern of Christ's.

11.8 Rather than be in any way financially dependent on the Corinthians, Paul had accepted support from other churches, the churches of Macedonia, as v. 9 makes clear, so as to minister to the Corinthians. In I Cor. 9.18 he gives as his reason for renouncing support from the Corinthian church a desire to give a clearer witness to the gospel of the grace of God. Here the reason suggested is the desire that his role in Corinth should be exclusively that of a servant.

As in the previous verse, there is a hint of a christological reference: Paul had acted in conformity with the pattern of Christ, the Servant *par excellence* (cf. Rom. 15.8; Mark 10.45).

In describing his practice of accepting support from other churches, Paul uses a surprisingly harsh word, 'robbed'. This is a word which can be used in classical Greek of stripping a fallen soldier of his armour on the battlefield. Here once again it is likely that Paul is picking up the language of his critics in Corinth. It is clear from 8.2 that the churches of Macedonia were poor, and yet Paul had accepted financial support from them and accepted none from the relatively well-to-do Corinthians. One can readily imagine some chagrined Corinthians protesting that Paul's acceptance of aid from the impoverished Macedonians amounted to robbery.

11.9 elaborates what has just been said. Paul acknowledges that he did run short, but he was determined not to become a charge

[9] For a full discussion see Marshall, *Enmity in Corinth*, pp. 323–25; Hock, *The Social Context of Paul's Ministry* loc. cit.

on anyone in Corinth, never to be a burden to them. And he is determined that things should stay that way.

This last statement may well have bewildered Paul's first readers, because it suggests that his policy was inconsistent.

'What is wrong with us?' one can imagine them asking. 'He accepts help from others but he will not accept it from us.'

One can partly account for this apparent inconsistency by supposing that Paul made a point of not accepting aid from a congregation so long as he was active in it as a missionary, but, if so, why this avowal that he will never be a burden on the Corinthians? Verses 7 and 8 suggest that the reason why he was treating them as an exceptional case was that they stood in special need of an example of self-denying service.

11.10   This refusal to accept help from Corinth is a point of pride with Paul, an object of legitimate boasting. We have already noted, in connection with II Cor. 10.17, that he recognizes both a godless boasting, which is of the essence of sin, and a godly boasting, which amounts to taking a legitimate pride in what one has been able to accomplish by the grace of God. Paul's refusal to accept help from the church in Corinth is a legitimate source of pride, and he is determined not to be deprived of it. The way in which he has expressed himself at this point is quite unusually forceful. He utters a solemn asseveration and clearly implies that some people are trying to silence this boast of his. Underlying the REB rendering 'bar' is a word which suggests the barricading of a road.

11.11   Then, as so often, Paul hears in his mind the voice of an objector.

'Why is he so determined not to be beholden to us? Does not his acceptance of help from the Macedonians, coupled with his refusal of help from us, smack of favouritism? Does he really care about us?'

In reply, Paul can only appeal to God, who alone knows the full depths of our inward motives (cf. I Cor. 4.5).

Sham apostles
11.12–15

Paul now reverts to the tone of the first paragraph of the chapter and attacks his opponents with invective unparalleled anywhere else in his extant writings. We have already discussed the relationship between the newcomer of v. 4, the super-apostles of v. 5 and the sham apostles of vv. 12–15 and have concluded that all three expressions refer to the same group, the intruders into the Corinthian community.

11.12   When Paul speaks of going on doing as he is doing now, he is presumably referring to his practice of not accepting financial aid from the Corinthians. His object in doing this is now stated to be *to cut the ground from under*, that is, to checkmate, these opponents, *who would seize any chance* of presenting themselves on the same level as Paul himself. The Greek text of v. 12 contains no reference to apostleship. The more literal rendering of v. 12b in the RV reads, 'that wherein they glory, they may be found even as we.' However, in the light of the next verse, which goes on to speak of false apostles and is introduced by an explanatory 'for', the insertion of the word 'apostleship' into the translation of v. 12 seems justified.

But how can Paul's continued refusal to accept help from the Corinthians frustrate the efforts of his opponents to make out that in their vaunted apostleship they are on the same footing as he is? It may well be that in some ways they felt themselves disadvantaged by his practice. He could, after all, fairly claim to be imposing no burden on the community. So perhaps they were hoping, by their tactics of denigration, to induce him to claim his right to material support, in order to demonstrate his apostolicity. In this way they would have wrested from him a secret advantage that he had over them and would be able to make a more plausible claim to be on the same footing as he.

11.13   Paul now tears the mask, so to speak, off the faces of his opponents and exposes them as *sham apostles, confidence tricksters* (the RV reads 'deceitful workers'), *masquerading as apostles of Christ*. In other words, 'they are counterfeits of the real thing' (J. B. Phillips), not to be trusted or acknowledged as apostles at all.

The term 'false apostles' was probably coined by Paul himself and suggested to him by the Old Testament term 'false prophets'. The word 'workers' is regularly used in the New Testament of people engaged in missionary work. These men are 'deceitful workers', because they are preaching a different gospel and thereby deceiving the church. When we add to the words 'apostles' and 'workers' from v. 13 the word 'servants' from v. 15, we have a triad of functional terms which Paul's opponents probably claimed for themselves and which Paul has placed in a totally different light.

11.14f.   Yet it should come as no surprise that evil men adopt the guise of apostles, for *Satan himself masquerades as an angel of light*, so that it is easy enough for his agents to masquerade as agents of good. In other words, like master, like servant (cf. Matt. 10.25). Quite unambiguously Paul is here calling his opponents agents of the devil.

But their end is sure. *Their fate will match their deeds.*

This 'satanizing' and demonizing of his opponents which Paul engages in here may well strike the modern reader as unduly harsh, even when one allows for a certain amount of rhetorical exaggeration. Is not Paul presuming to take upon himself the role of divine Judge?

We have no way of hearing the opponents themselves put their case nor of testing his accusations by their actual behaviour, but it is clearly his sincere belief that the Corinthians have been corrupted to such an extent that their salvation is at risk. He therefore sees no alternative before him but to appeal to them, as urgently as he knows how, to decide once and for all for him and against the intruders.

Give me the privilege of a fool
11.16–21a

11.16–18   Paul is acutely aware that, in listing his credentials and achievements, as he has been doing and is about to do, he has been boasting. He has not been *speaking like a Christian*, as the Lord's mouthpiece, but like a fool in his folly. The Greek words Paul uses in this chapter for 'fool' and 'folly' are not the words *mōros* and *mōria* (used in I Cor. 1.25, 27; 3.18), which are more pejorative, but the words *aphrōn* and *aphrosynē*, which suggest rather someone who is a lightweight, with no depth or sense of proportion and therefore not to be taken seriously. He still hopes, however, that the Corinthians will not think that he is acting in character, that this is the real Paul. He has put on the mask of a fool because he has been compelled to, because *so many brag of their earthly distinctions*. Verse 18a could be translated, more literally, 'Seeing that many glory according to the flesh,' 'flesh' here referring to all the credentials – all the things that people are or have or have done – in which they take pride. Paul is thinking specifically of his opponents, who, as we may deduce from other passages, were boasting of their letters of commendation (3.1), their rhetorical skill (10.10; 11.5f.) and their acts of spiritual power (12.11f.).

It is a striking fact that neither here nor anywhere else does Paul name his opponents by name. This is probably quite deliberate and corresponds to a Hellenistic rhetorical convention. Non-naming was a recognized form of invective.[10]

Paul cannot stress often enough that he is speaking only in an assumed role, but if, after all, his readers consider that, in boasting like his opponents, he is speaking in character, let them at least give him *the privilege of a fool* and let him have his *little boast like others*.

11.19f. It is not a big thing that Paul is seeking, in asking his readers to bear with him in a little foolishness. They can afford to *put up with fools* and do so with pleasure, since they themselves are *so wise*. This is another heavily ironical statement. From the heights of their superior wisdom, the Corinthians can smile tolerantly on a fool. Why, in their sublime tolerance they put up with what is far worse than folly. Though the form of expression in v. 20 is hypothetical, Paul is clearly talking about the actual behaviour of the intruders in Corinth, as in v. 4. They have reduced the community to abject slavery, by their domineering style of leadership, utterly opposed to the concept of leadership to which Paul himself is committed (cf. 1.24; 4.5). Furthermore, by exploiting shamelessly their right to sustenance, they have eaten the Corinthians 'out of house and home'. They have got them into their clutches by winning them over to their side and luring them to another gospel. They have put on airs of superiority and hit them in the face. The last phrase could be a proverbial expression for a severe insult, but Paul clearly believes his opponents capable of literal, physical assault.

So the cleverness of which the Corinthians are so proud turns out

---

[10] For a full discussion see Marshall, *Enmity in Corinth*, pp. 341–45.

to be illusory, since they have failed lamentably to see through the intruders and recognize them as the charlatans that they are. On the contrary, they have put up with all this tyrannical, grasping, arrogant and insulting behaviour, supposing, no doubt, that persons so exalted were entitled to behave in such a fashion.

11.21a   The RV rendering of v. 21a reads, 'I speak by way of disparagement, as though we had been weak.' This statement is best understood as it is in the REB, that is, as a continuation of Paul's ironical self-depreciation. He professes to confess with shame that he is not equal to 'strong' conduct like that which he has been describing. If 'strength' means displaying the violence that his opponents have shown, then he has been 'weak'.[11]

This all-out onslaught on the intruders is at the same time an urgent appeal to the church not to let itself be deceived any longer but to return to the preacher of the word of the cross.

This is another passage which acquires a heightened force, when read in the light of rhetorical conventions of the time. Forbes shows that irony was commonly recognized as an appropriate technique to use in contexts of invective and forensic oratory and 'was seen as particularly appropriate to a speaker who had been badly treated; whose achievements were being credited to others, and whose good name had been traduced.' He also observes that a finer example of irony than v. 21 it would be hard to find.[12]

The marks of a true servant of Christ
11.21b–27

11.21b   Paul has just protested his weakness. Nevertheless, any proud claim that anyone else may venture to make he can match. Now at last he lets himself go and begins 'boasting' in earnest.

The form of expression that he uses in v. 21b to allude to others is

---

[11] Forbes ('Comparison, Self-Praise and Irony,' *NTS* 32, 1986, p. 19) makes the interesting observation that in Paul's letters the terms 'weakness' and 'power' never indicate simple psychological states, like a sense of inadequacy, but rather carry strong social connotations. ' "Weakness" is the state of those without power or status, and "strength" is the state of those who do have status.' Here, however, weakness seems to denote conduct which is the reverse of the violence described in the previous verse.

[12] 'Comparison, Self-Praise and Irony,' pp. 13, 18.

once again quite vague, but, as in vv. 4 and 20, he is clearly alluding to the intruding apostles. Yet once more he apologizes for speaking as a fool.

This opening statement serves as a preface to the list of his credentials, as contrasted with those of his opponents, which follows. He begins by listing their credentials one by one and showing that at each point he can match them, but the moment he turns from their Jewish credentials to their Christian and apostolic ones, he is gripped by the conviction that his record far surpasses theirs. Thus what begins as a comparison turns into a catalogue of all the hardships he has undergone in the service of the gospel.

It is a remarkable fact that Paul bases his claim to be pre-eminently a servant of Christ not, at this point, on the successes with which his work had been crowned by God but precisely on his hardships, his sufferings and deprivations. These hardships had left their marks upon him, marks which, as he declares in Gal. 6.17, were the marks of Jesus branded on his body, signifying to all with eyes to see that here was someone who was authentically Christian and authentically apostolic. The present section leads up to the statement in v. 30, repeated in vv. 6 and 9 of chapter 12, that *if boasting there must be*, Paul will boast of the things that show up his weakness.

Once again, we note Paul's mastery of the technique of irony. Forbes describes the passage which follows as 'a ruthless parody of the pretensions of his opponents.'[13]

In form there is a superficial similarity between vv. 23–29 and inscriptions in honour of kings and emperors of the ancient world which list their triumphs and achievements. In the *Monumentum Ancyranum*, for example, which immortalizes the deeds of Augustus, the emperor speaks of having often conducted wars on sea and on land against foes within and without, over the whole world. Paul's chronicle, however, catalogues his sufferings in the service of the gospel.

Catalogues of hardships can also be found in Cynic and Stoic sources, but these lists characteristically emphasize the powerlessness of hardship to disturb the serenity of the true philosopher. Paul does not in any way minimize the intensity of his suffering and humiliation.

11.22 It is clear that Paul's opponents made much of their Jewishness. The way he addresses three different forms of what is

---

[13] 'Comparison, Self-Praise and Irony,' p. 18.

essentially the one claim shows how much importance they attached to it. No doubt in their eyes their Jewishness reinforced their claim to have the support of the original church in Jerusalem.

The three expressions Paul uses, however, are not exactly synonymous. 'Hebrews' is used of pure-blooded Jews (cf. Phil. 3.5), sometimes of people with a knowledge of Hebrew or Aramaic (Acts 6.1). 'Israelites' is a more religious designation of the Jews as members of the chosen people. 'Seed of Abraham' designates them as heirs of the promises made to the patriarchs. However, in whatever terms his opponents choose to assert their Jewishness, Paul is able fully to match their claim.

11.23   Paul now turns to the Christian credentials of his opponents and repeats a claim that they were evidently making to be 'servants of Christ'. This is close to the claim to be apostles of Christ, reflected in 11.13.

At this point the thought of simply repeating the rejoinder he has been making, which literally reads 'so I', strikes him as being utterly inadequate, and he exclaims, 'I more' (overliterally, 'more I'). In so doing, however, he slips in the parenthesis, *I am mad to speak like this*. Evidently the thought of *boasting* of being Christ's *servant*, and more truly Christ's servant than others, appears to him to be quite incongruous.

Paul then states in broad terms the grounds on which he can claim more right to the title, 'servant of Christ', than his opponents. What is striking about his statement is that, whereas they clearly based their claim to be servants of Christ on their gifts and accomplishments (5.12f.; 12.1–10), their rhetorical virtuosity (10.10; 11.6), their deeds of power (12.12; 13.3), Paul bases his claim to servanthood upon his sufferings – his toils, his imprisonments, his beatings, the occasions when he has looked death in the face. He and his readers know full well that his opponents cannot point to any sufferings which in any way compare with what he has undergone.

But how does this record of hardship authenticate Paul's apostleship? It is here that the profound difference between his concept of apostleship and the Christian life and that of his opponents becomes apparent. For Paul, apostles are authenticated by the conformity of their lives to the pattern of Christ's crucifixion and resurrection, that is, by signs that in their lives the dying and rising of Christ are being re-enacted. And what is true of an apostle is also true of any follower of Christ. The difference is that in the life of an apostle that pattern is writ large.

11.24   Paul now substantiates the broad claims of the previous verse by precise statements of how often he has undergone this or that punishment or hardship. He begins with a punishment inflicted by Jewish synagogue authorities, the thirty-nine strokes. Deut. 25. 1–3 prescribes that a person judged guilty may be given forty lashes but not more. It was evidently customary to stop at thirty-nine, in case of a miscount. This punishment therefore virtually represents the severest scourging that the Jewish law allowed. This had been inflicted on Paul five times, probably on grounds like disregard of the Torah or leading others astray.

The fact that Paul submitted to this punishment no fewer than five times shows up the wrongness of an assumption that is made unthinkingly by many readers of the epistles, viz. that Paul would have described himself as no longer a Jew but a Christian. He could have renounced his Jewishness and put himself outside the jurisdiction of the synagogue, but that he was not prepared to do, even though remaining a Jew cost him dear.

A remarkable thing about this first item and many of those to follow is that none of these scourgings are recorded in Acts – clear evidence of how selective is the record of Paul's career in that book. Many of the penalties and perils Paul mentions here could well have fallen within the fourteen years in which he worked in Syria and Cilicia (cf. Gal. 1.21; 2.1).

11.25   Paul now cites a form of punishment inflicted by Roman authorities. *Three times I have been beaten with rods*, probably on the pretext of creating a public disturbance. Acts tells us of one of these incidents, in Philippi (16.19–24).

Once I was stoned. This must surely be a reference to what happened in Lystra, recorded in Acts 14.19–20.

Three times I have been shipwrecked. Acts records one shipwreck, that which occurred when Paul was being taken in custody from Jerusalem to Rome, that is, several years after the completion of this letter. As for his being *twenty-four hours adrift on the open sea*, presumably clinging to some piece of wreckage, this again is an incident which Luke does not record.

11.26   With the mention of shipwrecks in the previous verse Paul's thought has moved from punishments to hardships in general, and to the dangers to which he has been exposed through being *constantly on the road*. The word 'dangers' is used eight times in the one verse.

We may think of the Roman Empire being safe for travellers, owing to the Roman roads and the *pax Romana*, but there was still the risk of drowning, as well as the risk of being robbed, especially if one was the bearer of funds. There were also particular reasons why Paul was at risk. His message aroused fierce antagonism from many Jews as well as some Christians, and Acts describes a number of occasions when groups of Jews tried to silence him either by recourse to the law or by more desperate means. There is also the account of the riot at Ephesus, precipitated by hostile Gentiles (Acts 19.23–41).

11.27   Paul now focusses on the physical aspect of his sufferings, beginning with two general terms for toil and hardship. What has caused the sleepless nights? Probably the need to work at his trade (cf. I Thess. 2.9) or anxiety over his churches, or both.

The references to hunger and thirst and the many times when he has *gone without food* suggest that, in spite of what he was able to earn by working at his trade and in spite of the help that certain churches gave him, there were times when he knew real destitution.

The last two items probably refer to journeys undertaken in wintertime or in mountainous regions like Cilicia. The RV rendering of the last phrase runs, 'in cold and nakedness', but the last word is probably not to be taken literally but rather as referring to the times when Paul has shivered with cold, without enough clothing to keep him warm.

'The world is my parish'
11.28–33

11.28   Paul has given the impression that he could go on and on, listing the hardships he has suffered and the dangers to which he has been exposed, but now he sets all these to one side and speaks of burdens of a different order, as heavy as the physical trials of which he has been speaking but far more constant in their pressure. There is *the responsibility that weighs* upon him *every day*, his *anxious concern for all the churches*. The Corinthian letters and other letters as well, Colossians in particular, show that there was a constant stream of people turning to Paul with requests for advice on questions of faith and conduct. Delegations with letters and questions were continually on the way to him, and we know that within a relatively short time he wrote at least four letters to Corinth. Commenting on Col. 4. 7–18, Eduard Schweizer observes that the passage points to 'a prolific activity – correspondence, reading of letters, talking, praying and thinking of one another – going on between the apostle and the community.'[14]

Paul speaks of his 'anxious concern for all the churches'. The latter phrase should probably be taken quite literally and therefore as including the churches which had been established by others. The church in Rome was one such church, and Paul's letter to it expresses an intense concern for its welfare. With the churches of his own founding, however, there was a uniquely close bond. To them he could say, *It is the breath of life to us to know that you stand firm in the Lord* (I Thess. 3.8).

11.29   The next verse provides a further illustration of the breadth of Paul's concern not only for all the churches but for every follower of the Lord. What brother or sister is weak in faith or life, without Paul sharing their weakness? What brother or sister is induced to fall away from their faith (the RV reads, 'made to stumble'), without Paul's heart burning with indignation?

In his analogy between the church and a human body in I Corinthians 12, Paul enunciates the principle, *If one part suffers, all suffer together*. Here we see how naturally it came to him to live out this principle in practice.

11.30   Paul has repeatedly expressed his reluctance to assume the role of a boaster. It is something that he has taken up only because it has been forced upon him by the tactics of his opponents. But he is determined that, if boasting there must be, he will do it in a way that is consistent with the spirit of the gospel and boast, not of his strength, of his triumphs, but of the things that show up his weakness, for it is these, as he is about to show in the following chapter, which provide scope for the fullest revelation of the power of God. In boasting of the things which display his weakness, therefore, he is really boasting of God.

Some editions and commentaries treat this verse as the beginning of a new paragraph, introductory to the account of Paul's 'thorn in the flesh'. It is true that he picks up the theme of boasting only of his

[14] Eduard Schweizer, *The Letter to the Colossians*, p. 243.

weakness in 12.5 and 9 but here he is not only looking forwards but backwards. In speaking, as he has been from v. 23 on, of all the hardships and humiliations he has undergone in the service of the gospel, he has been speaking of his vulnerability, of his weakness. We should probably take the reference to *the things that show up my weakness* as including also the embarrassing personal limitations which were the object of the ridicule of his opponents (cf. 10.10).

11.31   Suddenly Paul feels a need to vouch for the truth of what he is saying and invokes God, *who is blessed for ever*, as witness that he is not lying. Perhaps he has anticipated a rejoinder to what he has just said.

'So Paul is going to boast only of his weakness? He can talk in a very different vein. He can boast, when it suits him, of his commission as an apostle by the risen Lord and of his successes as a missionary' (cf. I Cor. 9.1f.; 15.8–10; II Cor. 3.1–3). But Paul is adamant that in the context of the present argument he will boast only of the things that concern his weakness.

11.32f.   The final item in Paul's catalogue of crises may well appear to be a bit of an anticlimax. He has spoken of being lashed, stoned, shipwrecked, of being exposed to innumerable dangers on land and sea, and now he brings the series to a conclusion with an account of how he managed to escape the clutches of the commissioner of King Aretas in Damascus by being *let down in a basket, through a window in the wall*. This incident may well strike the modern reader as being quaint and even comical. A comparison with Acts will help us to see how Paul understood it.

This is one of the incidents Paul mentions to which we have a parallel account from the pen of Luke in Acts, but the use that is made of the incident by the two authors is rather different. In Acts the story is presented as one more instance of how Paul, by the grace of God, surmounts all obstacles. Nothing can prevent the 'chosen instrument' (Acts 9.15) from fulfilling God's design.[15] Paul, however, in citing the incident at the climax of his catalogue of hardships, clearly sees it as a telling example of the humiliation to which, as a preacher of the gospel, he was constantly exposed.

It is quite possible that in these verses Paul is depicting himself as

---

[15] For an excellent description of Acts as the story of the triumph of the cause of Christ over all obstacles see C. F. D. Moule, *The Birth of the New Testament*, pp. 92f.

an anti-hero, in deliberate contrast to a Roman military custom to which Edwin Judge has drawn attention. One of the highest awards in the Roman army was the *corona muralis*, which was awarded to the soldier who was first up and over the wall in an attack upon an enemy city. Any Roman soldier would be proud to be the first up the wall. Paul is the first to be let down the wall as a fugitive.[16]

It is also possible that this was Paul's first experience of a persecution that was life-threatening, his matriculation in the school of persecution, as Calvin puts it, so that it was especially vivid in his memory.

A comparison may appropriately be drawn between the two ways in which Paul's escape from Damascus is depicted here and in Acts and the two selves of which Dietrich Bonhoeffer speaks in his poem, 'Who am I?' There was on the one hand the person whom others perceived, who would step from his cell's confinement 'calmly, cheerfully, firmly, like a squire from his country-house.' And on the other hand there was the person whom Bonhoeffer felt himself to be, 'restless and longing and sick, like a bird in a cage.' Unable to decide which is the true Dietrich Bonhoeffer, he finally reaches a conclusion which is thoroughly Pauline: 'Whoever I am, thou knowest, O God, I am thine.'[17]

The power that is most fully seen in weakness
12.1–10

Paul cannot refrain from apologizing once more for going on with his 'boasting'. Several times in the course of the previous chapter he has conceded that it is a sign of foolishness, something that he finds repugnant and alien to the spirit of the gospel. Here too he acknowledges that *it may do no good*, that is, to the community. Nevertheless, he sees no alternative to going on with it. The tactics of his opponents leave him no choice. And so he comes to *visions and revelations granted by the Lord*.

Why does Paul take up this topic at this point in the argument? It seems likely that his opponents were citing their own transcendental experiences of visions and revelations as serving to authenticate

[16] See Edwin A. Judge, 'The Conflict of Educational Aims in New Testament Thought,' *Journal of Christian Education* 9, 1966, pp. 44f.
[17] Dietrich Bonhoeffer, *Letters and Papers from Prison*, pp. 197f.

their ministry, and were meeting with an enthusiastic response from the Corinthians, who already had a particular predilection for ecstatic phenomena (cf. I Cor. 14). Paul will show that he too is no stranger to such experiences. Indeed, if he needed to, he could hold his own with his rivals in the matter of visions, as well as in that of speaking in tongues (cf. I Cor. 14.18). But he will show why he puts an entirely different value on such experiences.

12.2   After the opening verse, we expect Paul to go on to speak of some visions or revelations of his own, but for the moment he appears to be speaking about someone else, a Christian brother, 'a man in Christ'. Not until v. 7 does it become clear that this 'man in Christ' is himself.

Fourteen years ago, this 'man in Christ' had a profoundly mystical experience. He was *caught up as far as the third heaven*. The latter phrase suggests the highest heaven, the veritable presence of God.

How are we to conceive of this heavenly journey? Was it 'in the body', that is, was Paul's whole person, for the time being, transported to heaven? Or was it 'out of the body', that is, did his spirit travel to heaven, while his body remained unconscious on earth? Of the mode of rapture Paul professes himself entirely ignorant. It remains for him a mysterious event, the inner dynamics of which are known only to God.[1]

Whatever it was, this experience of rapture cannot be correlated with any incident in Paul's life known to us from Acts, and certainly not with the appearance on the road to Damascus. For one thing, the rapture has to be dated sometime around 42 CE, about a decade later than the date of the initial appearance. For another, the appearance centred around Paul's commissioning for mission and is something to which he refers frequently. The rapture evidently had nothing to do with commissioning and is an event of which he is reluctant to speak.[2]

12.3f.   With most modern scholars (but against most patristic com-

[1] For references to accounts of similar experiences in ancient literature see Barrett, pp. 309f.; B. H. Young, 'The Ascension Motif of II Cors 12 in Jewish, Christian and Gnostic Texts,' *Grace Theological Journal* 9, 1988, pp. 73–103.
[2] Cf. Knox, *Chapters*, pp. 121f. In an article in which he compares II Cor. 12.1–5 and Gal. 1.11–17, W. Baird writes that 'the former describes a revelation that disallows disclosure, the latter describes a revelation that demands proclamation.' See W. Baird, 'Visions, Revelation and Ministry: Reflections on II Cor. 12: 1–5 and Gal. 1: 11–17,' *JBL* 104, 1985, pp. 651–62.

mentators) we assume that Paul is now giving further information about the incident referred to in v. 2. Once again he disavows any exact knowledge of the nature of the experience.

He does not say directly that he saw the risen Lord or that he saw anything at all. Nor does he name Christ or God as having uttered the words that were spoken to him. All we are told is that he *heard words so secret that human lips may not repeat them.*

Paul has little more to say about this experience of rapture beyond the fact that it happened. Nevertheless, it must have been of profound significance for his inner life, deepening his knowledge of God and strengthening his assurance of the ultimate triumph of grace.

12.5 In vv. 7–9 Paul goes on to speak not of the revelation itself but of its aftermath. First of all, however, he reverts to the theme of boasting. He continues to speak as if the subject of the mystical experience he has just described were someone else. *About such a man* he is *ready to boast;* but he *will not boast* on his *own account, except of* his *weakness.*

The second half of the verse reiterates what has already been said in 11.30. Boasting of his weaknesses is the only kind of boasting in which Paul can appropriately engage, for it is not by extraordinary religious experiences that his apostleship is legitimated but rather by evidence that his life is being conformed to the pattern of Christ's dying and rising.

But why, both here and in v. 2, does Paul distance himself from 'such a man', if 'such a man' is really himself? And what is the point of his boasting about 'such a man'?

As for the first question, he may be wishing to stress that the experience he has described was quite exceptional, quite discontinuous with his normal experience, and also perhaps one in which he was totally passive. In being ready to boast about 'such a man', therefore, he is not really departing from the principle of boasting only of his weaknesses, because in either case he is really boasting about God.

12.6 If Paul were to boast of things other than his weaknesses, such as his mystical experiences, *it would not be the boast of a fool*, for he would be *speaking the truth*. Yet he chooses to refrain, because he wants people's opinion of him to be based on *the evidence of* their *own eyes and ears.* Let them be guided by what they hear from him in plain words and what they experience in their daily dealings with him, not by imponderables like visions, the genuineness of which no one can verify.

12.7 Now comes the great reversal. The ineffable, mystical experience was followed inexorably by Paul's sharpest trial, described metaphorically as *a thorn in my flesh* and mythologically as *a messenger of Satan sent to buffet me*. And all this happened *to keep me from being unduly elated by the magnificence of such revelations*.

This verse raises a number of problems. First, the trial is assigned to the agency of Satan, yet the words 'was given' imply that Paul attributes it ultimately to God's providential control – an impression that is confirmed by what follows. This concept of dual agency, for which there is precedent in Jewish and Christian literature (cf. Job 2.6f.), suggests an event which was intrinsically harmful but which has been used creatively by God.

As for the precise nature of the 'thorn in the flesh', this has occasioned a voluminous literature, which has yielded no certain conclusions. As Lietzmann has observed, a certain diagnosis is no longer possible, since the patient died more than 1900 years ago. In our judgement, the most likely reference is to some chronic, painful physical suffering.[3]

If one seeks to identify more precisely the nature of the sickness, if that is indeed what it was, one is presented with a bewildering variety of proposals, including epilepsy, acute ophthalmia, malarial fever, a speech impediment, hysteria and depression. As Klauck observes, to review the various sugestions that have been made is like turning over the pages of a medical dictionary.[4]

An objection that is often made to identifying the 'thorn in the flesh' with some form of sickness is that Paul must have been physically robust to undertake such long journeys and to survive the hardships which they entailed, like those listed in 11.23–33. To complete the journeys that we know about, he must have travelled some 7,500 miles. However, this argument does not rule out all chronic, painful ailments.

Some suggest that the thorn is a metaphor for persecution, and point to passages like Rom. 16.20; II Cor. 2.11; 11.14; I Thess. 2.18, in which Satan is represented as the author of opposition to Paul's apostolic efforts. An argument against this view is that the imagery

---

[3] Full surveys of the relevant literature are to be found in the commentaries of Allo (pp. 313–23), Furnish (pp. 548–50) and Martin (pp. 412–16).
[4] Klauck, p. 94.

suggests 'some affliction more directly personal than persecution, which Paul shared with the whole church'.[5]

A favourite view in the Middle Ages was that the thorn stood for sexual temptation. Against this theory we can set a fact which seems to be clearly implied by v. 10, viz. that in the end Paul ceased to pray for the removal of his 'thorn in the flesh.' It is hard to imagine him doing this, had it consisted of some sort of temptation.

The theory just mentioned affords an illustration of something that is a striking feature of the history of the interpretation of this verse, viz. the frequency with which commentators have understood the expression in the light of their own experience, in terms of their own 'thorn in the flesh'.

12.8–9a Whatever the precise nature of his trial may have been, Paul *begged the Lord* three times over *to rid* him *of it*. The expression, 'power of Christ', in v. 9 shows that 'Lord' here must refer to Jesus Christ, and that Paul did at times direct prayers to the exalted Lord (cf. I Thess. 3.13f.). Yet, in spite of his repeated pleas, Paul's prayer for deliverance was not granted. Thus, as W. Baird observes, II Corinthians 12 combines an apocalypse and a miracle story, but an apocalypse which does not do what it is supposed to do – provide a revelation; and a miracle story which does not do what it is supposed to do – provide a healing.[6]

Nevertheless, Paul's entreaty did not beat against a wall of silence. The Lord did respond, though not in the way that Paul had hoped.

The tense of the verb used to describe Christ's answer is the perfect tense, which indicates a present state resulting from a past action. This answer therefore still stands, as an abiding source of strength to Paul.

It can be that, because, while it amounts to a refusal of Paul's entreaty, it also has the character of a promise, a promise of Christ's grace, which will enable him not only to endure his 'thorn in the flesh' but to surmount any other trials he may meet in his ministry. Christ's answer is not (to adapt the rendering of the RV), 'My grace is sufficient for this extremity,' but, 'My grace is sufficient for thee.'

Indeed, Paul will know that grace in greater abundance than he would have done, had the thorn not been removed, for *power is most fully seen in weakness*. The switch from 'grace' to 'power' shows that the two terms are here essentially synonymous. Denney observes

---

[5] Furnish, pp. 549f.
[6] 'Visions, Revelation and Ministry,' p. 661.

pertinently that there are many to whom 'grace' means no more than 'a vague benignity', whereas 'grace in the New Testament is force; it is a heavenly strength bestowed on men for timely succour; it finds its opportunity in our extremity.'[7]

The answer of the risen Lord in v. 9 acquires deeper resonance, when read in the light of the contents of chapters 10–13. Klauck observes that it forms the secret heart of the letter of four chapters. It represents a basic principle of the life of faith. This principle has been verified in Jesus, who, at the point of ultimate powerlessness, was raised from the dead by the power of God (cf. 13.4), and also determines the fate of the apostle, over whom the shadow of the cross lies.[8] Paul's weakness, therefore, far from contradicting his apostolicity, is rather a sign of his fidelity to the way of the Lord.

12.9b–10   As Paul reflects on this experience of power-in-the-midst-of-powerlessness, he would not have it otherwise. Most gladly will he *boast of* his *weaknesses*, rather than bemoan them or pray for their removal, so that *the power of Christ* may *rest upon* him. His weaknesses, his limitations, have brought him a deeper experience of the powerful presence of Christ. So he is *content* with these humiliations of his, *with a life of weakness, insult, hardship, persecution and distress, all for Christ's sake*.

The last clause of v. 10 amounts to more than a repetition of the dominical saying of v. 9, it represents rather its appropriation by Paul. 'Power' in v. 9 becomes in v. 10, 'I am strong.' 'In weakness' becomes 'when I am weak'. This linguistic transformation shows that Paul is more than echoing the principle stated in v. 9, he has made it his own.

The signs of an apostle
12.11–13

12.11   Yet once more Paul acknowledges that he has been making a 'fool' of himself by writing in this boastful fashion, but he is not to blame for it. It is the Corinthians who have driven him to it, by succumbing in such a supine fashion to the propaganda of his opponents. So, against his will, he has been forced to commend

---

[7] Denney, p. 356.
[8] Klauck, pp. 94f.

himself, to produce his credentials. He had a right to expect that the Corinthians themselves would have rebutted the sneers and insinuations of his opponents and come forward to vouch for him, but few, if any, have done so.

In 11.5 Paul has already declared himself 'not aware of being in any way inferior to those super-apostles'. Now he asserts that that claim is fully substantiated by the outcome of his ministry in Corinth. He has no need to fear comparison with his rivals in any way. In all respects he is at least their equal. Indeed, the conclusion to be drawn from 11.23–33 is that in respect of the qualification that far outweighs any other, the conformation of his life to the pattern of Christ's dying and rising, he is by far their superior.

Paul is confident that he can claim equality with the super-apostles, even if he is *a nobody*. How are we to understand the last clause? Should the word 'nobody' be in quotation marks? In other words, is Paul quoting the words of his opponents? Or does his statement express his own conviction about his true standing in the sight of God? Probably he is quoting the contemptuous words of his opponents, but at the same time he would have readily acknowledged that, like everyone else, he had no standing in the sight of God apart from what God in his mercy granted him.

12.12   It is highly likely that, when Paul goes on to speak of *the signs of an apostle*, he is either picking up the language of his opponents or, perhaps more probably, the language of the Corinthians themselves. For one thing, he introduces the expression without any explanation, which suggests that it was already familiar to his readers. For another, it is a clear implication of the verse as a whole that 'the signs of an apostle' consist, in part at least, of *signs, portents and miracles*.[9] For the Corinthians to espouse such a position seems wholly in character. In the light of 11.23–33 and 12.1–10, it seems out of character for Paul to do so. And in fact he does not do so without considerable qualifications.

First of all, he gives us an important pointer to the right understanding of these 'signs' of his in the narrower sense, when he adds that they were *marked by unfailing endurance*. During his ministry in Corinth he had been subjected to attacks upon his person (see Acts 18.1–17), and in his ministry as a whole he had endured every kind of

[9] The word 'signs' seems to be used in a more restricted sense at the end of the verse, a sense close to that of 'portents' or 'miracles', whereas at the beginning of the verse it seems to be used in a wider sense to mean the marks of a true apostle. Cf. Furnish, p. 553.

suffering and abuse (see I Cor. 4.8–13; II Cor. 11.23–33). This is a claim which Paul can make and which his opponents obviously cannot, and it is one which makes all the difference. For this is above all the true 'sign' of an apostle, the evidence that in this person's life the dying and rising of Jesus are being re-enacted (cf. 4.7–12).

Paul is also noticeably reticent in his reference to the 'signs, portents and miracles' which he had performed. The contrast between his bare mention of them in v. 12 and the detail with which, in 11.23–33, he describes the hardships he had endured is most striking. It is the latter rather than the former which are the marks of the true apostle of Jesus Christ.

Furthermore, the actual Greek verb Paul uses with reference to the signs is in the passive voice. Thus the ultimate agent is not himself but God.

12.13   Paul now takes up again an issue which he has already addressed at some length in 11.7–11, one on which both he and the Corinthians were exceptionally sensitive and which his opponents had exploited to their advantage, the issue of apostolic support. He had never allowed the Corinthians to support him financially, and this refusal had caused bad feeling in Corinth, especially as he was prepared to accept help from other churches. His opponents had, no doubt, been quick to exploit this dissatisfaction.

'See,' we can hear them saying, 'he considers you inferior to these others.'

For their part, his opponents had accepted support from the Corinthians as their right, and had evidently argued, as we noted in our comments on 11.7–11, that their very act of acceptance served to authenticate their ministry as being, unlike Paul's, fully genuine.

Paul's response at this point is to resort to irony. Did I really treat you *worse than the other churches* by refusing to become a burden to you, by refusing to 'sponge' on you? Forgive me for being so unfair!

Not what is yours but you

12.14–18

12.14   Paul is now ready to come to Corinth for the third time. The second visit will have been the painful visit referred to in 2.1. As before, he is determined *not to be a charge* on the Corinthians.

The question of financial support has already been dealt with in 11.7–11 and touched on again in 12.13, but there are still misunderstandings to clear up. It is not their money that Paul wants, it is the Corinthians themselves, the renewal of their loyalty to him and, through him, to Christ (cf. 11.2).

Paul then cites an obligation commonly recognized to be incumbent on parents. As early as I Cor. 4.14–15, he had appealed to the Corinthians as to 'my dear children'. However many tutors in Christ they may have, he and he alone can claim to have 'fathered' their life in Christ and therefore to be their spiritual father. Well then, there is a recognized obligation incumbent on parents to save up money for their children rather than *vice versa*. As elsewhere in the Bible, the construction, 'not A but B', has here the force of, 'B rather than A' (cf. Matt. 12.7; Mark 2.17; Luke 10.20).

12.15   For his part, Paul would gladly spend all he has – his money, his time, his energy – for the sake of the Corinthians, and spend himself to the limit for their good (this verse is the source of the common English expression, 'to spend and be spent'). He is prepared to do that, however meagre their response. But he would not be human, if he did not yearn for an answering love. Plaintively he asks, *If I love you overmuch, am I to be loved the less?* The harshness of some of Paul's language in these last four chapters should not keep us from seeing the tenderness he still feels for these exasperating children of his. Denney calls this 'one of the most movingly tender passages in the whole Bible.'[10]

12.16   Not only has Paul met with misunderstanding and ingratitude, his personal integrity in money matters has been called into most serious question. As for the sequence of thought, he now appears to be anticipating the reaction of his opponents to what he has just said and to be imagining them saying to the Corinthians, 'We let that pass. We admit that he did not lay any charge upon you himself. But (to adapt the RV rendering) being crafty, he caught you with guile.' In other words, 'he is by nature a "con man" and he has taken you in.'

Just how Paul is supposed to have 'taken them in' is not yet clear, but the emphasis on the subject in the statement, *I did not myself prove a burden to you* (the Greek contains an emphatic *egō*), suggests the

[10] Denney, p. 363.

139

charge that he has contrived to fleece them of money indirectly. In other words, his renunciation of support is only a grand deception. Behind that façade of independence he has been lining his pockets with impunity.

12.17f.   The nature of the charge that Paul is refuting is now becoming clearer. It is to the effect that he has used the associates whom he has sent to Corinth, in order to defraud the Corinthians. His opponents may not have made this accusation openly and blatantly. They may have contented themselves with dropping damaging hints in various places that there had been some 'funny business' going on.

In response, Paul speaks of having *begged Titus to visit* them and having *sent* the (i.e. the well-known) brother with him (REB: *our friend*).

Obviously it would facilitate our understanding of this verse, if we could correlate this visit with other known visits of Titus to Corinth. Earlier chapters of II Corinthians speak of two visits of Titus, one completed, one in prospect. In 2.13 and 7.5–9 Paul speaks of a mission of Titus to Corinth, apparently on his own, which has just been successfully completed. Titus is able to report the welcome news that the Corinthians have taken Paul's Severe Letter to heart and acted accordingly. It is hard to imagine this visit giving rise to the complaint that the community had been exploited. In chapter 8, however, Paul is about to send Titus to Corinth, along with two other brethren, to organize the Corinthian contribution to the collection. Such a visit could well have given rise to the complaint that, through his emissaries, Paul had exploited the Corinthians. He had sent his friends to collect money for the poor saints in Jerusalem, and some of it had stuck to his own fingers. In other words, the visit contemplated in 8.6ff. and the visit referred to in 12.17f. could be the same visit.

It is true that in chapter 8 Paul speaks of sending two brethren along with Titus, whereas in 12.18 he mentions only one brother, but even in chapter 8 he gives the impression, to begin with, viz. in 8.18–21, that Titus will have only one companion, someone whom, as in 12.18, he describes as 'the brother'. The other companion is not mentioned until 8.22 and seems to have been less prominent in Paul's mind.[11]

---

[11] Barrett (p. 325) and Furnish (p. 560) consider that the brother referred to here is probably the brother mentioned in 8.22.

It is also worth noting that both in 8.6 and 12.18 Paul speaks of exhorting Titus (Greek: *parekalesa*) to go to Corinth.

But what about the difficulty that chapter 8 speaks of a visit in prospect, whereas chapter 12 speaks of a visit already completed? This ceases to be a problem, if we take the view (advocated by several recent scholars) that chapters 10–13 represent part of a letter written at a later date than any of the earlier chapters.

To revert to Paul's response, up till now he has relied on the messengers he has sent to Corinth, Titus in particular, to organize the collection there. Thus any fraud on Paul's part would have to have been perpetrated with their connivance. But the Corinthians have to admit that these messengers, Titus in particular, are recognized as trustworthy people. Paul knows that with Titus they have only had good experiences. Speaking of an earlier visit of Titus to Corinth in 7. 15, Paul speaks of Titus recalling *how ready you all were to do what he asked, meeting him as you did in fear and trembling*. But it is equally undeniable that Titus and Paul himself were at one in mind and conduct. What the Corinthians would not dare to impute to Titus, therefore, they should not impute to Paul either.

What I fear to find
12.19–21

12.19   The main clue to the interpretation of v. 19 is the contrast between *to you* and *in God's sight*. Paul's readers may well be thinking that all this time he has been addressing *them*, and making a speech in his own defence, trying to justify himself in their eyes. But he has no need to defend himself before the forum of the community, even if his 'fool's speech' could give that impression. What he has been saying is to be understood as a theological and christological utterance in the strictest sense, the speech of one who knows himself to be answerable to God and to be in communion with Christ.

This does not mean, however, that he has no concern for his readers. On the contrary, his *whole aim* in all that he has been doing *is to build* them *up*.

12.20   And indeed the Corinthians stand in dire need of being built up. Paul is afraid that, when he comes, he may find them different from what he wants them to be, and that they may find him different from what they want him to be. What these two fears imply is unfolded in the rest of the letter, the first fear in vv. 20 and 21, the second in 13.1–10.

Thus Paul is afraid, in the first place, that he will find that the Corinthians are at daggers drawn and are persisting in the immoral ways of paganism. He is also afraid that, in consequence, he will be forced to show them a new side of himself, an authoritarian side.

The eight vices which Paul lists in v. 20 are all destructive of community. In specifying them, he is drawing, no doubt, on lists of vices that were current in contemporary Graeco-Roman teaching and had been adapted by Christian teachers. The first four vices are all included in the catalogue of 'works of the flesh' in Gal. 5.19–21. Words related to items v and vi are found in Rom. 1.30. The verb *phusioō*, to inflate, puff up, which is related to item vii, occurs six times in I Corinthians. We have discussed its meaning at some length in connection with I Cor. 4.6.

Paul's fear that he may find these vices in evidence in Corinth, however, is real enough. This is the state to which he fears his opponents have brought the community – a state of turmoil, rent by rival factions.

12.21   Paul now discloses more fully the fears he harbours concerning his forthcoming visit. He is afraid he will have tears to shed over many members of the community, people *who were sinning before and have not repented of their unclean lives, their fornication and sensuality.*

The sins Paul is now singling out are all forms of sexual misconduct. In a slightly different order, they head the list of 'works of the flesh' in Gal. 5.19–21. In I Corinthians sexual misconduct is one of the major problems Paul has to address, but, apart from 6.14–7.1, the authenticity of which is doubtful, this is the only passage in II Corinthians in which he alludes to it. Indeed, the misgivings which he expresses in both of these verses, as well as in the chapter to follow, stand in marked contrast to many of his utterances in the first nine chapters. He has, for example, described the Corinthians as a letter that has come from Christ, written by the Spirit of the living God (3.3). He has declared them to be rich in spiritual gifts of every kind, as well as in the love they have for him (8.7). He has professed his complete confidence in them (7.16).

Is he therefore now giving expression to fears which he has hitherto suppressed? Or does he have reason to fear that the evil effects of the activities of his opponents extend to sexual relationships? The sharpness of the contrast with Paul's earlier utterances in praise of the Corinthians could be taken as pointing to the latter possibility. In that case, the verse could count as evidence that the opponents were Hellenistic Jewish Christians who had soft-pedalled the moral implications of faith, in order to gain a readier hearing from Gentiles. On the other hand, Paul's actual words – 'many who were sinning before and have not repented' – suggests persistence in sin rather than relapse into it. So it seems that in v. 21b Paul is thinking of people whose immoral behaviour grieved him before and who, he fears, have not changed their ways, and in v. 20b of all those who, under the influence of the opponents, are now causing disharmony in the community.

If Paul's worst fears are realized, it will make his forthcoming visit as painful as the second one had been, as painful and as humiliating. Not that he would begin to doubt the legitimacy of his own apostleship. He believes that behind such an experience he would be able to see the hand of God, but of God acting in judgment, showing him, to his shame, how far his converts still fell short of what they were called to be.

Empowered to deal with you
13.1–4

13.1f. Paul now repeats from 12.14 the announcement of his imminent third visit to Corinth and then proceeds to unfold the implications of the second fear he expressed in 12.20, viz. that on the forthcoming visit he would be forced to show the Corinthians a side of himself which they would find unwelcome. The structure of v. 2 is complex,[1] but the main point is clear: Paul is repeating now in his absence *the warning* he gave in person on his last visit that when he comes *this time* he *will show no leniency* (cf. I Cor. 4.21).

On the earlier visit the warning was evidently addressed to *those who sinned before*. In 12.21 Paul has expressed the fear that he will find that many who were 'sinning before' (the same word as in 13.2) have

---

[1] Klauck (p. 100) suggests that the verse consists of two statements interwoven with each other in an a b a b a b pattern, thus: a: 'I have given a warning . . . when I was present the second time . . . to those who sinned before'; b: 'and I give a warning . . . being absent now . . . to all the rest. . . .'

not repented of their unclean lives. He had wanted to take them to task on that earlier visit, but the situation had worsened in a way that made that impossible, so that he had to leave the city with a warning on his lips. The present warning is again addressed to that group of sinners but also *to everyone else*. The latter expression probably refers to all those who, in the spirit of the catalogue of vices in 12.20b, have succumbed to the influence of the opponents and are causing disharmony in the community.

The point of the quotation from Deut. 19.15 in v. 1 has often been taken to be that Paul is planning to hold a formal, judicial investigation, put all wrongdoers on trial and call witnesses to establish the truth of any charges, but there is no reference to any such court of enquiry anywhere else in this letter. It is therefore more likely that Paul is applying the text with a certain freedom and that the mention of two or three witnesses should be taken as referring to his three visits to Corinth and the two warnings on separate occasions referred to in v. 2. Van Vliet has shown that in Palestinian Judaism this text from Deuteronomy was widely taken to mean that anyone suspected of wrongdoing should be carefully warned about the possibility of future punishment.[2]

13.3   This stern disciplinary action that Paul is prepared to take will provide the Corinthians with incontrovertible evidence that he is indeed Christ's spokesman. That has clearly been called in question.

'Where is the proof, ' the Corinthians have been asking, 'that Paul does speak with the authority of Christ, especially since outwardly he compares so unfavourably with these impressive newcomers?'

The kind of 'proof' they were awaiting was probably some demonstration of power, perhaps some miracle of punishment that deprived an opponent of his sight, as Paul is reported to have done to Elymas in Acts 13.11. The kind of 'proof'[3] Paul himself is talking about is likely to be something less dramatic but no less rigorous, viz. exclusion from the community.

When Paul comes to Corinth this time, the Corinthians will have all the proof they are asking for. They will not be able to gainsay that Christ is indeed speaking through him, and it will be no weak Christ with whom they have to deal but a Christ of power. They already

---

[2] Hendrik van Vliet, *No Single Testimony. A Study on the Adoption of the Law of Deut. 19 : 15 Par. into the New Testament*, pp. 53–62.

[3] The Greek word here translated 'proof' (*dokimē*) is a key word in this letter. It also occurs in 2.9; 8.2; and 9.13. For a full discussion of its connotations, see Young and Ford, *Meaning and Truth* , pp. 98–101.

have evidence of Christ's powerful presence in the church, in the preaching of the gospel and the conversions that have resulted from it (cf. I Cor. 2.4) and in the rich abundance of their charismatic endowments (cf. I Cor. 1.5–7; II Cor. 8.7). They will see further evidence of that power, if Paul finds himself compelled to take disciplinary action.

13.4   The moment Paul says this, however, he seems to sense the danger of appearing to endorse the triumphalism of the Corinthian community and of his opponents. All through his correspondence with the Corinthians, and especially in this latest phase, in which he has been contending with the influence of the intruding apostles, he has been confronted with an interpretation of the gospel which placed all the emphasis on the resurrection and saw the cross as a mere prelude, now happily left behind.

This distorted concept of Christ is associated with a distorted concept of the Christian life, according to which believers enjoy already the fullness of Christ's resurrection power.

But it is only in a carefully qualified sense that Paul can speak of Christ being powerfully present among believers or of himself exercising Christ's power towards them. Christ's way was marked by both weakness and power, because it was a way of both cross and resurrection, which belong inseparably together.

So it is with believers. Their way too is marked by both weakness and power, dying and rising. Indeed, weakness, dying with Christ, is the dominant note, not power, living with Christ.[4]

It is significant that in this verse it is the affirmation of our weakness in Christ that comes first, and that it is this affirmation which is in the present tense, whereas the affirmation of our living by the power of Christ is in the future tense. Our participation in the life of the exalted one will not be fully consummated until he comes in glory (cf. Rom. 6.5, 8; I Thess. 4.14; 5.10). We cannot therefore enjoy already unbroken resurrection glory but experience the divine power in suffering – a truth which is demonstrated with particular clarity in the life of Paul himself.

Nevertheless, even in the weakness of our present existence we do experience something of the power of Christ's risen life. The REB

---

[4] Cf. Barrett (*Signs*, pp. 43f.): 'Paul's ministry bears the imprint of the resurrection too, but, just as the crucifixion of Jesus was a public event, known to all men, whereas the resurrection was known to few, so what is generally visible in Paul's apostleship is the sign of the cross.'

translation of v. 4b suggests that Paul is thinking here only of the future consummation, but this is to do less than justice to the last phrase of the verse in the Greek, which is translated by the RV 'toward you'. The inclusion of this phrase shows that Paul cannot be thinking at this point of the resurrection promised to believers but of the strength which Christ will lend him to reform the church. The Corinthians will find that he, like Christ himself, is alive with the power of God and therefore well able to deal decisively with the troubles in the community.

Put your own house in order
13.5–10

Paul has observed in v. 3 that the Corinthians are seeking 'proof' of the Christ who speaks through him. The underlying Greek word, *dokimē*, is a characteristically Pauline word, which also occurs in 2.9; 8.2; and 9.13. It denotes testing, and then the quality of what has been tested and not found wanting, solid worth, character.

These ideas dominate vv. 5–7. Perhaps the central theological question in the letter of four chapters is, What are the marks of a true apostle? The Corinthians have been asking, 'Where are the signs of Paul's apostleship? Where is the proof that he is indeed Christ's spokesman?'

For Paul himself, as we have noted several times, the sign above all is a life lived in conformity with the gospel, a life in which the dying and rising of Christ are being re-enacted. Verses 5–7 suggest a further, but related, answer to the question: an apostle is legitimated by the way that the message he or she has preached bears fruit in the lives of those to whom it has been preached. Have the Corinthians been asking for evidence that Christ's power is at work in Paul? Then they must allow Christ to have his way in their own lives.

13.5   In v. 5 Paul uses a verb which corresponds to the noun, *dokimē*, along with a synonymous verb, and applies them both to the Corinthians. They have been putting Paul to the test. In a counter-move, he summons them to self-examination; it is their own selves that they should be putting to the test (the pronouns are in an emphatic position), to see whether they are *living the life of faith*.

A literal rendering of v. 5a would run, 'Examine yourselves (to see) if you are in the faith.' With its rendering, *Examine yourselves: are you living the life of faith?* the REB brings out well what Paul seems to mean by 'faith' here, viz. a way of life, a life lived under the guidance of the Spirit of Christ. In the second half of the verse, the crucial question which the Corinthians are being called upon to consider is expressed in terms of whether Jesus Christ is among them (cf. Rom. 8.9). 'In you' is equally possible as a translation instead of 'among you', and indeed is preferred by both Barrett and Furnish.[5]

The force of the last clause of v. 5 (the last sentence of the verse in the REB) seems to be, 'Surely Jesus Christ is in you, unless (as I refuse to believe) you should turn out to be counterfeit Christians.' Paul uses here the Greek word *adokimoi*, which is related to *dokimē* in v. 3 and to *dokimazō* (used earlier in v. 5) and denotes something which has been tested and found wanting. What the Corinthians must realize is that it is not just a personal dispute that he is engaged in; ultimately it is the salvation of the church in Corinth that is at stake.

13.6   It is Paul's hope that, in the process of putting themselves to the test, the Corinthians will *come to see* that he too has *not failed*. With himself he appears to associate his fellow-workers in the founding of the church in Corinth, particularly Silvanus and Timothy. He here applies to himself and his colleagues the same word (*adokimoi*) that he has used of the Corinthians at the end of the previous verse. The question of the standing of the Corinthians as Christians and that of Paul's standing as an apostle are intimately related, in that a positive answer to the first question necessarily implies a positive answer to the second question as well. If their way of life is authentically Christian, then that is clear evidence that the ministry of those who brought them to faith is authentically apostolic.

13.7   In this battle for Corinthian loyalties, Paul knows that only God can direct the hearts of men and women. That is why it is his constant prayer that God will bring them back to the right way, so that they *may do no wrong*.

In all this, Paul is well aware that his primary concern could well appear to be to vindicate his own apostolic status, but anyone who supposed that that was what it was would be completely failing to recognize his true motives. If only the life of the community is repaired, Paul will gladly renounce the use of his apostolic authority

[5] See their commentaries on pp. 338 and 572, respectively.

to discipline the Corinthians, even if this means that the reputation of being weak still clings to him. What matters is that they should *do what is right*, not that he should refute any criticisms that have been made of his apostolic style.

13.8   Out of its context, v. 8 could easily be taken as a declaration of the power of truth, in the broadest sense, to prevail in the long run over error. In its context in this letter, however, 'the truth' must refer specifically to Paul's controversy with his opponents. He has been commissioned to preach the revelation of the truth of God in the cross and resurrection of Jesus Christ (cf. 4.2). This verse is not an assertion of the power of truth in an abstract sense to establish itself against all untruths and half-truths; it is rather a declaration of Paul's incapacity deliberately to act in a way that would be prejudicial to the gospel. He can do no other than act to further the gospel. And he would be working against this gospel truth, if he were to make the refuting of criticisms of his apostolic style the central issue.

13.9   Once again, as in v. 7, Paul declares that it is the spiritual good of the Corinthians that he is concerned about, not his own status. He is *happy to be weak at any time, if only* they *are strong*. Like v. 7, this verse too should probably be understood in terms of discipline. Paul is glad not to have the opportunity to show his strength by exercising discipline, if this should mean that the Corinthians are in no need of it. The word 'strong' here does not appear to have a pejorative nuance but to denote moral strength.

For this, Paul continues, is what we are praying for, *your amendment*. The underlying Greek word here implies not a continuous progress on an upward path but rather the putting right of something that has gone wrong.

13.10   Between the arrival of this letter and Paul's coming to Corinth in person a certain amount of time will elapse. Let the Corinthians use this time to send the intruding apostles packing, and let them return to the practice of the faith as they have been taught it by Paul himself. If only they would do that, *any sharp exercise of authority* on his part would then become superfluous. He has the power to discipline the church – of that he has no doubt – and he is quite prepared to use that power, if necessary, but he is most reluctant to do so.

The ultimate purpose of the authority he has been given by God is to build up communities of faith, not to pull them down (cf. 10.8), though it may sometimes be necessary to pull down a building that has been built awry, in order to rebuild it.

The overall tone of this paragraph is more conciliatory than that of the earlier chapters of the four-chapters-letter, and even than that of the previous paragraph. Perhaps part of the explanation is that Paul now has only the community of believers in Corinth before his eyes, which he has in no way written off and which calls for a different treatment from that due to his opponents. It is also understandable that towards the end of the letter a desire to part in peace should make itself felt.

Finally, brothers and sisters . . .
13.11–14

13.11   Paul now brings the letter to a conclusion with a few succinct admonitions, greetings and a closing benediction. This conclusion is notably shorter than that of other letters of his, particularly I Corinthians and Romans, which is perhaps an indication of his continuing apprehension, in spite of the cordiality of his tone.

This is the only passage in the letter of four chapters in which Paul addresses the Corinthians as 'brothers and sisters' (REB: *my friends*). The only other passages in II Corinthians as a whole in which he addresses them in this way are 1.8 and 8.1. His use of this address at this point is another sign of the more conciliatory tone which we detected in the last paragraph.

Equally revealing is the way Paul uses the words 'us' or 'our' four times over in the space of two verses in Gal. 1.3f, as well as the way he concludes that letter also, apart from the final *Amen*, with the word 'brothers and sisters' (REB: *my friends*). He has no wish to exclude either the Corinthians or the Galatians, for all their folly, from the community of faith and love.[6]

The next word could be translated 'rejoice', but is probably better translated, as in the REB, *farewell*. This is the word that is normally used by Greek speakers for conveying greetings. There is a clear example of its use in this sense in Acts 23.26. In II Cor. 13.11 the

---

[6] In my book, *Striking Home* (p. 35), I have cited Paul's use of the first person pronouns in Gal. 1.3f. as an instance of barely conscious or unattended meaning which is yet revealing and characteristic.

rendering 'rejoice' would sound rather incongruous after the severity of warnings like that of 13.2.

The next verb is related to the noun translated 'amendment' in v. 9. Here, as there, it refers to the putting right of something that has gone wrong. Commentators are divided over whether the actual form of the verb used here should be understood as a middle (hence renderings like 'put yourselves right', *mend your ways*) or as a passive (hence renderings like 'be perfected'). However, the middle voice can be used in the sense of allowing something to be done to oneself, and that is perhaps the shade of meaning that fits the context best. The Corinthians are to let God have his way with them and allow themselves to be put right.

The same problem arises with the translation of the next verb, which can also be understood as a middle (hence renderings like 'exhort one another') or a passive (hence renderings like *take our appeal to heart* or 'listen to the appeal we make'). Since the verb is used to denote both exhortation and comfort, the translation, 'take courage', is also possible.

The admonitions to *agree with one another* and to *live in peace* are especially timely, in view of the fear Paul has expressed in 12.20 that he may find the community torn apart by internal strife.

In the final clause of the verse Paul adds that *the God of love and peace will be with you*. There is a rich background in the Old Testament to the notion of the divine presence. There it is stated close on a hundred times that God is, or will be, 'with' a person. Again and again the context makes it clear that what is meant is an active, not a static presence, involving protection, help and deliverance.

By itself the statement in v. 11 might suggest that God's blessing is consequent upon our reformation, but Paul would surely also insist that it is only by God's grace that anyone is able to fulfil the injunctions he has just spelt out.

There is a certain correspondence between the last two admonitions in v. 11a, 'agree with one another; live in peace,' and the description of God in v. 11b as 'the God of love and peace'.

13.12   It is quite likely that the *kiss of peace* was already an established part of Christian liturgy. In contemporary Judaism the kiss was a recognized symbol of reconciliation but not – so the evidence suggests – a liturgical rite.[7]

---

[7] For a survey of literature on the meaning and forms of kissing in the ancient world apart from the Bible, see Furnish, pp. 582f.

Paul's inclusion of this admonition at this point serves to remind us that the letter he is now concluding would have been read in public worship. By exchanging such a kiss immediately after the reading of the letter, the Corinthians would be enacting liturgically the injunction just given to 'live in peace'.

13.13   Paul is confident that he can send the Corinthians not just the greetings of himself and his associates but those of *all God's people*. Older versions read 'all the saints'. This expression may not be quite as comprehensive as *all Christ's churches* in Rom. 16.16, but Paul must be including at least all the Christians who were in his company when he wrote chapters 10–13.

13.14   It is Paul's usual, but not invariable, practice to end his letters with the blessing, 'The grace of our Lord Jesus Christ be with you' or 'be with your spirit.' Only here does he use a triune formula in a blessing, although there are several passages in which he refers to God, Christ and the Spirit as different agents within the one economy of salvation (see Rom. 8.9–11; I Cor. 12.4–6; II Cor. 3.3f.; Gal. 4.4–6). It may be that he began by dictating his usual blessing and then felt impelled to extend it. That would explain why he speaks of *the grace of the Lord Jesus Christ* before he speaks of *the love of God*. If so, his expansion of his usual formula may be due to his perception of the special need of the Corinthians for the fullness of the divine blessing.

It is generally agreed that the first two genitives should be understood as subjective genitives – the grace which Christ bestows, the love which God shows – though the sense of origin is surely also present. As for the third genitive, in the phrase, *the fellowship of the Holy Spirit*, scholars are divided over whether it should also be understood as subjective – the fellowship which is produced by the Spirit – or objective – fellowship in the Spirit and in the gifts which the Spirit confers. To pose the question, however, in terms of an 'either . . . or' is not only to fail to recognize that categories like 'subjective genitive', 'objective genitive' and 'genitive of origin' are the creation of grammarians but also to fail to do justice to the richness of Paul's thought. Grammarians may divide syntactically what is theologically one. The Spirit of God brings about in believers a common participation in the Holy Spirit and binds them together into the community of the body of Christ.

The word 'fellowship' is a key term in the eucharistic text, I Cor.

10.16f., to our discussion of which the reader is referred. In II Cor. 8.4 and 9.13 Paul uses this word for the collection for the saints.

The only other letter in the Pauline corpus in which the closing benediction is extended to *you all* is II Thessalonians (see II Thess. 3.18), which may well not be the work of Paul.

So at last the storms of anguish and anxiety, of yearning and reproach, subside, and Paul is able to end the letter with a blessing, a blessing, moreover, addressed to all the members of the Corinthian community, with all their faults, without exception.